SURVIVING SOLITARY

SURVIVING SOLITARY

Living and Working in Restricted Housing Units

DANIELLE S. RUDES

with SHANNON MAGNUSON *and* ANGELA HATTERY

STANFORD UNIVERSITY PRESS
Stanford, California

STANFORD UNIVERSITY PRESS
Stanford, California

© 2022 by the Board of Trustees of the Leland Stanford Junior University. All rights reserved.

No part of this book may be reproduced or transmitted in any form or by any means, electronic or mechanical, including photocopying and recording, or in any information storage or retrieval system without the prior written permission of Stanford University Press.

Printed in the United States of America on acid-free, archival-quality paper
Library of Congress Cataloging-in-Publication Data
Names: Rudes, Danielle S. (Danielle Sheldon), 1971- author. | Magnuson, Shannon, other. | Hattery, Angela, other.
Title: Surviving solitary : living and working in restricted housing units / Danielle S. Rudes with Shannon Magnuson and Angela Hattery.
Description: Stanford, California : Stanford University Press, 2022. | Includes bibliographical references and index.
Identifiers: LCCN 2021033165 (print) | LCCN 2021033166 (ebook) |
    ISBN 9781503614673 (cloth) | ISBN 9781503631236 (paperback) |
    ISBN 9781503631243 (epub)
Subjects: LCSH: Solitary confinement—United States. | Prisoners—United States.
    | Prisons—United States—Officials and employees.
Classification: LCC HV9471 .R85 2022 (print) | LCC HV9471 (ebook) |
    DDC 365/.644—dc23
LC record available at https://lccn.loc.gov/2021033165
LC ebook record available at https://lccn.loc.gov/2021033166

Cover art: Shutterstock

Text design: Kevin Barrett Kane

Typeset at Stanford University Press in 10/14 ITC Galliard Pro

To my children DEVIN, DYLAN, *and* JACE
for their enduring strength, love, resilience, and hope

CONTENTS

Acknowledgments ix

Abbreviations and Glossary xv

1 Living and Working in the RHU   1

2 Risk   17

3 Relationships   42

4 Rules   80

5 Reentry   112

6 Reform   130

7 Reversal and Revision   152

BEHIND THE WALLS: About This Book   185

Notes   223
References   229
Further Reading   239
Index   245

ACKNOWLEDGMENTS

Although this book is dedicated to my three spirited sons, my first acknowledgement belongs to the residents and staff at the prisons who graciously granted me and my colleagues access to their lives. While they easily could have shut us out and refused our requests for conversations, they overwhelmingly did not. In fact, they readily accepted us into their living and working world and provided answers to our questions and thoughtful insight on topics we did not even think to ask about. Residents endured strip searches to meet with us, a full shackling of wrists, legs, and bodies, a walk on a leash, and sometimes a wait in cages and visiting bays for an hour or more after talking with us before being transported to another strip search followed by return to a lonely cell. Staff could have seen us as an interference to their work and a cruel time-suck, but instead they brewed us sweet tea and coffee, made sure we were safe and fed, and spent time talking to us while the tasks of the day piled up, which sometimes meant they might not leave work on time. Staff also answered our follow-up phone calls and emails during off hours (one time even while on vacation) and they opened their working world to us in countless ways. To both the residents and the staff, *thank you*, with all our hearts. We sincerely hope the narratives in this book provide some knowledge that you are not unseen, you are not alone, and at least a few people (though I suspect it is many more than that) truly care about your experiences, your perceptions, and your lives. And, of course, thank you to my favorite major who answered numerous emails and phone calls, talked me through methods, protocols, and policies, and always helped me find a way to do the research with as little disruption to staff and residents as possible. Also a huge thank you to this state's secretary of corrections and director of research (you know who you are). I honor your commitment to reform and change and I thank you for your trust, time, and support. In honor of our promise to keep your information anonymous and confidential, we do not name any individual in this book. We also do not name the state of study, although many who know us may already know what state we conducted our research in. This was a purposeful choice as we are trying to tell the narratives without a particular emphasis on any state system.

Next, I give my profound and deepest gratitude to my spectacular doctoral student and friend Shannon Magnuson and my friend and collaborator Dr. Angie Hattery. Shannon, Angie, and I have spent countless hours talking about prisons, staff, residents, and restricted housing units (RHUs), and there is no doubt that these conversations have enriched my understanding and perceptions of our data and my understanding of carceral environments immensely. Both Shannon and Angie read every chapter of this book as I wrote it and were formative in the project's origins. The interplay of ideas between us often leaves me wondering where one brain ends and another begins. Additionally, Shannon's and Angie's thoughts and guidance were instrumental in the creation of the "about this book" chapter. Thank you both for the profound impact you have on my thinking and my life. Although I wrote this book, the amount of work and heart both Shannon and Angie pour into everything we do together in the RHU studies left me wanting to honor their commitment to the work, our team, and RHU studies by listing them on the cover of the book. Stanford University Press graciously agreed. Thank you Mags and Ang. Here is to many more years of work, learning, and friendship.

Now, to those spirited boys: Devin, Dylan, and Jace. Being your mom is truly the greatest of all gifts and I probably tell you this way too often for your liking. I learn so much from each of you and I find myself teary even writing these words. Devin, you are literally the strongest person I have ever known. You inspire me and everyone around you to live life on your own terms and to fight to overcome all challenges in a way that is true to yourself. Dylan, you are such a beautiful soul. The kindness in your heart exudes even when you try to keep it to yourself. I am in awe of the man you are becoming and so in awe of your wit, wisdom, and empathy for others. Jace, your love is absolutely unparalleled. You are gentle and kind and funny and sweet. Watching you watch your brothers and the way you look deep into my soul are the highlights of every day and of my life. These three amazing humans graced me with the time and sanity I needed to write this book during a global pandemic. They watched me work, interrupted me (for dinner and snacks) regularly, but also reminded me that I needed to get up from my desk and live a little here and there. I love you all—more than the universe, more than anything.

To my energetic and unconditionally loving mom, Joanne, you are my rock, my salvation, and my amazing companion through life. Thank you for always, always, always having my back and springboarding my dreams. To my life partner, Eric, thank you for your love and support and for listening to me talk endlessly about my work (and everything else). Meeting you and loving you is a beautiful gift and one I will never take for granted. To my sister (in-law, but not really), Betsy, you are my family—now and forever. I love you infinitely.

Big, happy acknowledgement and praise also goes to my amazing team of researchers and collaborators for this project. We have built a remarkable group of folks and I could not possibly be prouder to know each of you. It is absolutely my honor to work with you. I always say "teamwork" as a way of recognizing the source of all our accomplishments and I truly mean it. *We are a team* who learns from and gives to each other continually. Thank you: Shannon Magnuson, Angie Hattery, Earl Smith, Taylor Hartwell, Sydney Ingel, Lindsay Smith, CJ Appleton, Chelsea Foudray, Cait Kanewske, Esther Matthews, Kristen Huete, Bryce Kushmerick-McCune, Casey Tabas, Liz Rosen, Kaley Regner, Karlie Berry, Liana Shivers, Sabrine Baiou, Beau Coleman, Taylor Whittington, Cady Balde, Heather Pickett, Sewit Beraki, Dakota Daughtry, and Elizabeth Schray. Also, to the graduate students and colleagues who do not work specifically on the RHU studies but are part of my/our team and inspire us all: Ben Mackey, Lynnea Davis, Madeline McPherson, Lauren Duhaime-Bush, Lina Marmolejo, Daniela Barberi, Heather Toronjo, Esther Matthews, Teneshia Thurman, Jen Lerch, Amy Murphy, Sara Debus-Sherrill, LaToshia Butler, Arden Kushmerick-Richards, Jordan Kenyon, Stacey Houston, Rob Norris, and PJ Houston. Thank you to Kevin Wright and the Center for Correctional Solutions at Arizona State University for your amazing work and for the pathway you forge toward carceral reform. Finally, thank you to the powerful women who are my "go to" for love, strength, cocktails, and encouragement: Jen

Sumner, Lori Sexton, Edi Kinney, Keramet Reiter, Kim Richman, Hollie Nyseth, Sarah Lageson, Liz Chiarello, Renee Cramer, Jinee Lokaneeta, Hadar Avarim, Ashley Rubin, Shannon Portillo, Alesha Doan, and Chrysanthi Leon. Also a special thank you to Sydney Ingel for her help assembling the Further Reading section of the book.

My growth and development as a scholar and researcher is in large part due to a variety of brilliant and wonderful folks who I am proud to work with and receive mentorship from. In my years as a doctoral student at the University of California, Irvine, I received phenomenal training, time, and support from Dr. Calvin Morrill (now at the University of California, Berkeley). Cal taught me to think, to conceptualize research studies, to conduct ethnographic fieldwork, to write, and perhaps most importantly, to believe that this rural, small-town girl deserved to be and in fact belonged in academia. Dr. Joan Petersilia also mentored me at UCI and all the years beyond. Joan, I miss you and I am so grateful for every moment we shared. Your strength and ability to see solutions to problems before others even noticed the problems still inspire me today. My gratitude also goes to Dr. Faye S. Taxman, my enduring friend and colleague at George Mason University and the group we co-direct, The Center for Advancing Correctional Excellence (ACE!). You are truly an extraordinary scholar, researcher, collaborator, partner, and friend. Thank you for opening doors for me (even when I did not see a door), for supporting me, and for your incredible and endless kindness. Much love, Famous Faye, much love.

Additionally, this work would have been much more difficult without the generous financial support provided by the Provost Office via a faculty development grant, ACE!, and the Office for Student Creativity, Activities, and Research (OSCAR)—all at George Mason University. This funding helped me pay an awesome group of students to work on this project, put my weary team up in prison-town motels after long fieldwork days, paid for gas and rental vans to get us there, and afforded us the opportunity to do work we all believe in.

I also offer generous thanks to the many professional organizations that have allowed me to speak and write about this work over many years and provided me with generous opportunities to tell this story. These include the American Society of Criminology, the Law and Society Association, and the Western Society of Criminology. The feedback and critique from the audiences at these presentations undoubtedly shaped my thinking and helped me see how all the pieces of the RHU puzzle fit together. And a heartfelt thank you to my editor, Marcela Maxfield, and all of Stanford University Press for taking a chance on this first-time book author and to the anonymous reviewers who read the proposal and manuscript and offered salient advice and critique.

Finally, thank you to the readers of this book. Thank you for trusting me to be the storyteller who brings the voices of those living and working in RHUs to life (at least on the pages here). Despite its often sad and perhaps overwhelming content, there is also hope in this book. Hope for individual, organizational, and systemic change. Hope for a better life for those living and working within RHUs and for everyone who knows them and loves them as well as those who have not yet had the great privilege of meeting them. We all hope for more than survival. Piece by piece, together, we can learn to thrive, not just survive, and enhance the world with this long-overdue reward.

ABBREVIATIONS AND GLOSSARY

Prisons have a language all their own. This language is overrun with acronyms and carceral vernacular and slang. The following glossary defines some of these terms.

AC	administrative custody
ADHD	attention-deficit/hyperactivity disorder
AdSeg	administrative segregation
BIU	behavioral intervention unit
belly chains	series of chains and locks that secure around resident's waist for transport
block	group of units in a prison/jail
bubble	the control room of an RHU housing all monitors, equipment, and switches to open and close cell doors electronically
cellie	cellmate; person living in same cell with another
central office	main headquarters of a DOC; mostly administrative
CIT	crisis intervention training

CM		contingency management
CO		correctional officer (also called guard), custodial-staff member
commissary		in-custody place for residents to buy limited goods from DOC lists using their own funds
cosmetics		items residents can purchase from the commissary such as deodorant, shampoo, toothpaste (not makeup, which is generally unavailable in RHU settings)
cover room		place in some prisons where staff can go during a shift to discuss challenging situations and mental health with professionals or just to calm down and be alone for a while; may have other names too
CPS		certified peer specialist; resident with special training to assist other residents through mostly talking and listening
DC		disciplinary custody
DOC		department of corrections
double celling		cell containing two residents, generally with bunk beds
DTU		diversionary treatment unit
fishing		process residents use to send or receive items via string or lines between cells; also called kites or "throwing a line"
gen pop		general population; the units within a prison or jail that are without enhanced restriction; also called GP, pop, or population
hard cell		cell that contains only a bed, toilet, desk, and sink, without amenities such as sheets that a resident may use to harm themselves
hole		slang for RHU or any other housing unit that is restricted in some way

IRB	institutional review board, which oversees all research with human subjects to ensure ethics including confidentiality, informed consent, and safety
leash	leather or other material fashioned into a tether that attaches to a resident during transport; is held by correctional staff
leg irons	chains and cuffs that fit around a resident's ankles and shackle them for transport
lifer	resident who has a life-in-prison sentence
LT	lieutenant
meds	prescription medications
MHFA	mental health first aid, a training course for correctional staff about mental health issues and challenges
misconduct	a violation committed by a resident within a custodial setting; also called a violation
NIC	National Institute of Corrections
OC	oleoresin capsicum made from the oil of a pepper; also called pepper spray or mace
OSHA	Occupational Safety and Health Administration
PC	protective custody
POC	psychiatric outpatient cell
pod	group of cells in a unit on a block
PRC	performance review committee
PREA	Prison Rape Elimination Act
psych	psychological staff
PTSD	post-traumatic stress disorder
resident	more humane word for prisoner, inmate, convict who is in a custodial setting
RHU	restricted housing unit
RHU School	training course or program for custodial staff who are or will be working within RHUs

SEAP	state employee assistance program
SHU	special, security, or secured housing unit
SMU	special management unit
super	superintendent; top manager within a prison; also called warden
tablet	personal electronic device possessed by some residents (institutionally issued or self-purchased) that operates using a secured intranet system; like an iPad
unit	group of cells on a block in a prison or jail
WHO	World Health Organization
wicket	hinged opening in cell door that may be locked from the outside
yard	place for recreation within a prison, block, unit, or pod; may be outdoors

SURVIVING SOLITARY

CHAPTER 1

Living and Working in the RHU

THE RHU, or restricted housing unit, is a separate location within a prison or a jail that houses residents* whom prison staff feel need additional control or punishment or who require private and separate housing for a variety of reasons, including safety. Some entire prisons—supermax facilities—contain only RHUs and no general housing units. However, other prisons operate general and restricted housing units within the same institutional complex. While some states and jurisdictions use other monikers for their restricted housing units, such as administrative segregation (AdSeg) or special, secured, or security housing unit (SHU), the colloquial term *solitary confinement* is no longer common within correctional institutions. Instead, the US government and many correctional departments prefer the umbrella term *RHU* as less pejorative and more specific. Additionally, due to overcrowding and suicide prevention efforts, these units often double-bunk residents and the unit is full of staff, making everyone's time in the RHU decidedly not solitary.

---

* Throughout this book, we use the term *resident* to represent current, not lifetime status in custody, and to acknowledge individual rights; we use the terms *inmate* and *prisoner* throughout this book when we use the words of other scholars, residents, media, and prison staff.

RHU Residents

On any given day in the United States, there are between 60,000 and 80,000 individuals locked inside RHUs within prisons and jails. This equates to roughly 20 percent to 40 percent of prison residents spending time in RHUs during their carceral stay, with all residents eligible to serve time in the RHU without exception.[1] RHU sentences range from a few to thirty, sixty, or ninety days at the low end to years or decades at the high end. An RHU resident is never guaranteed a specific release date unless they are maxing out (reaching the mandatory end of their prison sentence) and will be released directly to the community. For most residents, a thirty-day RHU sentence for example, may become much longer if the resident gets into any trouble while housed in the RHU or if, as their RHU release date approaches, there are no available beds in general population or the institution is short-staffed in a way that may inhibit, slow, or prevent resident relocation.

Many of the folks housed within RHUs are purported as the "worst of the worst," yet numerous reports and studies find RHU residents often receive RHU confinement for nonviolent acts including possessing contraband (such as cell phones or inappropriate pictures), screening positive for drugs or alcohol, or even for being disrespectful to staff or residents in the general institutional population. Individuals sent to RHUs as punishment for misconduct are often placed on a disciplinary custody (DC) status. Additionally, many individuals end up in the RHU as a form of protective custody. This occurs either to guard them from the general prison population if they are in danger of harm because, for example, they are transgender, are gay or lesbian, or are charged with a sex offense, or to protect the general population and/or staff from them if they have, for example, high-notoriety gang affiliations and/or have hurt or killed a correctional staff member, a law enforcement officer, or another resident. These individuals are housed in RHUs on administrative custody (AC) or protective custody (PC) status. Individuals housed in RHUs, particularly those with DC status, are not generally afforded any opportunities for programming or treatment services from prison staff or volunteers. AC-status residents may begin or continue correspondence (educational) courses, but because of property rules or staff decisions, DC-status residents often do not have access to these courses and their accompanying materials while in the RHU. RHU residents on DC status are also not allowed to work at any prison job while housed in the RHU and may, in fact, lose any prison job they had prior to RHU placement.

Sentencing to the RHU from the general population is an internal prison process that occurs without attorneys, judges, or any outside assistance. As a result, residents and staff report that most RHU hearings within prisons end with guilty verdicts and RHU placement. Additionally, the decision to release an individual from the RHU to the general population occurs via a performance review committee (PRC)—another internal institutional process. This process pulls residents from their cells about every thirty days for a formal evaluation in front of a team including correctional and psychological staff. It includes a case review of the resident's performance within the RHU to assess appropriateness for release. Like RHU placement, this process occurs without any legal or other representation for the resident. Numerous residents report not understanding this process and the subsequent decisions and consequences.[2] Many residents also report their time in the RHU is extended at these meetings. Staff generally concur with these sentiments.

RHU Staff

Staff come to work in the RHU through a variety of pathways. For many staff, someone on the current RHU team (generally the lieutenant or sergeant) requested that they receive posting within the RHU. Lieutenants and sergeants often assemble their RHU team with custodial staff they know and trust. These leaders note that building their team in this way ensures staff collegiality and comradery—which helps make daily activities and tasks more efficient and perhaps more safe in the RHU. If they are not requested by a supervisor, prison staff may bid for an RHU post through the prison's formal bid-posting process or they may fill in for someone in the RHU during an absence and receive a request to stay on.

The perceived dangerousness and intensity of working in the RHU leads many prisons to create policies regarding the maximum number of months or years that staff may work within the RHU. These policies, when they exist, delineate a rotation out of the RHU to another prison post and may also dictate if or when someone may return to an RHU post after another post rotation. Not all prisons do this, and there is no scholarly evidence suggesting when exactly this shift rotation should (if indeed it should) occur.

Many custodial staff in US prisons have a high school education, some have some college, and many come to work in corrections after military service. The work is hard and demanding but may come with its own rewards. Many RHU staff see their time working in the RHU as akin to time in combat for military service. It bolsters their resumé and provides a pathway toward upward career mobility and higher-paying and better carceral jobs that may eventually include promotion.

The following quotes from both staff and residents provide a sense of living and working in an RHU:

> The RHU is full punishment. You will lose yourself back here. It's easy. I don't wish being back here on anyone. It institutionalizes you. This prison hands out RHU time like candy. It may change you for the worse or for the better—it depends on who you are.
>
> This place can be war on you.
>
> Changes [in people] here don't happen overnight. They happen over years. They become more jaded, cynical, vigilant. There's more divorce and family discord. High blood pressure and anxiety.
>
> They don't have trust with me. I don't have trust with them.
>
> Dear God, please give me the strength to deal with this.

In these quotes, residents and staff describe the RHU as a punishing place that is analogous to a battlefield, where emotions harden, trust evades, and strength is desired but often elusive. As you read the quotes, did you wonder who said each of them: a resident or a staff member?[3] Either could be correct, as both residents and staff suffer greatly in RHU environments and, interestingly, in many of the same ways.

As a residence or a workplace, the RHU is no place to call home. Risk abounds, rules register as unfair and ambiguous, relationships suffer, reentry haunts, and reform is a fantasy or a nightmare depending which direction it takes. Present-day RHUs cause immense and often untold mental and physical harm to both residents and staff, yet they also, perhaps surprisingly, yield a sense of hope among both those living and working there. The hope emerges from deep within the boundaries of forced coping and an overwhelming desire to live a better life.

In the state where we conducted our study, the RHU staff-to-resident ratio is approximately one staff member for every thirty-one residents. If this holds nationally (these numbers are not available), there are approximately

1,800 to 2,400 staff working in US RHUs daily. Additionally, there is typically just one psychological staff member for an entire RHU (with up to four or more resident pods), with an occasional rotating psychological staff member also providing some services. There are no posted religious, treatment, educational programming, or medical staff members specific to the RHU. Any additional staff who come to the RHU do so as part of their workday rotation within the broader prison. Some RHUs do employ peer assistants (current general population residents) to occasionally talk with and assist RHU residents, but these are relatively rare.

Although the National Institute of Corrections (NIC) hosts a four-day training course for correctional staff working in RHUs, and the state we studied provides a five-day training course commonly called RHU School, many states do not provide additional formal training for correctional staff who move from working in general population units into RHUs. Yet, the context, circumstances, rules, policies, and procedures are vastly different for staff working in restricted carceral space. Most correctional staff we interviewed said they learned "on the fly" or informally once on the job within the RHU. Many reported simply following other RHU staff or using a trial-and-error approach to challenges and problems and hoping for the best. Without adequate training and resources for RHU work, correctional staff endure a steep learning curve in a place where the risks of suicide and mental illness for both staff and residents are often heightened, and the heavy workload and one-to-thirty-one staff-to-resident ratio leaves very little time for interacting, building rapport, and aiding each other or the residents.

Challenges for Researchers

Despite a distinct lack of scholarly attention to RHUs, there are a few notable works and some emerging studies of residents and staff in these carceral locales. Perhaps a primary reason for the slight attention to RHUs is the difficulty of access. For many years, prison researchers faced a distinct and pronounced lack of access to prisons and jails. Many correctional systems and their upper management are not excited about having researchers traipsing around their institution, interviewing, observing, and surveying residents and staff. Of primary concern are both safety and exposure. Carceral institutions are responsible for all the people within them, both legally and otherwise. Prisons and jails can be dangerous places. Although security abounds in many correctional institutions, many researchers are inexperienced about navigating these settings and their presence may put both themselves as well as staff and residents at risk. At least one state prison system, for example, requires all researchers to sign a waiver before entering any prison, agreeing that they understand if there is a hostage situation during their visit, neither the state, the prison, nor the staff will negotiate on the researcher's behalf. While some argue this concern is overblown and just a way of keeping researchers out, it is a very real concern for many correctional administrators. Additionally, labor unions and associations who often support correctional staff regularly take issue with researchers interrupting the work of their members. For example, should a staff member be busy with a researcher and miss a major event on the block, this may reflect negatively on the union and the staff. And, what if a staff member takes too long during their interview, leaving another staff member to cover their post or shift in a way that extends overtime, workload, and associated issues? Union concerns abound. So, even when prisons grant access to researchers, unions may not follow suit.

Then, there is the issue of exposure. Many prison staff make one or more of three arguments in defense of their employer. First, they are doing the best they can with their limited resources. If this is the preferred narrative, researchers pose a threat to expose just how limited those resources are and just how harmful the lack of resources may be. Second, the place is a disaster. If this is the perceived narrative, researchers pose a threat to expose just how bad things really are. Third, the prison is an efficient, effective, well-oiled machine. Although this narrative is far less common, some carceral staff do make this perception known. If this is the perceived narrative, then justifiably, research is unnecessary. Generally, researchers confront a mix of these arguments—and all three perspectives typically view research as not necessary, important, or helpful. Sociologist Loïc Wacquant eloquently outlines a similar perspective in his 2002 article on what he calls the curious eclipse of prison ethnography.[4] Wacquant found that it had become harder for researchers to do traditional ethnographic studies (in-person observations) during the age of mass incarceration largely due to funding and access. However, in more recent work, sociologist Ashley Rubin examined over nine hundred dissertations focusing on prisons. She found an increase in qualitative work within prisons over time. However, she notes that these studies do not show the same increase for classic ethnographies as for other qualitative methods (e.g., interviews, focus groups). All told, prolonged data collection in prison is iffy at best—even with these slightly mixed findings.

The vast majority of books and articles on RHUs typically focus on residents, covering a wide array of topics including mental health and other effects of solitary confinement,[5] historical and legal issues,[6] and daily living experiences and conditions.[7] Written by scholars, former residents, psychologists, and journalists, these offerings generally paint a picture of how we got here, what legal harms occur and what remedies exist, and what a day in the life of an RHU resident looks, feels, smells, and sounds like. With some limited exceptions, staff are largely missing from the daily life narrative and when discussed, they are typically cast as the harmer, not the harmed, too.

Most studies of correctional staff examine staff in prisons in general, not RHUs specifically. Research on RHU staff includes a study by criminologist Daniel Mears and his colleague Jennifer Castro at the Urban Institute. In this study Mears and Castro surveyed wardens of supermax facilities. They found that most wardens think supermax facilities are successful in achieving the intended goals of safety, order, and control. They suggest that supermax is good option for segregating, incapacitating, and controlling violent and disruptive residents. However, interestingly, they also found that many wardens believe there are alternatives to supermaxes, which include rehabilitation, increased training for staff, and perhaps disbursement of particular residents to other facilities as a way of increasing safety and control. A related study is criminologist Robert Johnson's 1990 book, *Death Work*. This book examines living and working on death row in America's prisons with considerable attention to the psychological and physical demands on and harms to custodial staff. However, death row is just one type of RHU and in many ways is decidedly different from more generalized RHUs. Additionally, there is a litany of scholarship on burnout and stress among correctional staff, primarily correctional officers, but few of these works consider these ills for staff within RHUs specifically.

A Preview of This Book
The story in this book is mostly one of intense and prolonged pain, frustration, sadness, worry, fear, and confusion. However, sprinkled into these negative experiences are glimpses of hope via coping, reflection, agency, and sheer grit. The harms endured in the RHU are acutely felt by both residents and staff. In no way do we mean to belittle or make light

of the fact that one group (staff) gets to leave prison and go home, perhaps to their family and loved ones, at the end of each working shift—to a home they *do* call their own, outside the walls, fences, and razor wire. They get to see the sun and feel it warm their skin. They may attend religious services, visit friends, eat the food of their choice, kiss their children goodnight, hug their spouse or partner, and sleep in a comfortable bed, feeling relatively safe. While these perks of daily living are inaccessible to RHU residents, the damage to both mental and physical health caused by living and working in the RHU is real, and it is in so many regards exceptionally heart-wrenching.

To cage or be caged is not the only question worth asking. Instead, examining how these cages (that we already have in place and use readily) affect both the keeper and the kept is perhaps what matters most immediately. But these issues are complex and nuanced, and sometimes they defy logic and rational thought processes. Psychological indices on surveys and narrative accounts from only one side of the bars do not present a holistic picture of RHU harms; they do not allow for perception or incongruent thinking—yet that is precisely what residents and staff often wrestle with during their time in RHUs. One day, things seem easier and fear lessens, and another day (or perhaps within just an instant), fear intensifies, grief abounds, and life looks arguably more difficult. Exploring these perceptions nestled within the complexity of staff members' and residents' lived experiences yields a fuller, if sometimes more confusing picture of the impact of RHUs. To really understand and grasp the complexity of RHUs requires a thorough understanding of and an intense reflectivity regarding their purposes and goals. Without this degree of rigor, we cannot, and will not, create and adopt any informed and humane change. Living and working in RHUs provides a steady dose of risk; it hinders relationships of all kinds. The rules are unclear and often misunderstood. Reentry (or the eventual leaving of any kind) is hard to imagine, and virtually no one, not staff or residents, possesses a strong belief that anything will ever change for the better.

The central argument of this book is that RHUs create and maintain a sense of *masked malignancy* for both residents and staff. Malignancy is something that tends to produce deterioration and death. The RHU malignancy is the intended and unintended harm that comes to both staff and residents nearly every moment they spend in the unit. It is a disease, a cancerous growth that may exist for years without notice, and yet it is still present, lurking, harming, debilitating, and potentially killing. RHU harm is masked in several ways. The mask or cloak the harm wears is intentional, hiding behind the guise of safety and security. It is also masked purposefully to deceive or fool those within the RHU into believing that they deserve to be there, that it will help them learn and grow, and that it is for their own good.

In addition, there is what the residents and staff do to contend or cope with the masked malignancy. Even before its presence is confirmed, most understand the malignancy is both possible and probable—and much more likely in the RHU than in other carceral spaces. At some point, the malignancy becomes known in one or more ways, but it is often too late or too difficult to fully remedy. The harm is already done, and although staff may leave the unit and residents may also exit at some point, both groups take with them the inevitable pain, anguish, and suffering caused by or correlated with their RHU experience. Yet, both residents and staff persist. They fight internal and external battles to live and thrive with the malignancy haunting them at first and then later staring them in the face.

Within the RHU, residents and staff develop a *tenacious resilience* that guides them through the RHU experience and helps them cling to the hope that something better awaits; it must. The resilience is also masked in some ways because many staff and residents do not know or understand they are, in fact, coping. Their narratives, though, make it clear that each group finds interpersonal, personal, relational, or spiritual support within themselves and from others while in the RHU. Some of this occurs internally—in their own hearts and minds—and is thus difficult to discuss or describe. Some happens via conversations and interactions (even if limited) with others. Other strategies for resilience emerge via particular experiences or interactions that manifestly or latently reveal to residents or staff an external and, at times, tangible pathway toward resilience. These may arise from mundane events such as a book passage or a word, a nod, or a shared experience. Or they may occur through more obvious events such as a conversation with an RHU resident or staff, a visit from a psychological staff member, or a chance to talk with researchers about their experience in the RHU. These moments can breathe life into an individual and make the masked malignancy seem tolerable, surmountable, or even absent—if just for an instant.

Life in the RHU as a staff member or a resident is not easy to understand because it is often not easy to explain. Capturing the narratives of

RHU time can provide insight into the harms and coping that occur in these carceral spaces, locked away from the rest of the prison and from what feels, to many, like the rest of the world. To start the journey toward understanding, really understanding, the next sections provide an overview of both living and working in the RHU.

Living in a Hole

By both resident and staff accounts, RHUs are prisons inside prisons. On the unit, residents and staff are in near complete isolation from the outside world, with no contact with friends and family and with little or no natural light. The grey concrete or cinder-block walls remain cold to the touch no matter the temperature inside or outside. Each RHU generally contains multiple pods (groups of cells), and each pod includes two or more tiers of cells along the walls with strong steel doors that make loud metal-on-metal sounds when they slide open or closed. Each door contains a small rectangular window (roughly six by ten inches) and a similar sized rectangular locking metal slot with a hinged door that only opens from the outside. There is slight gap where the cell door meets the wall, enough to pass a paper through or talk and be heard, but not wide enough for a finger or pen to poke through. Cells on the unit's perimeter sometimes have windows, but while some external light may filter through, the thickly frosted glass often eliminates any view of the sky, clouds, stars, grass, or trees. The black metal-grid staircase leading from the unused day room in the center of the RHU's first floor gives way to a raised walkway to the upper tier's cells. The walkway, too, is a metal grid so that anyone on it, as on the stairs, is always visible. The dayroom reveals its former purpose for the unit, when residents were free to mingle, play games, and watch television in each other's company. Today, the metal tables and benches (all bolted to the concrete floor) remain, but years of nonuse render them obsolete. Each floor contains two shower cells at one end of the upper and lower tiers. At one end of the unit, large, shatterproof, one-way windows look into the dayroom. Staff in the hallway outside the unit can see onto the unit through these windows, but residents cannot see out. There are also strategically placed cameras at the corners and on the ceiling of each pod and the broader unit, which make all cells and areas visible from the unit's external control room. Cameras point directly into a few cells so their residents can be watched 24/7. These camera cells are used primarily for suicide watch or violent residents. Depending on when you visit, the RHU air carries scents of bleach, chow, remnants of OC spray, or sweat. There are often no visible clocks in the RHU so except for wristwatches on staff members, residents must rely on their senses, meal and count times, and television programming (if they are in a unit with a communal TV and it is on) to determine what time it is.

Residents' cells contain roughly 98 square feet of living space and contain a steel-framed bunk bed with two thin mattresses, a metal writing desk and stool, and a steel sink and toilet (no seat). All of these are bolted to both the floor and the wall. Residents are allowed minimal property (more for AC residents than DC residents), but all property must fit into one or more filing boxes or footlockers (depending on classification status). Residents typically receive one pillow, one blanket, one sheet, one towel, and unless they are on AC status, standard hygiene products including powdered toothpaste, a bar of soap, and an institutional toothbrush (roughly three inches long and flexible). After intake, residents also receive a copy of the RHU handbook, an institutional pen (also about three inches long and flexible), two pieces of paper, and perhaps a couple envelopes. While AC-status residents may also have televisions, some commissary, tablets, and radios (if they had them previously or can purchase them), DC-status residents are allowed none of these amenities within their cells.

Count time occurs at least three times a day. During count time, residents must remain locked in their cells (no movement for showers, yard, etc.) and must stand at the door to be counted. The count process in the RHU is generally quicker than in general population (due in large part to the lower number of residents and immobility), but count is not cleared (so that residents can return to whatever they were doing before) until it clears in the entire institution. Typically, this process takes forty-five minutes to an hour, but on days when residents in general population cannot be found easily, a count may take several hours.

Food and prescriptions arrive at the unit from dining and medical services at designated times. Meals are served on hard plastic trays unless the resident has used their tray as a weapon, "held it hostage" by refusing to give it back during collection, or is on suicide watch. In those cases, the resident receives a Styrofoam meal tray for an amount of time deemed suitable for their infraction. Correctional staff deliver meals through cell door wickets and collect them the same way. Residents generally have about twenty minutes between tray drop-off and pickup to consume their food. All residents eat the same meals, prepared by the prison kitchen staff, with a few exceptions for special diets such as Muslim, kosher, vegetarian/vegan, diabetic, and low salt. Psychological or medical staff deliver prescriptions in small paper cups through cell wickets too, at specified times, with a cup of water. Food and medicine delivery times do not include much chatter or interactional conversation between staff and residents. With some occasional talk of logistics, these processes are largely transactional.

All movement in the RHU is also relatively transactional. Residents receive an opportunity to shower three times a week, to attend yard five times a week in an outdoor cage with concrete flooring, roughly ten by twelve feet, and AC residents are allowed one noncontact visit with a nonlegal professional (i.e., a family or friend on their visitation list) once a month. DC-status residents do not receive any nonlegal visits. Depending on the institution, AC residents are allowed a certain number of phone calls (typically one) per month with family and loved ones. When staff transport a resident to yard or shower, the resident is placed in handcuffs (for men this is usually behind the back, and for women, in front of the abdomen). Men are also placed in leg irons and belly chains and tethered to a waist chain (leash) prior to movement. Movement of residents generally involves two correctional staff. If a resident finishes shower, visitation, or yard and no correctional staff are available to transport them back to their cell, the resident will wait for the correctional staff to return for them. In our experience, this process can take as little as a few minutes but in extreme cases may take over an hour.

RHU residents receive reading materials by filling out a request for books, which are delivered in about a week. A book cart is stocked with the requested books and wheeled to the RHU. In most RHUs we visited, residents may only have one borrowed book a week. Several residents report that if a book they request is not available, they will not receive any book that week; no substitutions are offered. Residents are not allowed to share or trade their library books or any of their other possessions. In some RHUs, correctional staff have installed thick plastic anti-fishing mats in front of all cell doors to prevent residents from attaching a string (generally pulled from bedsheets) to an item and casting it to another resident's cell. In places without these mats, fishing (also called throwing a line or a kite) is prohibited, but an RHU can, on occasion, resemble Spiderman's web with all the lines crossing the dayroom. Residents report sharing items via fishing, including books, toiletries, paper, pens, envelopes, stamps, and among AC-status residents, commissary items (including better hygiene products and snacks).

Working in a Hole

Staff working in the RHU experience it in many of the same ways as residents: no natural light, gray concrete floors and walls, lots of steel, and for all intents and purposes, locked on the unit, although not within a small cell. Each cell locks, each pod of cells locks, and the unit itself remains locked for most of every day. Staff do not have the ability to unlock unit doors; rather, they must stand in front of a camera for identification or press the call button to enlist an officer in a control unit far from the RHU to open external doors. Although staff can open wickets in cell doors, the cell doors themselves can be opened only by someone in the RHU control room.

Two additional locales for RHU staff are the control room (commonly called "the bubble") and the lieutenant's office. The bubble is a small room that looks like the inside of an electrical closet. The room is generally hot because of all the electronic surveillance equipment running in the room. To get to the bubble, staff wait for entry through a locked door in the unit's main corridor and then travel up a narrow staircase. Typically, one CO is assigned to work the control room on every shift. This officer sits behind a shatterproof-glass window overlooking the main hallway in the RHU (the hallway that contains the doors to the RHU pods). On the table in front of this CO are a host of monitors and lighted buttons. The monitors show live feeds from every camera in the RHU pods and the broader unit, and the buttons open every locked door except the main unit door (which is controlled by staff in the prison control room). The walls are adorned with hooks holding waist chains (leashes), handcuffs, leg irons, and belly chains. You may also find other equipment in the bubble such as flashlights, walkie-talkie radios, OC spray, and other supplies. In several bubbles we visited, Styrofoam cups littered desks and filled trash bins, and the smell of brewed coffee and cigarette smoke wafted through the air. Supervisors regularly puffed cigarettes (against the rules in all of this state's buildings) in the bubble's bathroom or storage closets.

The other room frequented by staff is the lieutenant's office. Sometimes the lieutenant and sergeant share a larger room, and sometimes there is a separate lieutenant's office with an adjoining space containing one or more desks or a small conference table, or both. Staff use this space most often, gathering during downtimes and breaks, drinking coffee, talking, and making shift plans. The lieutenant's office typically houses the cell assignment board, which contains small identification cards with pictures of every resident on the unit (in all pods and cells) and their cellie (if they have one). The board also has particular codes that indicate if a resident cannot live with a cellie or if they have a special diet. In a process that staff call the "inmate shuffle," "the dating game," or "match.com," the lieutenant and other staff members make changes to cell assignments on this board and add notes relevant to securely supervising each resident. In these offices, staff also find bulletin boards or papers and posters taped to walls that include information about new or existing policies, trainings, and prison events (such as potlucks, picnics, retirements).

The RHU also contains an office for psychological staff; an intake room complete with a strip-search cage, a psychiatric counseling room (with a small steel cage for residents during therapy); a property cage where resident belongings from general population are examined, logged, and, depending on AC or DC status, distributed to residents; a room for resident performance review meetings; and a law library. There is also a bathroom and a drinking fountain for staff in the main RHU hallway.

Researching and Organizing This Book

The narratives in this book come from data collected by a large research team (directed by the author) of twenty-six faculty, graduate students, and undergraduate students. We interviewed 351 RHU residents (26 percent) and 95 RHU staff (62 percent) in seven prisons in one US state. We also observed the RHU staff performing their duties, including working in the bubble, doing cell-to-cell rounds, serving meals, counting residents, intaking and classifying new RHU residents, attending performance review committee meetings, signing up and transporting residents to the shower and the yard, and killing time through intense conversation in the lieutenants/sergeant's office. Five of the institutions were medium security, and two were maximum security. One prison housed female residents.

We collected data on every shift, even overnight, but we interviewed residents only when movement to secured and confidential interviewing locations such as visitation rooms or strip-search or psychological cages was possible (primarily between 8 a.m. and 4 p.m. but not during meal, count, shower, or yard time). At times, we interviewed staff in private offices (for confidentiality), but generally staff interviews took place off and on throughout the workday as we accompanied staff members during their shift. Instead of using a formal, rigid interview questionnaire, each research team member memorized a list of interview foci and conducted what we call conversational interviews, weaving in the focal areas throughout an informal and casual conversation. We recorded all fieldnotes by hand on paper in a private area of the RHU immediately following each interview and at the end of the day because recording devices are prohibited in the prisons we visited. We did keep a pen and paper on hand during interviews to jot down quotes or any information we wanted to follow up on or not forget. Our data collection totaled 1,666 hours in the field and exponentially more hours recording, coding, and analyzing data. The last chapter, "Behind the Walls: About This Book" provides greater detail about the data collection and analyses processes.

Each chapter of this book presents the perceptions and views of both residents and staff in seven US RHUs. Whenever possible we provide full verbatim quotations from both residents and staff. In some cases, we paraphrase conversations to help readers understand the context and weight of the spoken words. Each substantive chapter is broken into sections containing narratives first from residents and then from staff on the chapter's topic. The five thematic chapters cover subjects that emerged as a conglomeration of both researchers' foci and research subjects' interest.

Chapter 2 highlights the immense risk that both residents and staff feel inside the RHU. This risk manifests both mentally and physically and extends far beyond the confines of the RHU and into personal lives outside prison. Chapter 3 considers how residents and staff perceive relationships with each other, broader management and administration, and individuals and communities outside prison. Here, the stories reveal raw truths about loss and love that painfully highlight the ever-reaching tentacles of the RHU. Chapter 4 exposes the dark underbelly in RHUs where neither residents nor staff holistically understand, believe in, or uphold rules, policies, and practices with any consistency or regularity. This amorphous and ambiguous understanding of rules yields great uncertainty among both residents and staff and contributes to feelings of risk and unstable interpersonal connections. Chapter 5 provides insight from residents and staff regarding reentry (broadly defined as the eventual exit from the RHU or prison). In this chapter, many residents tentatively long for a return to the general population and achingly (yet cautiously) desire post-prison life. However, most staff (all but one) do not regularly or with much hope ponder RHU or prison exit for residents. Their sentiments on reentry suggest a crucial, yet missing, link between RHU and post-RHU and prison and post-prison life that potentially endangers residents, staff, and whole communities. Chapter 6, the final substantive chapter in this book, considers the hopes and dreams of residents and staff regarding RHU reform. The cavernous differences between resident and staff perspectives in this chapter are eye-opening. Although residents dare to only minimally imagine RHU reform, their thoughts center on humane treatment that could provide or restore dignity. Staff, however, overwhelmingly want RHU reform that further incapacitates, sanctions, punishes, controls, and indeed harms residents. The final chapter in the book offers closing comments summarizing the overall themes and offering a healthy dose of suggested avenues for advancing carceral policy and practices to help, not harm, both residents and staff in US RHOs. This last chapter focuses on human beings—on their treatment and care and the ability of a containment and employment system, like prisons, to operate in ways that *provide* rather than *withhold* opportunities for the growth and development of all humans. Finally, "Behind the Walls: About This Book" offers a roadmap for future researchers considering prison or jail investigations. It pulls back the curtain on our research team's thoughts, considerations, actions, and reflections in the hopes that this book will mark only the beginning of a long line of scholars, scientists, students, activists, and everyday people who think about—and work toward the betterment of all people—even those largely forgotten in the holes society rarely recognizes or acknowledges, like the RHU.

CHAPTER 2

Risk

RISK, OR THE FEAR OF IMMINENT DANGER, is both a survival instinct and a potentially debilitating emotional response to the unknown. In nature, this might look like what prey experience as they contend with the risk of predators. This space—where prey engage in daily living while navigating potential harm or death from a hungry predator—is commonly called the "landscape of fear." Coined by Y. F. Tuan in 1979, the landscape of fear is the conscious or unconscious perception of risk.[1] In knowing (or perceiving) one's risk, an individual (or animal) may estimate the cost of the risk and make decisions regarding the actions or behaviors necessary to avoid or lessen risk. While the landscape of fear emerges both intrinsically and via learning, it is a decidedly difficult concept to measure scientifically. In some ways, the landscape of risk (or fear) is aligned with spatial qualities, but in others it emerges internally as a type of cognitive map. For example, antelope may have both an innate concern about the risk of predators such as lions *and* may operate to avoid increasing risk. They may also feel or sense danger or see the lion and react accordingly. To reduce or stop risk, prey like antelope may travel in groups, forage near an area of cover, and possibly even signal alarms to other antelope if a lion is near. For humans, the landscape of fear includes additional dimensions because humans are capable of more advanced cognitive reasoning than are animals. In his book *The Landscapes of Fear*, Tuan notes that in addition to fear stemming from alarm and anxiety, for humans, fear also stems from shame and guilt. These cognitive and visceral responses to fear add additional layers to risk perception and complicate the landscape of fear overall. Tuan contends the landscape of fear exists in the mind and in physical and measurable space. As such, the landscape of fear occupies both the cognitive/psychological and tangible environments.

The carceral environment is a definitive landscape of fear. In correctional institutions such as prisons and jails, risk is a part of everyday life and a constant reminder of where you are. For many residents and staff in RHUs, risk takes on additional meaning. It is a defining factor of who you are: I. Am. At. Risk. I. Am. A. Risk. To feel at risk, to show fear or worry is considered by many (particularly in these environments) as a sign of weakness. To be a risk is to show fear or worry about harming self or others and the stigma that accompanies the perceived label of being risky. Both RHU residents and staff regularly maintain a tough exterior persona to signal to others that they can take whatever the RHU world dishes out. A common belief in this world is that if there is a place for weakness in prison, it is certainly not within the RHU.

The challenge of understanding risk within RHUs is that we have no universal definition for the term.[2] Risk is the gray space between something negative with the potential to occur and something negative with a good probability or likelihood of occurring. For those experiencing feelings of risk—or the landscape of fear—the unknown is a large part of the problem. Because risk is difficult to define or conceptualize, it is often unnecessarily simplified or unduly complicated in an individual's perception or fear of danger. It is a masked malignancy.

It should come as no surprise that prisons are dangerous places, places that evoke feelings of risk for both those living and working behind the walls. The very image of a prison with its fortified enclosures, razor-wire fencing, and armed towers signals for many that it is a place where bad things happen. But such imagery just scratches the surface of life inside. For both RHU staff and residents, risk involves concern for ongoing or eventual physical and mental harms. These include the psychological deprivation of spending day after day confined within small spaces, with little or no natural light, few opportunities for human contact or communication, and a highly regimented schedule that provides routine via a heavy dose of monotony. The well-documented, if somewhat controversial, literature on the negative effects residents endure in supermax or RHUs (including death row) reports new or exacerbated mental health conditions such as anxiety, depression, suicidal ideation/tendency coupled with some evidence of increased loneliness, anger, agitation, and irritability.[3] Other studies suggest physical effects including headaches, shaking, heart palpitations, and palm sweats—all linked to distress.[4] In other research, residents report feeling overly sensitive, having difficulty with focus and memory, and experiencing a variety of mood disorders. In extreme cases, some residents experience psychopathy in the form of "hallucinations, perceptual distortions, and thoughts of suicide."[5] Although these effects exist in prisons generally, the likelihood of their developing or worsening in RHUs increases exponentially.

For staff working in RHUs, the negative effects are much the same, although scientific inquiry into correctional officers and other carceral staff specifically within RHUs is limited. One study found intense and pronounced alienation present among surveyed and interviewed correctional officers broadly.[6] That study connects alienation to feelings of normlessness (not knowing or understanding the rules, and existing norms breaking down and no longer guiding behavior), powerlessness, and meaninglessness that occur via an occupational role that limits teamwork and comradery with everyone they come into contact with: supervisors, coworkers, and residents. Although that study considers prison staff in general—not specifically within RHUs—it lays the groundwork for understanding, investigating, and interrogating the emotional and physical harms staff endure working in a unit housing those referred to as "the worst of the worst."

If both staff and residents feel devastatingly at risk in RHUs and in prison more generally, the nature of that perceived risk is elusive and difficult to define. Risk comprises the real and the imagined—the wondered about and the experienced before. It represents a black box of apprehension facing both RHU residents and staff regarding their own and others' mental and physical safety. In its immediate form, the risks to self and others living and working in RHUs are most prominent, but lurking in the background is the risk of harm to others in the outside world—the free world, including families and children. Residents wonder, "Are they OK? Is someone harming them when I'm not there to protect them? Do they even miss me?" And staff worry, "Will my family/friends leave me because I work too much? Is working in this prison affecting my mind? I hope I don't bring home what I experience in here. Will I survive another day in this place?"

Moreover, risk determines the way residents and staff interact with peers and each other. Suspicion or fear of risk creates, among both groups, heightened awareness and intensified sensibility that danger is just a moment away. In the narrative accounts that follow, residents and staff detail some of the causes and consequences of living or working in temporal locales where the consistency of risk overwhelms thinking and subsequent actions to a point of acute redundancy. Perhaps most interesting in resident and staff tellings are the pronounced and fortified links between both groups' experiences and perceptions of risk. That is, two groups spend significant time in the same environment, but with different positions and power, yet both groups experience heightened worry, fear, and unease and both cite similar origins for these feelings: the very unit where intensified protocols and practices are supposed to quell, control, and subdue risk but instead deepen perceived risk and harms beyond good reason.

Residents on Risk

One of the first things you notice when talking to RHU residents is the absences on their faces and bodies. Skin tones that may once have seemed full of color and vibrant now appear dim, faded, and lackluster. Many body frames are skeletal, with hunched postures, and features are gaunt with eyes lowered or haunted. It may remind some of caged animals in a zoo pacing back and forth, longing for a different life. While this is certainly true for many penal environments, the stark contrast of RHU life is palpable. Even the staff seem different. They are somehow languid, and the heavy burden on them is nearly visible as they walk the halls and move around the unit. They barely speak to anyone, including each other. They too have faces that only faintly gesture to a life lived outside these walls. Their minds seem busy with thoughts about the tasks at hand and the rawness of the reality here. The recirculated air is thick, and echoes ripple ominously from the cages beyond the locked unit doors of men banging, yelling, murmuring, and shuffling. The RHU residents are in prison because they were a perceived risk to their external or carceral communities. They are in the RHU because they were a risk, or were at risk, in the general population. But containing them here does not negate risk; in the RHU, risk becomes enhanced and takes on new, sometimes hidden or masked forms.

Physical and Mental Health Risk

For RHU residents, risk is overwhelmingly expressed as a condition born of not knowing. This includes not knowing if or when they might receive food, go back to general population, be physically harmed, harm themselves, or see a psychological or medical staff person, as well as the not knowing what comes from witnessing an unexplainable harmful or negative event. It is notable that, despite the many rules and policies for RHU living, life for residents is still unknown. This causes great worry among RHU residents as even the most taken-for-granted events like meal and medication delivery may, at times, seem unreliable. When asked to describe his life in the RHU, resident Jericho thoughtfully replies:

> I was recently not fed and went to bed hungry. . . . I'm hurt and scared and beyond tears. I been in the RHU for two years—the hole. They gave us a TV back here. Well, it's supposed to go off at 12 a.m., but a 10-to-6 officer [an officer working on the third shift, from 10 p.m. to 6 a.m.] . . . already let us know he's upset they put the TV back here, so he turns it off at 10 p.m. when he come in on his shift. [Last night] he did it and we all covered up our windows to get a lieutenant 'cause they don't respect just asking for one. They respect violence. . . . But I'm scared to death. I have no family or friends to tell. I can't tell the higher-ups here. Not only won't they believe me, they already knows what goes on. How we are abused, harassed—sexually also. How guards bring their problems to work. They know. So, I can't go to them. I don't have a life. I should be released by 2022, but maybe I should kill myself.* You know, to escape the racist attacks, the starvation, the harassment, [and] my mental health depression that the psychologist won't help me with no matter how much I beg for help. I'm just scared and don't know who to go to.

Jericho expresses fear and concern over what he perceives as physical and mental abuse. He worries about being hurt or having to physically defend himself. He worries whether and when his next meal will come.

---

* Whenever residents express thoughts of self-harm or harming others, our research team takes these concerns very seriously. We clarify all language and thoughts with residents and if the thoughts seem to move from casual thinking to actual planning, we inform correctional staff. This practice aligns with good ethics and our IRB (human subjects) protocols.

He expresses a distinct lack of hope in the process of being heard and having his concerns remedied. He feels alone, scared, sad, and hungry.

Other residents note the same. The risk of mental health problems triggered by the RHU is deeply concerning to them. "I feel at risk of losin' my mind," confides Froame, an RHU resident who has been in the unit for many years. Cook, another long-term resident, confesses, "Never thought about killing myself before coming to RHU [but] knowing [I'll be] in here a long time [and not] see family . . . so, every day I think of killing myself. Every day." A third resident, Stiles, reports, "When a person's been in the hole for so long, there's only so much you can do to bring them back." These quotes reveal residents' pain of not knowing if they are, or will be, safe or if they are, or will be, forgotten. While some residents suggest they feel safer in the RHU than in general population—largely due to heightened security and decreased movement and interaction with correctional staff and other residents—it is largely a paradoxical predicament. It is clear from residents' narratives that there is *no safe place* within prisons.

Risk and Trust

It is not just thoughts of risk that plague RHU residents. They also witness and experience harm in many tangible ways, which contributes to intense feelings of risk and fear. Many residents suggest that physical risk comes from letting down your guard and being or becoming vulnerable. RHU resident Kinder notes that risk is "the opposite of not being vigilant. . . . It's possible you could be harmed in the shared cage." It is unclear if Kinder is thinking of the "shared cage" as the RHU or his cell within the unit, but either way, the fear emanating from the unknown is pervasive.

RHU residents contend that one of the most dangerous situations is being handcuffed because it renders them unable to defend themselves against harm from staff or other residents. Handcuffing is a safety protocol to keep staff safe from residents during moves and transit within RHUs, but for residents it creates an uncomfortable level of vulnerability stemming from a general lack of trust and much experience. Resident Randell notes, "If you're cuffed up, you can't defend yourself from inmates who are violent. I'm worried the guards won't defend us from them [other residents] either." Similarly, resident Worell remarks, "I don't trust the COs, I have seen grimy things. You can be cuffed from behind and get tripped by the CO and pushed around. There has been no time where I have trusted the CO." These examples suggest that an RHU safety protocol designed to minimize risk actually exacerbates it by creating the perception of safety for staff but enhancing perceived risk for residents.

Handcuffs are only one part of the larger story of physical risk though. Residents repeatedly recall incidents of physical harm they witnessed or personally experienced. RHU resident Sorrell admits he did wrong in the RHU, but complains that the process for rectifying that wrong created undue harm to him:

> I was assaulted by five COs when I came here. I was in the wrong because I had drugs, but how they got me was wrong. I still have bruises and can't get medical. It was the wrong way because there was no investigation. I was told to strip and when I was taking my pants off, they thought I was going for something. CO choking me trying to get the drugs out of my mouth. Went about holding me wrong with like eight COs holding my limbs. I wasn't given meds or an X-ray. I was having chest pains and pressing my button [an in-cell emergency button residents may use to call medical or psychiatric staff], and it took two days for them to take me out. Could have been having a heart attack, so I don't feel safe.

Residents regularly retell stories of incidents that they do not seem to fully understand. In these shared narratives, residents reveal much about their hidden fears of harm within the confines of the RHU. RHU resident Jackson recalls an incident where another resident accidentally spilled food on a CO and the aftermath that he endured:

> Yeah, the other day, an inmate splashed a CO with his tray and it was an accident. First reason to come onto the cell, he [the CO] did. No camera, no lieutenant. Fifteen minutes later, they run in with a shield and nail him [the resident]. When the camera was coming, the other COs started yelling "Camera! Camera!" to let him know the camera was coming.

In relating this incident, Jackson describes how an event that he believed was accidental was mishandled with power and abuse by COs. He explains that the COs did this without oversight (without the lieutenant or cameras). The lack of protection left Jackson feeling uneasy and at risk in the RHU environment. Jackson fears that an incident like this may one day happen to him. For Jackson and others, even an accident may have dire consequences.

Other residents tell similar stories of perceived mistreatment by correctional staff leading to emotional distress or physical harm. RHU resident Motes recalls:

> A brother needed toilet paper. He waited for five hours for the toilet paper. The CO threw it up to him and let it roll on the floor. Then you have to use it to blow your nose—that's dirty, that's abusive. Another guy got maced and they shut his water off in his cell so he couldn't wash it off. They [COs] asked me on the way here (to the visitation room to do this interview just now), if I'm going to tell you about them or if I'm going to tell you about someone else. Staff in the RHU are handpicked because they have an aggressive attitude.

Likewise, RHU resident Connelly talks about correctional staff treatment:

> If you tried to kill yourself [in another prison in this state], they would just mace you. They do that here. . . . I don't know why you mace someone who tried to kill themselves. You know, like the guy's just hanging there—I don't know what he's going to do to you. It's demoralizing. They spray you [with mace] and then put you back in a cell where they stripped your bed—sheets, everything. Psych staff takes all of your property out of your cell when a guy tries to kill himself. Some people fake [suicide]. . . . One guy right now, he has refused to eat until they shut his light off. The COs have control over that because only certain cells are able to turn their lights on and off. They never turned his light off. For seventeen days he hasn't slept. They took the toilet paper out of his cell for punishment. They refused him socks, boxers—things a man needs here when it's cold. He hasn't eaten in seventeen meals. They just took him to medical this morning because you guys [the researchers] are here. They were supposed to take him to medical after nine days [the policy is after three]. Now, they're going to take him to medical and force-feed him. He'll come back dead. He just won't be there mentally. Totally dead.

It is abundantly clear in Connelly's narrative that he does not understand several RHU rules regarding policies and punishment. He sees residents who are suffering in pain receiving control rather than comfort. A resident who attempted suicide was pepper sprayed and left without sheets or other items to keep him warm. A resident enduring many sleepless nights in cell where the light remained constantly on was starving himself to get attention. His act was not working in the way he intended. Instead of earning darkness so he could sleep, he was going to be force-fed and suffer as a consequence. Connelly's concern for these residents is evident and heartbreaking. But it is not just about altruism. Connelly's statements conjure feelings of worry that these residents are him, that he, too, will experience control, punishment, and negative consequences if or when he seeks comfort, attention, or humanity.

Other residents describe the physical harms they have endured and the scars these harms have left both mentally and physically. Resident Relic recalls, "I don't feel safe around the COs either. They use excessive force. An example of this would be continuing to assault someone after they've been pepper sprayed. And then they don't even let you shower after you've been pepper sprayed. They throw you in your cell." Resident Houser has similar feelings and experiences:

> It really weighs in on my mental health. My anxiety is worse because I'm not around people. They won't release me because of my misconducts, but only some of them are true, and some of them are false. The COs have physically assaulted me multiple times, one of them knocking me unconscious on my birthday. Another time they threw me in a cell with nothing for three days for no reason. I was also sent to POC for punching a wall, and then I was supposed to go to the doctor because of my hand and I never did. One time I tried to give the COs a Mother's Day card to send to my mom, and they sprayed me, saying I was trying to attack them. I've been sprayed over ten times since I've been in the RHU.

In these examples, RHU residents wholeheartedly express fear of the unknown and the perceived known. When pressed for explanations regarding why or how these incidents occur, residents do not have easy answers. For some specific incidents, the policies regulating them are misunderstood, confusing, or unknown. In cases for which specific policy does not exist, correctional staff discretion takes over. Residents express both fear and exasperation over not knowing how correctional staff will handle a particular event. It seems to be anyone's guess how things will unfold; even for similar incidents, the reactions are not always the same. This uncertainty weighs on residents as they try to navigate the RHU in the hope of surviving it with their physical and mental health at least moderately intact.

Risk and Unmet Needs

Finally, given the risk-inherent nature of the RHU, residents seem acutely aware of their needs for programs and services. They also holistically understand that they are not receiving the help they require. This mismatch of perceived needs and available or delivered treatment and services creates a feeling of risk among residents that yields pain and emotional harm. Many residents, such as Howlen, recount not receiving medications or psychiatric or medical assistance and fearing they could possibly die without anyone noticing:

> My mental health has gotten worse. I've been sick and throwing up. I'm peeing blood. You might not want to know this, I'm HIV positive. There's no treatment here, and I don't get any help. When I ask for help, they say I only do it for attention.

Likewise, resident Delancy openly discusses his substance addiction and the need for continuing his medically assisted treatment program while in the RHU. He says, "I'm going through withdrawal because I'm not on suboxone, which I think is what's causing my suicidal thoughts. I'm losing weight, I can't sleep, and I'm claustrophobic." Resident Johnson discusses his hearing loss, noting that he is waiting for his hearing aids but correctional staff have not brought them after many days in the RHU. "Whenever they feel like giving me hearing aids, I'll get them." RHU residents Cox's and Jiles's comments concur as both fear major medical inadequacies or suffering without anyone noticing. Cox remarks:

> Physically, I feel safe in here, but mentally no. We don't have much contact with staff or inmates so I'm not afraid of getting hurt, but I am worried about my mental health. It's tough in here. I also see so many people die of heart attacks in here. Now I'm not a doctor or anything, but I know heart attacks come in stages, right? Like there are signs over time? And yet no one seems to notice a heart attack in here until it's too late, and the dude's dying. There's a real lack of care in here—seems scary to me that no one is really looking out for me. That I could be near death or die, and no one would know or care.

Jiles expresses a similar sentiment:

> Something happens and they put you on meds, but don't give you no groups, no coping mechanisms. I got no therapy after stitches. Just meds. The vast majority don't. . . . At what point do you notice that something

is wrong? Two weeks ago, an inmate committed suicide (*shakes head sorrowfully*).... To hear staff laughing and joking—that's someone's family member.

The narrative tales of fear, risk, and worry in the RHU paint a desperate picture of humans enduring immense suffering within the confines of a specialized unit where intense and regimented rules and regulations are supposed to incapacitate those who were not doing well in the general population units and keep them safe from self and others. But what does safety entail? In spite of all the rules and regulations, so much is still in a constant state of flux for RHU residents. The continual worry about what may happen or what is happening is not an easy problem to rectify for the hundreds of individuals held captive in these units. With safety protocols in place to ensure basic survival (life), much of the life is draining out of the residents in countless other, seemingly unnoticed or masked ways. This is not a malignancy or a burden that residents alone face, however; correctional staff working in RHU units carry similar risk burdens with them daily and the effects may be as critical for the mental and physical safety of the correctional team as for the residents.

Staff on Risk

It should come as no surprise that staff working in custodial environments feel and experience risk. After all, prison is where society incapacitates the people who many believe cannot or should not remain in the community. Correctional staff technically have the role of the confiners, but experientially they are also incarcerated. In the prison workplace environment, there are not only coworkers and supervisors whom they find troubling, but the job itself entails supervising individuals that society feels are unsafe, unable to follow societal norms and rules, and unwilling to control their own actions and emotions. Moreover, the RHU is filled with a siphoned-off portion of those folks who also could not follow *prison* rules. Many staff refer to RHU residents as "the worst of the worst, "the severely troubled, and "those who must be babysat."

Staff working in an RHU, like residents living there, describe the unit as dangerous, hectic, under-resourced, and chaotic. Although some claim to become desensitized after days, weeks, months, or years of working there, others note the toll the RHU takes on their personal and professional lives. They gibe about or ruminate on their anxiety, panic, and loathing while grimly detailing resident attacks they or others have suffered.

Many discuss troubles at home with children and family; some recall visits with therapists or psychologists; and yet most admit they put up with the day-to-day pains they endure for a secure salary, benefits, and a nicer-than-most pension. It is worth mentioning that no correctional staff we spoke to (in this or any other study) ever declared corrections as their first or favored employment choice. Yet, they continue to enter the gates, walk the hallways, don the equipment, and suffer the anticipated and actual risks of a workplace that endangers their physical and emotional health from the very first day they punch the time clock; throughout the decades, they work to earn a long-awaited and hard-earned retirement.

Physical Risk

Of all the risks correctional staff face in their daily work, physical risk is the most discussed and perhaps the most outwardly feared. Although many staff suggest that the RHU is in fact safer than general population units because residents are locked in their cells nearly twenty-three hours a day and cuffed and chained during all transports and movements, this feeling of safety goes only so far. Nearly every correctional staff person relayed vivid narratives of resident-to-staff violence that signal the real dangers in this work space. CO McConnell recalls a particularly violent incident that still bothers him:

> About a year and a half ago, an inmate attacked a guard here and slit him badly on the arm. It still hurts me to think about when that happened. I was sitting on my couch at home at 9 a.m. on a Saturday and I got the call. My family member also works here [at this prison], and she's actually the one who called me, and I came right in. The guard had to be triaged here before going to the hospital because the cut was so deep and he was losing so much blood that he would have died if he was not treated here first before going to the hospital. That incident still haunts me because he easily could have died. Things changed in the wake of that incident. You really learn a lot from a situation like that. You learn that you never know what could happen on any escort [accompanying a resident somewhere]. You learn that you have to handle any escort as if it is a situation in which someone's life could be in danger. It still haunts me to think about that day. It also makes me wonder how police officers can possibly do their jobs—any car that they walk up to could have someone in it who is armed and aiming to kill them. You just realize

that things could go south at any minute. In public, I am super-vigilant, because there is much more randomness out there—anyone could have a weapon; anyone could be violent.

Several residents expressed a sentiment similar to McConnell's. The risk stems from unknowing. Because anything can happen in the randomness of RHU living, McConnell, like the residents, is always at risk. This risk, in turn, manifests through worry and fear, and McConnell understands that much of this risk is outside his control. He just has to endure it, live with it, and wait to see if and in what ways he will experience harm.

Correctional staff note that despite security measures, residents are still a constant and continual risk and a reminder that the RHU is dangerous and vigilance is required. Interestingly, this sentiment is nearly identical to risk identified by residents. Officer Jones states: "Most guys are cuffed when they come out of their cell, but they can still kick, punch, etc." He says he isn't really afraid of that, though. What he is most afraid of is "inmates pissing or shitting on you and giving you HIV or hepatitis through bodily fluids, or not being able to retaliate if they hurt me."

Likewise, Officer Kent notes, "I didn't sign up to have a cup of shit thrown in my face," and Officer Cade reports, "I wouldn't say that this unit is safe. I've been hit or slashed. I mean, recently one of the inmates hit me with a food tray. I thought we were cool, but he got agitated about something and decided to take it out on me with his food tray."

Officer Kelley remembers, "Last week, I was spit on, I got hit by an inmate when I had to go into their cell to cut them down [they attempted suicide by hanging], and I got a tray thrown at me. I mean, it's hard, but these guys down here are at their lowest right now. Can't take it personally."

CO Smith remembers, "We found a whack [homemade weapon or knife] buried in the food a few weeks ago. Someone had stuffed it in their tray. You constantly have to be aware and check everything."

Even a prison chaplain notes the likelihood of violence, saying, "There's always a chance that an inmate will take an opportunity to hurt someone."

CO Vox adds that it is not just danger from residents that concerns him. The RHU takes a physical toll in other health-related ways. He says, "It's like freshman year for us. We eat bad food and there's a lot of stress. Lots of us die young. You retire and that's it."

In these numerous examples, both custodial and noncustodial staff working in the RHU relay personally receiving an injury at the hands of a resident or hearing of an incident where resident-to-staff harm was possible or imminent. These narratives graphically detail risk via the constant concern of the unknown—what might happen or what might happen again. Staff, like residents, face this risk every minute in the RHU. Over time, it wears on their mental and physical selves—bearing down like an ever-present ache without an easy remedy. But worry about possible physical harm is only one way staff feel at risk. There are countless RHU risks lurking.

Personal Health Risk

As in many institutions, safety protocols forbid correctional staff from bringing food from home into the prison (to stop contraband). Instead, they eat their meals in the staff dining hall—food prepared by residents and made from government surplus stocks. In prior times, the prisons in this state and others had bakers and chefs (mostly residents with these skills) prepare both resident and staff meals. However, cost-cutting to food budgets eliminated this perk. While meals are still prepared in house, no special training or expertise is required to work in institutional kitchens. The menus are pre-planned, and the portions and ingredients are tightly controlled and dictated by DOC menus. Correctional staff in most of the prisons in this state do have access to a daily salad bar in their dining hall, complete with iceberg lettuce, carrots, eggs, cheese, croutons, cherry tomatoes, cucumbers, mushrooms, and a variety of dressings. At times, there is also cottage cheese, coleslaw, macaroni salad, or fruit (generally bananas and apples—the same fruits available to residents as they spoil less quickly and cost much less than other fruits.) While these offerings may give the impression of healthy choices, it is far from a gourmet selection. With very few nutrients in the slim offerings, dark leafy vegetables, nuts/legumes, whole grains, and the like are a rarity. Staff receive milk, coffee, concentrated lemonade, and water as beverages, white bread slices, and the high-sodium, high carbohydrate food options provided to residents. Standard hot fare includes fried and breaded chicken patties, partial-beef patties (made with soy filler), white buns, ketchup, mayonnaise, canned veggies (such as corn or green beans), and instant mashed potatoes with instant gravy. Eating this type of cuisine two to three meals a day for five or six days a week for twenty years definitely takes its toll on cholesterol levels, weight, and heart function. Correctional staff commonly report related health conditions. Couple these dietary choices with very little physical movement on a shift, and you certainly have a recipe for a host of chronic health issues.

Mental Health Risk

It is not just the actual or anticipated physical health harms that feel risky to correctional staff. Staff, like residents, also face and experience very real mental and emotional harms. These risks are often unnoticed or are in some cases, too difficult or too complex to understand, let alone discuss. For the many correctional staff who put words to these risks, the intense burden placed on them via working in the RHUs affects them personally in a myriad of ways. They readily discuss stress and burnout, and some go further into the accompanying anxiety, post-traumatic stress disorder (PTSD), depression, anger, irritability, and sadness.

Sergeant Lenox notes some of the causes of these mental health risks: "For the officers, they are working directly with inmates one on one, nonstop. It's loud. They have a lot of documentation to do. And then you throw crisis elements on top of that."

CO Michaels worries about events that may occur: "It can get frustrating. It's more mental for me than anything. Because I do sometimes wonder what's going to be next. What are they going to do that puts me in danger?"

"I'm constantly on edge here," says CO Taylor.

CO Kincaid describes some specific incidents: "If I told you all the things I've seen, you'd probably cry. I saved a guy once—he cut open his stomach and started pulling out his guts trying to get to his heart. Another guy cut open his artery and by the time I got there, there was blood all over the cell."

Many staff shared their battle wounds with researchers during our visits. Long or deep scars, bruises, and formerly broken bones, as well as the anxiety that accompanies contact with blood, urine, semen, and feces.

Some correctional staff add raw details to their perceived and actual emotional risk, noting their struggles with mental illness. CO Madar details his personal struggles with panic and anxiety:

> I once had a panic attack here. I think the environment here probably triggered anxiety I didn't know I had all my life. I went to my personal doctor and got antianxiety medication. I mean, they probably won't tell you, but most of the staff working down here right now

are on antianxiety medicine. I started seeing a therapist. I stopped seeing her because I didn't really care for her, but I'm definitely open to going again.

It's a hard thing to get used to because you're going from one life to another and having to find a way to draw a hard line between the two. And, when you're using two to three unplanned use of forces a week, you have to look at it as amusing—you have to have a raw sense of humor to be able to get through it all.

CO Ault concurs: "The longer you're there, the worse it gets. You get depressed, agitated quicker."

CO Tanner goes a bit deeper into what he considers a crucial ongoing issue for correctional staff, PTSD: "A lot of us are open about our PTSD and how we manage it. But I will say, there's a lot of guys working in the unit that turn to booze. I think you see higher rates of alcoholism, suicide, and divorce from guys not getting help." This narrative turn from self to family, or how the RHU affects correctional staff when they are not at work, reveals a deeper layer of risk or harm that RHU correctional staff face. These concerns highlight the importance of correctional staff relationships with their family via staff perceptions of risk.

Family Risk

If it is not enough that correctional staff experience work-related mental health issues that may affect their family life, they also, at times, endure threats to the physical safety of their family. Although threats from residents to harm correctional staff and their families once they are released may seem far-fetched and unlikely, stories of such incidents rest heavily with corrections personnel. Almost everyone working in corrections knows of a story where the nightmare of post-release violence came true. In 2013, in Colorado, a released prisoner disguised himself as a pizza delivery man and violently murdered the highest-ranking correctional official in the state. Just over a week earlier, the released prisoner had told a fellow prisoner via recorded phone call that he was going to do something that would help inmates on the inside and that the event he was planning would likely end in his own death.[7] There are countless reports from correctional staff of residents threatening them and their wife and children. Although very few actual incidents exist, they represent an unknown risk that correctional staff endure and take seriously.

CO Ripper recalls, "I once had an inmate down here tell me he was going to fuck and rape my family members and then kill them." CO Vock reports, "When I enforce the rules here, there are repercussions on me. It's putting my reputation and potentially family life on the line because I try to do my job."

The effects on correctional staff's mental health are not confined to their homes. Staff also experience changes in the way they behave in their neighborhoods and communities. These changes weigh heavily on them as they come to realize how much of their work life etches prison on them, comes home with them, and becomes a part of them. For many, this is the part they are not particularly proud of. They express the details of these changes in matter-of-fact ways that signal their desensitization or their acceptance of their new normal after beginning work within the RHU. Perhaps most telling is CO Blake's recollection:

> You don't notice changes in yourself. Others do, like your family. But that's corrections. Doesn't matter if you're in [general] pop[ulation] or the RHU, you change. Like, most people when they're in public see happy people. I see people who could attack me. . . .
>
> [One time I went to a] comedy show, and a guy who was walking in front of me had been tased and "wasn't cooperating." [I] jumped on him. It was an *immediate* reaction—an instinct. The cop thanked me after. But normal people wouldn't do that.

CO Normandy concurs: "I isolate myself more now. I'm antisocial. I don't like crowds. I like my back to the wall. It's part of the job, but if I could choose? No, I wouldn't do it."

CO Countryman adds: "I have noticed that I've changed. . . . I always sit with my back towards the wall and facing the door. I find myself scanning public spaces more. And, like everyone around here, humor gets darker."

CO Wilder expresses similar sentiments: "Yeah, I've changed. I can't stand people anymore. My sense of humor has changed—more twisted now. And I can't sit with my back to any door. I always have to be facing it. I also have a hard time trusting people on their word or on face value."

CO Able discloses: "I stereotype at the grocery store. . . . I think every fat white guy I see is a pedophile."

In these quotes, COs share narratives about the ways working in the RHU affects them during nonworking hours. They are more cautious, more vigilant in public environments, and they worry about their safety and that of their family. Although stories like this are common in many law enforcement occupations, COs are often left out of these conversations, as workers who exist on the fringe of law enforcement, seemingly operating as keepers of those whom other law enforcement arrest, detain, and send to carceral environments. COs describe their role as being babysitters, zookeepers, and parents of RHU residents. But their stories of punishment, control, fear, and worry suggest that their roles are far more diverse and often require a heavy lift, one that is beyond their training and expertise.

Risk and Organizational Trust

It is not just the mental strain of supervising residents that causes mental and emotional risk for correctional staff. Some department of corrections (DOC) or managerial decisions and policies intended to better secure both residents and staff and provide relief from harm may have an opposite effect on staff. For example, numerous RHU staff complain about the lack of staffing and other resources that plague RHUs and that they feel puts their physical and emotional safety at risk. Some of these decisions may stem from the changing tide in corrections as the metaphoric pendulum swings from more punitive resident treatment to more rehabilitative options. In this regard, many correctional staff fear for their job and reputation and resent new or reformed policies, such as using pepper spray more sparingly.

CO Inger reports:

> We shifted. . . . You used to have a problem, crack the door and regain compliance. Now you're lucky if you can even spray guys you need to, and then you have to do a ton of paperwork to even spray a guy. Then they're down here several more months before they get transferred, and they're still causing problems.

Other correctional staff note that COs may feel their power and authority is at risk with the new DOC policies that include incentives for RHU residents. A prison chaplain says: "I know that the use of incentives leads to frustration with line staff [COs]. They view this as their authority is in jeopardy, and this could lead to their safety being in jeopardy."

For other correctional staff, the problems with the system begin with their supervisors. CO O'Conner says his stress comes from upper management. . . . Honestly, I've been deployed twice and it's worse than combat. . . . At least in combat you know what you're up against every day . . . you're not just fighting inmates, you're also fighting upper management [about] policy . . . they don't give you enough staff to do what they want . . . it's nonstop and it comes into your home . . . you see things other people don't see . . . it's just like combat . . . It's morbid . . . am I even [mentally] right anymore?

CO Cole responds to a question about any changes he would like to see in the prison, noting:

Honestly, I'd get rid of the super[intendant]. He'll come down here and tell us all that we are the hardest working guys in the jail. Then three weeks ago, there was no AC [air conditioning] in here. There isn't a water fountain down here either. They don't take care of us. There's a real disconnect because the administration doesn't know what we're going through. They like to say they do, but they don't. Neither of the deputies have been a CO.

Numerous correctional staff suggest that the lack of policies, or at least the lack of policy follow-through or enforcement, creates risk for them. For example, there is a policy that all residents are to be double-bunked for their first seventy-two hours in the RHU. This policy stems from the DOC studying and determining resident suicides most often occur when residents first enter the RHU. To combat this, many DOCs now require new RHU residents to be housed with existing RHU residents in a type of informal "suicide watch." One unit manager, Merreck, explains, "We have to put an inmate in a cell with a cellie for the first seventy-two hours. There's a directive in place. But it's not easy to do because of restrictions." These include formal and informal policies about which residents can cell together based on considerations such as past criminal involvement, codefendant status, and prior prison misconducts. "I haven't seen a policy," he says.

As this conversation continues, Merreck and other correctional staff begin talking about a resident whom they believe will most likely hurt or kill someone or himself. The psychiatric staff member says, "Sometimes we care about suicide; sometimes we don't." Merreck expresses confusion about how to implement a policy when there are restrictions about who can cell with whom in the RHU. He also reveals another aspect of policies that he finds confusing: the policy is not uniformly enforced and in this case, he has yet to even see the official policy. Without having read the policy, Merreck is unclear about what the formal rules are. When the psychiatric staff member notes that sometimes they do not care about suicide, Merreck is left wondering what those times are. He feels at risk of not implementing or wrongly implementing policy regarding celling residents because he has never actually seen the policy.

Other correctional staff express feelings of being overwhelmed in the RHU by the amount of work they do, the high volatility, and even the many different roles they play. CO Jamison says:

> It's a stressful place. Management seems like they're out to get you rather than the inmates. They dump so much on RHU officers. When we cut corners to get stuff done, we get reprimanded. We're short-manned. We're expected to do med and psych's job and transport, feed, yard, shower, run groups, and whatever else gets thrown in there like (*he motions to the side, where we can hear an inmate kicking his door repeatedly*). We'll probably have to suit up a team to go in there and deal with him. He's a repeat cutter [a resident who frequently self-harms by cutting his skin]. We'll have to go in in and change his bandage.

Correctional staff also discuss a litany of other policy and DOC concerns. They regularly complain about the inadequacy of their options for medical or psychiatric assistance. When asked about his health, CO Kendal sarcastically comments: "The medical care for the inmates is better than the care I have."

CO Tellez notes: "There were more staff suicides in [this state's prisons] last year than there were inmate suicides."

CO Kent concurs: "You don't realize how stressful it is inside the walls. You're in jail too. You feel like an inmate. Inmates are running institutions, and you have to do things to take care of them, and no one is taking care of us."

Although several correctional staff mention DOC options for mental health such as the State Employee Assistance Program (SEAP), a hotline accessible via web or telephone for correctional staff and their families for help with mental health issues, most feel this service is inadequate in a number of ways. For example, CO Normandy suggests:

> There should be some kind of immediate help. If you call SEAP, it can take up to a week before they get you set up to see a psych. There's nothing immediate. We just had a staff member commit suicide. If you're in that situation, you need help right away.

One particular policy that spurs a lot of talk among correctional staff regarding the ways it affects their perceived risk in RHUs is the Prison Rape Elimination Act (PREA). PREA, which focuses on organizational and individual response to rape and sexual violence inside carceral institutions, passed Congress with unanimous bipartisan support in 2003. While in theory, PREA provides oversight and an avenue for residents to officially complain about sexual violence in prison, it creates a heavy load of administrative issues for correctional staff. In addition to the bureaucracy that accompanies PREA, correctional staff also complain of false claims made against them by residents in what they perceive as attempts by residents to harm them. A PREA claim—even one that is unfounded—goes on a correctional staff member's record. During an open investigation (which can take months), it is visible in any background check by outside viewers. The chapter on relationships discusses PREA's effect on correctional staff's family life in more detail, but in this chapter on risk, we offer a few examples of the perceived harm and potential fear and worry PREA causes as an institutional policy.

CO Thompson describes his stress and frustration regarding PREA:

Honestly, they use lots of things against us. For example, the PREA process. They will PREA us in retaliation for not passing things across the pod or doing them other favors. The PREA process needs to be completely overhauled. I have more PREAs filed against me than anyone else down here because I follow the rules. I have even gotten a few PREAs on my day off.

(Interviewer nods.)

Yeah, it doesn't make sense to me either, but essentially, the inmates get mad at me about something and make something up. I've had a few of them date an "event" that happened on a day that I wasn't even working. For a while, they were PREAing us so much, that we had to put up a board saying which inmates had PREAs against us because we couldn't go on the pod that they were on while there was an open investigation. It was getting so out of hand that the board was necessary to figure out who we could ask to go on the pod with us to do movement or pass out trays. At one point there, every one of us had at least one PREA filed against us. It's their way of keeping us off the blocks. It's actually really disheartening as an officer because effectively the inmates can choose who works around them by doing this. I'm essentially getting PREAs filed against me for doing my job. Because I do property a lot, I get PREA'd a lot because I really enforce the property rules.

In this example, CO Thompson describes residents using what he feels are largely illegitimate PREA claims to manipulate staff policies or procedures that residents do not like. He relates his anguish with PREA to how resident property is handled and delivered.

COs Meeks and Mendell have similar concerns. Meeks states: "So, I got PREA'd off the block, which means that an inmate filed a PREA allegation against me. Immediately, I have to be taken off the block for an investigation. That's why I've been floating" between positions and posts within the institution. CO Mendell adds a bit more context to a similar PREA story:

> Oh yeah, I've been PREA'd down here before because I didn't let someone go to the library. Can you believe that shit? When you get PREA'd, you are put on PREA restriction while there is an investigation. Which means you can't work on the post you're on and you have to move, all because of a flagrant accusation. Honestly, when you get PREA'd, it's really stressful. First, it's always going on your record, which is stressful. Then, you're assigned to a new unit or post, so it's stress to be doing something new. Stress of what if you get more and it looks like a pattern when it isn't? The stress of what if the administration thinks it's a legitimate claim?

For CO Mendell, the risk of receiving a PREA complaint is high, but perhaps higher is the risk of stress that comes with someone believing that complaint, finding it true, and the damage just an accusation can do to a career and reputation.

Although correctional staff express in great detail how the RHU produces real and perceived risk, they are also quick to point out how ill prepared they feel in this immensely challenging environment. The DOC in this state and in many US states provides a variety of training (via academy or continuing educational classes) for correctional staff. These include some standardized and widely used courses, such as Crisis Intervention Training (CIT), which focuses on de-escalation communication techniques, and Mental Health First Aid (MHFA), which emphasizes understanding mental health disorders and techniques for intervention. Additionally, individual DOCs offer some localized training, including the RHU School. This week-long, in-person mini-academy teaches recruits the ins and outs of working within an RHU. Although these courses are available and common, many correctional staff working in RHUs suggest they have not received many of these trainings before or while working there, or the trainings are not all they feel they need. In several examples, like the ones below from COs Trotter, Casey, and Malek, these correctional staff perceive risks doing their RHU jobs without adequate training and skills.

CO Trotter notes: "I didn't get training or anything to work in the RHU. I'm supposed to go to this class [RHU School] but I haven't gone. They just gave me the policy and said, 'Read this.' It was all stuff that you learned on the job anyways."

CO Casey recalls: "I did go to RHU School after seven months of working down here. They paid me to go, so I didn't mind that, but it was a joke. Half the class was about what we should do in situations which I knew most from working in the unit. And the other half was about how they (Central Office) would burn us if we didn't do it that specific way."

CO Malek provides more detail about how he feels undertrained for the situations he faces in the RHU: "You have to be able to adjust. A lot of the inmates here are mentally ill. You have to be stable and be able to deflect." During our interview, an inmate was kicking the door very hard, and Malek said: "Like that. You can't get aggravated. You just have to be ready to do your job if it escalates." Malek referred to interpersonal communication (IPC) skills and emphasized their importance in population. He said: "You use the same IPC skills, but it's different back here. It's quite the adjustment. I'm not trained for mental health. I don't know the first thing about cooling a schizophrenic person down." Malek also noted he'd never been to CIT, MHFA, or RHU School trainings.

Although the correctional systems of this and other states do place a priority on training staff, administrative and other burdens create gaps between the date a staff member begins a position and the days that trainings are available and open for their participation. For example, even though the DOC notes it ideally likes to provide staff with RHU School training before they start working in RHUs, this rarely occurs. Typically, RHU School is not on the work site. For most staff members, going to RHU School means spending several nights in a local hotel and spending a work week in training rather than on their RHU post. With staffing shortages and shifting resident numbers in RHUs, security takes precedence over training. As a result, COs often work in the RHU for many months, or longer, before receiving training via RHU School.

Many COs also have family obligations that inhibit their ability to travel away from home for training. So, a CO may postpone scheduled training to a date that works better with family commitments. As a result, COs may work within RHUs for a long time without having had much or any formal training. This lack of training leaves them open to several risks: the risks involved with not knowing what they do not know; the risk involved with relying on coworkers and supervisors for formal policy guideline interpretation; and the risk involved with facing complicated and often dangerous RHU situations without having the mental and tangible tools to adequately handle them.

Risky Living, Risky Working
The US Department of Labor's Occupational Safety and Health Administration (OSHA) defines workplace violence as "any act or threat of physical violence, harassment, intimidation, or other threatening disruptive behavior that occurs at the work site. It ranges from threats and verbal abuse to physical assaults and even homicide."[8] For both residents and staff in RHUs, workplace violence is the norm rather than the exception. While violent acts (physical or emotional) may not occur every day in these carceral spaces, the threat is ever present and the memory of past harms continually haunts. For both residents and staff, the not knowing, the not understanding, and the inability to prepare for what they may face wreaks havoc on both bodies and minds. Residents and staff report similar patterns and concerns regarding risk including receiving (or fear of receiving) physical harm such as punching, kicking, hitting, slashing, and killing. Both groups also report similar real or perceived psychological harms. Science overwhelmingly reports that real or perceived risk may trigger a range of physical and emotional symptoms including frustration, anger, agitation, difficulty sleeping, fear, anxiety, stress, depression, and annoyance.[9] These ongoing threats are often linked to PTSD.[10] In correctional contexts such as prisons, much research finds these environments operate as "high risk, low safety" environments,[11] where physical and psychological threats greatly affect residents in a innumerable ways.[12] Moreover, rather than PTSD—which may be present for many RHU staff and residents as a result of or as a precursor to time in the RHU—some research on children living in dangerous environments posits a concept called "ongoing traumatic stress" that plagues dangerous environments where individuals constantly and continually face traumatic experiences and events and the resulting effects:

> Chronic danger imposes a requirement for developmental adjustment—accommodations that are likely to include persistent PTSD,

alterations of personality, and major changes in patterns of behavior or articulation of ideological interpretations of the world that provide a framework for making sense of ongoing danger, particularly when danger comes from violent overthrow of day-to-day social reality, as is the case in war, communal violence, or chronic violent crime.[13]

In persistently dangerous environments, such as the RHU, residents and staff fear, worry, and expect harm. While it might be argued that this is true for carceral institutions in general, the RHU exacerbates these fears for many residents and staff as security is heightened, movement is further restricted, and more safety precautions taken, because at its core, the RHU houses those who cannot behave or live in general population units. What is left is a population of the kept whom no one else wants to deal with and a population of keepers who must secure them to prevent harm to themselves and others.

One irony, however, stems from the fact that while a primary RHU goal includes protecting residents from themselves and others and punishing residents for misconducts and maladaptive behaviors, the exhibited control creates intensified feelings of risk for both residents and staff, perhaps more intensely than anywhere else in the prison. These feelings of risk emerge for both staff and residents from similar circumstances. Staff feel the risk of not getting nutritious food, while residents feel the risk of no food at all. Staff mental health problems lead them to express a macabre sense of humor about their job, while residents feel the risk to their safety amplified because of the sense of humor of the staffers. In the RHU, risk lives, it thrives, and it incapacitates everyone in this space with a fear and a strain of worry that no human should endure for a day, a week, or for any portion of their life. Here, risk transforms from something individuals fear to something they become.

CHAPTER 3

Relationships

HUMANS ARE A DISTINCTLY SOCIAL SPECIES. For most of us, this means we form and develop relationships with other people. These relationships serve a variety of purposes. For example, infants and small children are nearly entirely dependent upon caregivers for survival. As we age, our relationships generally grow, deepen, and mature, just as we do. Interpersonal relationships commonly provide emotional sources of support and love, and they may also provide functional support by way of networking and learning and physical support through touch and intimacy. Except in extreme cases, most humans need and desire relationships with others (or at least one). However, in RHUs where risk is ever present, forming, building, and maintaining relationships is decidedly difficult. Issues related to trust and authenticity edge up against the challenges that come with fear and worry. This paradox leaves many RHU residents and staff in a critical conundrum: in a living/working space surrounded by people, the desire for relationships exists but the possibility of finding and keeping positive relationships is deeply difficult.

With some methodological challenges (of sampling, operationalization, conceptualization),[1] numerous studies in psychology, medicine, and nursing, among other disciplines, detail the many benefits of positive interpersonal relationships, including decreased depression, anxiety, and stress, as well as improved immune function and mortality.[2] Studies on meaningfulness also find relationships to be a key factor for individuals to achieve happy, productive lives.[3] In his somewhat limited and occasionally controversial work, Eric Klinger reported that 89 percent of the college students he surveyed responded that personal relationships are what most makes their lives meaningful.[4] Subsequent work found 85 percent of survey takers ranked friendship over power, excitement, achieving recognition, and comfort in life. For individuals living in free society, finding, forming, and maintaining interpersonal relationships is often a challenging, if usually greatly rewarding, endeavor. However, for individuals confined or working within carceral settings, the processes of maintaining a relationship with those they left outside prison and building or sustaining relationships with those within prison are infinitely more difficult. Behind the razor wire and the walls relationships represent potentially dangerous undertakings for many reasons.

For RHU residents, the ability to have relationships with anyone and the ability to find individuals to engage in meaningful relationships with are extraordinarily limited due to mistrust and fear. In most circumstances, residents are locked into a one- or two-person cell for roughly twenty-three hours a day, seven days a week. There are no programs, there are no activities (save shower and yard, which generally occur only three to five times a week and for short intervals), and for many in an RHU, the world feels smaller with few, if any opportunities to really connect with anyone. With removal from general population, RHU residents encounter a different penal environment. In some ways, this is akin to moving to a new neighborhood or attending a new school because RHU staff and residents are mostly unknown to newcomers (unless, of course, the resident has been to the RHU previously). The rules and policies are different inside the RHU; movement is largely curtailed, always beginning and ending with strip searches, and the resident wears handcuffs, belly chains, and leg irons throughout. RHU residents walk a foot or so ahead of their escorts—typically at least two staff—tethered by a leather leash. Virtually alone in every way, residents struggle to secure meaningful, positive relationships with individuals within and outside of their carceral confinement environment.

Staff in correctional systems receive training and frequent reminders about boundary violations, which include strong warnings never to reveal anything personal about themselves to residents or within their earshot. Staff are also acutely aware of the reasons not to develop personal relationships of any kind with residents, such as friendship, doing favors, or sexual or intimate relationships. Although this constraint may seem intuitive, it is anything but simple. The RHU is a work environment unlike almost any other; correctional staff work alongside each other knowing very little, if anything about each other personally (save friendships built during after-work activities). At work, they are trained to avoid talking about their kids, their spouses, their sick dogs, or their mothers. They cannot share a meal with the several hundred residents they are paid to control, contain, and supervise, in contrast to the way that many workers in the for-profit and nonprofit worlds share meals, celebrations, or comradery with their clients or customers. For all intents and purposes, it is an anomic (normless) space for social interactions, where the standard rules of human and personal engagement simply do not apply. Given these incredibly rigid limits coupled with the work of confining humans in dehumanizing ways, relationships often suffer or are ill formed. This is the case for all categories of relationships, including staff-resident, resident-resident, staff-staff, resident-family/friends, staff-family/friends, and staff-DOC.

Residents on Relationships

Despite the tremendous overlay of fear, risk, and confinement, RHU residents can and often do form relationships within the broader prison environment, and specifically within the RHU. Most often, their relationships are with other residents (commonly cellies or neighbors), but at times the improbable occurs, and residents form relationships with correctional staff members. Additionally, RHU residents regularly try to establish or maintain familial relationships with kin and friends outside prison. This is overwhelmingly difficult while they are in the RHU because visitation is exceptionally limited for AC-status residents and disallowed for DC-status residents. Phone calls (for AC-status residents) and mail (for all RHU residents) are still possible though, so RHU residents sometimes attempt meaningful relationships with free folk in these ways.

Residents' Relationships with Cellies

Although it may seem counterintuitive, the RHU environment is anything but solitary for many residents. Due to overcrowding and suicide-watch protocols (requiring new RHU residents to be bunked with existing residents for at least their first seventy-two hours in the unit[5]), many RHU residents share a cell with another resident (a cellie). For many, the cellie relationship is the only, or the closest relationship they have within the RHU. This may be a positive and fruitful relationship (someone to talk to, share items with), or it may be a total nightmare. The cells in the RHU are roughly eight by twelve feet, and a double cell will have a bunk bed, a sink, a toilet, and a writing desk. To share this space in general population—where out-of-cell movement is much more routinized and regular—is challenging. But in the RHU, where both cellies are confined to this small space about twenty-three hours a day, it is definitely cramped and privacy is unheard of.

In the RHU, the cellie policy works a bit differently than it does in general population but has some similar features. Prison staff do not house residents together if they are members of different or rival gangs, if one has a sexual offense, or if one is considered a danger to other residents (for example, if they have seriously harmed or killed a cellie), and residents with certain classifications for mental health are not housed with other residents. Where the RHU differs though (at least in the prisons we studied) is that staff generally (although not always) ask residents if they will take a cellie and generally provide some information about the incoming cellie so that the current resident may make an "informed" choice. It is a bit of stretch, though, to say that RHU residents have a choice. In fact, if they refuse a cellie, they risk receiving additional RHU time or a reprimand, or both. Many residents do, however, refuse particular cellies for a variety of reasons and risk the repercussions.

For example, resident Kelley states: "I don't want to be in a cell with a murderer/rapist." Resident Matta says he refuses homosexual cellies. Resident Baraka articulates what a number of other residents also stated: "If he looks suspicious, looks like a pervert, child molester, [or] rapist, I don't take him." Baraka, who is Black, adds that there is a racial component to his decision making: "I take him if he's Black and then I figure out if he's a nut or not." Although these examples do not cover all the reasons residents accept or deny a cellie, they do yield a window to some of the factors residents consider.

In the staff office in the RHUs we visited, staff constantly reconfigure a bulletin board hanging on the wall that lists all cells and current residents. It is a bit of a matching game to read incoming residents' files and figure out who they can cell with and who they should be kept away from. The data on the board resemble the complicated algorithms at work in an online dating program. Staff consider a resident's history of predatory behaviors or risk of victimization, institutional misconducts, race/ethnicity, gang affiliation, sexuality, religious affiliation, temperament, and any other demographic or personal features before making cellie requests and placement. Moreover, placing a new RHU resident is not as simple as finding an available cell. Other residents may need shuffling to find the right matches, so current residents move often and get new cellies with some regularity.

Residents colorfully describe what makes a good or bad cellie. These narratives resemble college-roommate or apartment-mate narratives, but with the addition of a perceived potential risk of harm. Good cellies are those who keep to themselves, keep the cell clean, are interesting to talk to, respect property, provide (relative) privacy, and are not mentally ill or violent.

Resident Booth describes his preferred cellies like this: "Somebody who showers, who's not aggressive, not a pedophile. Somebody you can trust. You gotta be compatible 'cause you're locked in twenty-three hours a day."

Resident McElhone similarly notes that a good cellie is someone compatible, who "has the same interests—gives us something to talk about."

Resident Roker adds that a good cellie is someone who "shares commissary, laughs together, watches TV, and smokes cigarettes, too." (Smoking in this prison system is banned, but contraband exists, even in the RHU.)

Additionally, resident Campbell notes that good cellies level him out and keep him calm. He says, "Everything makes me upset. I might not get bread on my [meal] tray, and I might blow up about that. When I have a good cellie, I don't care about stuff like that."

Regarding bad cellies, residents describe the same character flaws repeatedly. Resident Rooker sums it up best when he says a bad cellie "don't wash his ass. Snores. Annoying. Gets on my nerves. And eats everything up that you buy [with] nothing to put on the table to pay you back." In general, good cellies are compatible, at least relatively trustworthy, and friendly. By contrast, bad cellies are dirty, annoying, greedy, and have little or no respect for personal boundaries.

For most residents with cellies, the experience bifurcates into good or very bad. In basic terms, resident Copes explains: "I've had a cellie for about a month, and he's a good cellie. He's clean, and there are no arguments. We respect each other's space."

Resident Trotter concurs, adding this about his cellie:

We're on the same page; had the same traumas. We've been in the same places. We're both from [the same city]. We can relate more. We're always talking about stuff. We talk about [our hometown]. We get along really well. [On a typical day I] wake up, eat, do some writing, talk to my cellie . . . more writing and then the same stuff over again.

Resident Gleason and his cellie do things together: "We wake up, do puzzles, watch TV, tell stories."

Resident Lopez states that his cellie "is respectful, clean, lets me sleep, not yelling out the door. He's got a good character. He gives me someone to talk to, relate with. We have similar morals; schedules. We have great stories. Time goes by fast."

Perhaps one of the most interesting aspects of cellie relationships is the rarity of deep and fulfilling relationships. For most, the cellie relationship is surface level—an acquaintance rather than a friend. Despite the close quarters and near continual interaction, for many RHU residents there is a level of trust and friendship they will not attempt with cellies.

"The cellie I'm with is cool. I don't trust him though," remarks resident Scott.

Similarly, resident Thompson states: "My relationship with my cellmate is all right. We talk, but I'm on edge. I don't trust him or anyone."

Resident Michelson adds: "Some cellies are OK, but they have to not be from where I'm from on the streets. I don't want him to know what I did."

In these conversations, residents openly discuss the limits to cellie relationships. For many RHU cellies, talking (without including too many personal details), watching TV, playing games or doing puzzles, writing, and sharing goods are mostly positive, but deep, meaningful conversations and relationships are uncommon. Most RHU residents do not forget who they are housed with and try to avoid situations where they may be physically or mentally hurt or taken advantage of. Most RHU residents have experienced a bad cellie in the RHU or in general population and have layers of visible and invisible scars from those experiences.

Bad cellies abound in prison, and the RHU is no exception. Residents regularly describe systemic issues such as the lack of privacy, but they also discuss the mental and physical pain that comes from harmful interactions with cellies.

Resident Cullen presents a detailed picture of his current negative cellie relationship:

> I don't like him. You get no privacy. I don't like anyone down here. I'd rather be by myself. I tried to refuse, but they [COs] threw me in . . . threatened to spray me. Try living in a bathroom with another person for forty-five days. The little shit bothers you. Like the way he presses the button on the sink. There's no privacy. I don't like anybody down here. My cellmate was already in the cell when I got down here. There is never really a good cellie in the hole. I'm sure I do stuff that bothers him, but I'm just doing my own thing, you know?

Resident Kent reports similar problems with his cellie: "To be honest, it hinders me. He sleeps early, and I like to read at night. But I can't because I'm trying to be respectful. . . . They just don't shut up. They yell and scream. They bang on stuff. I don't like noise."

Resident Tucker's experience resonates as well: "I don't like my cellie now. I have to worry about him touching my stuff when I'm out of my cell. I worry about what he's going to do to me at night. It's good if I don't have to worry about it."

And resident Wallace's cellie story gets right to the point:

> He's a problem. The one thing I can't stand is uncleanliness. Let me tell you this: a dog in a kennel knows when and when not to use the bathroom before it eats. That space is where it eats, sleeps, goes to the bathroom—everything. When [meal] trays come around, my cellie decides that's when he needs to use the bathroom. That's disgusting.

While the cellie relationship is the most common interpersonal interaction between RHU residents, it is far from the only one. RHU residents also interact with non-cellie residents, staff, and family and friends outside the carceral environment. These relationships also elicit both positive and negative feelings and provide only limited opportunities for or comfort within social interactions.

Residents' Relationships with Non-Cellie RHU Residents

The good-and-bad-relationship bifurcation extends beyond the cellie relationship within the RHU. This is the case even in an environment such as the RHU, where residents rarely leave their cells and have exceptionally limited opportunities for interacting with other residents or anyone else. In search of human connection, some RHU residents report forming and maintaining positive relationships with other RHU residents who are not housed in their cell. Because of limited out-of-cell time, some of these relationships occur in creative ways such as talking through air vents and toilets, and others first started in general population or even outside of prison. These relationships help pass the time, imbue a sense of connectedness or belonging, and provide assistance that formal institutional pathways or staff cannot, such as through talking, counseling, programming, or treatment.

Some resident perceptions of relationships with other residents are tales they perhaps tell themselves—thoughts regarding relationships they would like to have, relationships they once had, or relationships that may or may not be the same to the other person or persons. Other resident relationship narratives provide more concrete evidence of relational interactions and the outcomes of these encounters. For example, numerous residents talk about their positive, comradely feelings toward other RHU residents, saying things like "I believe these individuals won't sit by and watch something bad happen, but they're locked behind doors" and "Certain inmates with vibes like he might got my back. Doesn't have to be physical, it could be mental. We would keep a good relationship." These examples are about perceived comradery or group cohesiveness by one resident without the benefit of input or verification from all other RHU residents. But some RHU relationships bear the evidence of actual connection, rather than just private beliefs that a relationship may exist.

One important way to generate or sustain relationships is via talking. In the RHU, this occurs most commonly (aside from talking with cellies) by yelling through the doors and talking through vents, toilets, and the small space between the cell door (a heavy sliding door) and the wall. This type of communication often irritates staff, seemingly violating quiet rules in RHUs, but for residents, communicating with other residents may be deeply beneficial. Resident Trainer describes these RHU chats as valuable: "Certain guys all right. You might hear his voice, but not see his face. Next you know, you think he's all right." Again though, most of these relationships are surface-level and not overly personal or trusting, and they are often not private because others may overhear these interactions. Resident Kanter describes this form of interaction with some skepticism: "Some people I'm cordial with, but no real relationships."

In some cases, the resident-to-resident relational interaction goes a bit deeper than just the surface. Providing help to or receiving assistance from other residents illuminates a tangible way that relationships form and perhaps are sustained within the RHU. Many residents recall needing help when they first arrived in the RHU. They were unfamiliar with the rules and policies; they did not yet have any of their property; and they were often unsure of how to proceed. Resident Gasparis summarizes this experience:

> The staff don't tell you anything. I learn from the inmates. The staff wanna burn you. I didn't get a setup when I came to RHU. A setup includes a handbook and a blanket. I've seen guys laying in their cell in a jumpsuit, no blanket, nothing. I got [my setup] late at night. It happens where guys are left overnight without one though. [In cases like this] inmates help each other. The COs yell really low [softly when they're coming by with trays or for yard or shower sign-ups], and the inmates will holler it loud [so everyone hears and can get what they need]. You might not hear [a CO], and someone will yell, "Yard!" This happens at other jails too, because the COs want to do as little as possible.

Resident Ayer expands upon this helping behavior when he notes that other residents are "your only conversation—I wouldn't say trust. You bond. They're your information. They tell you, on Tuesday we do this, Thursday we do this. The staff don't tell you. The person next door does."

Resident Leeson reports he tries to help other residents in numerous ways because he (and others) feel they do not receive the help they need from correctional staff. "I talk to my neighbors. I try to be of assistance—if someone needs paper. The COs won't give it. We have to learn to fish it [pass a line between cells with an item attached]. If I notice someone isn't eating or is pacing in their cell, I'll ask them what's wrong?"

Sometimes, age is a factor in these relationships. For example, resident Spooner notes that he mostly enjoys talking to the "older generation. You can't learn anything from young inmates besides don't be stupid. The older guys have the jewels and gems [important things to say]."

Resident Timon expresses frustration with talking to younger residents despite his best attempts to help them:

> I talk to my neighbor. I keep it to a limit . . . talking to people. There's a lot of young kids. I try to talk to them. They listen to me for a minute, then they go back to their jitterbug shit, gang war. The younger generation is dangerous and they don't care. Some can be reached. The old days wasn't like this . . . you had to fight for your manhood. When I see them taking

the same route I did, I talk to them. Some listen. I tell them to stop calling women bitches. . . . I tell them to think about their mom, sister, aunt, cousin. They will learn. All they have is each other. Just have to get one [who] a lot of them look up to, they're eager to learn. People around them take them to the corrupt side. They're only sorry when they're in the hole.

Other residents detail how they help with legal or other practical challenges. Resident Jacks says, "I'm helping a guy in [cell] 22 with his legal work, and the guy in [cell] 9 helps me with mine."

Like many residents, resident Keller notes, "We all try to help each other. If someone's starting a gang war with a CO, we try to talk him out of it. We try to help each other with pens and deodorant. We hide it in the shower or yard."

Resident Tarik broadens the relational scope, saying residents often work to help certain individuals for the greater good. "There's no [personal] TVs on the pod [for DC residents]. So, we try to give everybody an opportunity to watch what they want on the [unit] TV. It keeps everyone calm to watch TV. If people bang on their door, we can't watch TV."

Other residents like Clayton, discuss the help they receive from fellow residents. He notes, "If my sugar's low, I yell to them from the door and they'll fish something back." Because fishing is a clear rule violation, RHU residents often risk more RHU time or other sanctions to help one another in this way. However, residents' comments on the connection such actions build between and among residents suggest that the risk of possible punishment is worth helping each other survive in this desolate place.

In terms of physical comfort or safety, very few residents express feeling fully safe in the RHU. However, numerous residents say they believe that if things were to turn violent, some or all RHU residents would likely defend one another. Resident Booker says, "There is one person on my [RHU] pod that I'm on good terms with. We can't talk through the vents [because their cells do not connect]. We say something to each other every now and then. I can depend on that one guy to have my back if shit hits the fan, [but] anything short of a guard beating me, I don't expect him to do anything." Booker, like others, reports that although he has faith that a fellow resident would defend and perhaps protect him, both context and circumstance create severe limitations on the depth of this relationship.

Resident Trunker iterates how he would help others if needed:

I don't trust inmates, but there are certain things I can't go for. I don't have to be friends. I'll stand up for that. In some places, inmates are loyal to COs, not to inmates. They get violent with other inmates. Would I sit back and let something happen to you? No. People have families. I could dislike you and [still] do that.

In rare instances, residents do express a deeper level of friendship forged in the RHU. These kinship-like bonds seem deeper, more completing for residents, and at times, even extend beyond carceral control. A few residents note they have solid friendships within the RHU.

Resident Zeller says, "I had one friend. He left here in April. I call him two or three times a week. He was a jailhouse junkie. He would stab someone for a strip of Suboxone. He's doing awesome now! He's running NA [Narcotics Anonymous] meetings."

Other residents note that their RHU friendships may extend beyond their time in prison. Resident Axel says, "I have one friend on DC. I'm engaged [to be married], and he's getting transferred [to another prison]. We have plans to move to New York together. I need to make sure he's OK and doesn't cut himself."

For other residents, a deeper relationship comes from other affiliations or previous knowledge of individuals. Resident Bryans says:

> Some of these dudes are like family. I'm a gang member. I'm a known gang member. We help each other. Some of these dudes have life and are more kind-hearted and caring people than people I've met on the streets. A lot of people do fucked-up things to each other, but a lot of people help each other [too]. We just happen to be in the same gang, like when we identify that you're one of us, you're automatically family, and you're expected to treat them as such.

Despite the relative positivity of some RHU resident relationships, residents have a nearly equal concern about the lack of or nature of relationships in this unit. Residents talk frequently about feelings of risk (as discussed in chapter 2) and the perceived lack of safety. They exude a lack of trust in everyone around them, including other RHU residents. For many residents this distrust precedes a type of self-isolation within the RHU that they use to keep themselves safer and even saner—a type of tenacious resilience.

Resident Nathan states: "No, I don't trust inmates. Sometimes the closest people to you are the quickest to turn on you. . . . As soon as you let your guard down, someone will disappoint you. And then you're disappointed in them and in you."

Resident Hanna agrees: "You give them the shirt off your back and then they ask you for your pants. You know the saying 'Birds of a feather flock together?' There's some slimeball people in here."

Resident Kelsey adds: "I don't trust anyone for real, *for real*. It goes against what jail stands for."* Likewise, residents Barufka and Thanos each report specific instances where trust was broken for them and led to a general mistrust of other residents.

> Barufka: You never know really. They could be your friend one day and enemy the next. Nobody can be trusted here. . . . I don't go to yard. It's really nasty out there. They get naked and throw shit on each other. I'm like, yo, we can fight each other and stab each other, but I'm not getting shit thrown on me. . . . A little while ago an inmate at another prison stabbed a CO in the neck and killed him over a towel. A fucking towel! You never know what these guys are capable of. You even have gang members fighting their own kind. The staff get mad at us for carrying weapons. Like, I changed my life around, but my reputation forces me to carry a weapon because when people get transferred here all they knew was the me before. You can't trust no inmate. The same dude that you trust is the same person that will stab you. I've been stabbed in the stomach and the head before (*shows interviewer the scar on his head*).

> Thanos: Majority are cons. I don't lie, but I had to learn to for persistence. An inmate would be persistent, and I would have to lie. That says to me I can't trust him. I was OK with this one guy—I was his tutor. But this guy attacks me for no reason. I had to defend myself. I got hole time for throwing a punch. I never expected it. We was cool. Shows me that I can't trust anybody. I helped him for months, then one day . . . boom! Where did that even come from? If that can happen, anything can happen. I thought we were all right.

As these quotes reveal, RHU friendship-like relationships are often heartbreaking and are sometimes physically damaging. Residents may

---

* A note about vernacular: prison residents regularly use the term *jail* to mean prison; they are simply discussing institutional or carceral settings. All residents in this study are in state prison, but many refer to their locations as jails.

be unpredictable and sometimes violent. These experiences help solidify many residents' beliefs that no one can be trusted. Resident Tully relays a heartbreaking moment in his RHU experience: "I used to talk to an old friend through the vent on the top of my ceiling, but one day I didn't hear from him from lunch until dinner. It ended up he'd killed himself from mental health issues." The thought that a relationship ended this way is overwhelming. Tully expressed intense sadness when relaying this story, and his retelling of the story seemed to suggest he believed their friendship had a level of trust preventing this type of event. But then, maybe all friends and loved ones of individuals who have died by suicide contend with these feelings of grief and guilt. Everyone may wonder, "What could I have done?" However, in the RHU, the answer is usually truly nothing.

Locked in a cell for nearly every hour of every day with no physical contact with other humans (except possibly a cellie) and no specifically sanctioned communication, residents face dark and lonely hours and the monotony of living in the hole. For those with cellies, that relationship can help cut through the boredom, or it can create new or exacerbated fears and stressors. This leaves many RHU residents without viable options for human interaction and relationships. It is a form of masked malignancy even if, at times, the mask is fully removed, making the harm obvious and foreboding. The malignancy is the harm caused by the longing for and absence of authentic relationships. Some of this harm is identifiable and known, but much of it hides in plain sight with residents leveraging coping mechanisms like closing themselves off and embracing symbolic mental toughness while they live among many others but remain virtually alone. The malignancy of solitude weighs on residents, and the harms of the absent relationships may not be obvious to the residents, staff, or anyone else, yet they persist. If residents are not, or cannot be there for each other, might correctional staff or external family members fill this void?

RHU Residents' Relationships with Resident Prison Workers

Certified Peer Specialists (CPS workers) are a particular group of residents whom other residents generally have positive relationships with. Peer specialists are resident workers with a trusted status within the prison so they are technically residents, but as workers they also carry a status that resembles staff. They receive training via an accredited national program in communicating with residents and de-escalating conflict among them. They do shift work throughout the institution, walking cell to cell asking residents if they would like to talk. While many RHU residents express not wanting to talk to peer specialists, those who do want to talk generally report positive relationships with them, such as resident Marx, who notes: "The peer specialists are trustworthy. They're old heads who know the system." Likewise, Resident Tunco says, "I chat with him [the peer specialist] as much as I can. It's very positive help. If I'm talking a lot of nonsense, they can calm me down. They can relate. They've been in the same spot."

One peer specialist reports: "I do everything I can to help them, and I don't care what they did to get into prison. I don't trust them though, but I feel physically safe regardless. I could walk through hell and still feel safe. They're bees without stingers." In this statement, the peer specialist gets to the heart of the surface-level relationship other residents overwhelmingly report. Even for peer specialists, it is their job to listen and help, but trust, in a risk-filled environment, is a luxury they simply cannot afford within the RHU.

Peer specialists in RHUs are relatively rare. While they are often present on the unit, there may only be one peer specialist assigned to a unit of several hundred residents. So, even if they are there, many residents may rarely see or interact with them.

RHU Residents' Relationships with Correctional Staff

RHU residents overwhelmingly describe their relationships (if they can be called that) with correctional staff negatively. Residents describe these relationships as untrusting, rife with poor interpersonal dynamics, and even physically or mentally harmful. For RHU residents, the chief barriers to relationships with staff, particularly COs, stems from three challenges: lack of confidence and privacy, the unequal power dynamics between staff and residents, and a perceived loss of dignity.

RHU residents consistently tell stories of COs revealing personal information about them to other residents or lying. This data breach often puts residents at great risk in the RHU. In carceral institutions, gossip is rampant and knowledge is power.

Resident Melek says: "If an inmate is having problems with one of the COs, there is nowhere that inmate can go. So, they get sent to solitary confinement for protection. The COs snitch on other inmates, and this makes inmates not want to trust the COs or want to be around them. You are risking our own life if you decide to trust a CO."

Resident Lugget agrees and adds: "I've heard COs gossiping about inmates. This is part of the reason I am not trying to befriend them."

Similarly, resident Marshall says: "If I tell them something, they'll use it against me."

And resident Giles says: "The COs will talk about you, what you did to get into prison, and that's not cool. I don't want people knowing what I did to end up in prison."

Residents report COs lie to them or about them to others in ways that suggest they are not trustworthy. Resident Bennet says, "They lie all the time. You know, they're [like] a gang. They don't care. Psychologically, they kick us in the ass and then smile to our faces. Everything they do is to tear us down. Forty-seven years in prison, and this is the worst place I've been. No one to talk to or trust."

Events like the ones described here are common, according to residents, and create an us-versus-them mentality among residents that puts a strong inner wall between the two groups. These perceived negative and potentially harmful actions by correctional staff lead residents to feel even more alone and isolated, with no one to turn to for comfort, protection, or interaction.

Perhaps the biggest issue negatively affecting residents' relationships with correctional staff, particularly COs, is the power imbalance inherent in carceral institutions. This power plays out in numerous ways for residents including loss of rights and privileges and sometimes results in violence or the fear of retaliatory actions. Residents describe grim scenes with such detail, intensity, and regularity it is difficult to imagine these are made-up stories.

Resident Paul describes being threatened by a lieutenant: "One time I got two threats from a LT [lieutenant]. He pushed my intercom and threatened me and said he wanted me to swallow my teeth. Like, are you serious? You can't use your professional oath to make those comments!"

Another resident, Canner, says,

> They burn you for these small things because they like the power dynamics. It's like they get some form of orgasm after they do something like that to you. Then, all of a sudden, they'll start playing with you like they're your best friend. It's another way to control you; it's another

agenda of theirs. If they're nice to you, they're hoping you will just behave.

Resident Kato describes relationships with RHU COs:

> It's a madhouse in here. COs will say, "Go kill your effing self. The COs mess with my next-door neighbor. . . . Ask me if I have lube in my cell. The CO says he will come up and do things to me. It happened on Saturday. I tried to call my uncle. [The CO] said, "Take the banana out of your effing blank [referring to his butt]."

Resident Lalonde gives another example:

> It's hard to feel safe when you're cuffed. Some of the COs like to start things, so that's why I don't talk to any of them. For example, if your cellie is coming back from yard and you're in the cell, you also have to get cuffed for them to open the door to let him back in. One time my cellie was sleeping and didn't wake up when he was supposed to. The CO told me, "Maybe you can say something to him or I'm going to spray both of y'all."

In these examples, residents express fear, dismay, and worry manifesting through their powerlessness within the RHU. The threat of physical violence, or at least the perception of it, weighs heavily on RHU residents and is a common reason residents provide for not engaging in relationships with staff.

Pepper spray is a common concern for residents, and its use signals an institutional power that significantly hinders residents' trust of and overall relationships with COs. Residents complain about its use, but more often its misuse or overuse.

Resident Magna says, "The other day they threatened a guy in the shower because he was in there too long. They sprayed him for twenty seconds, when it's only supposed to be three seconds. That kind of stuff makes me feel like, damn, that could be me, you know."

Residents' complaints about COs using pepper spray frequently merge with their concerns over power and dignity. RHU policy requires COs to spray a resident who attempts suicide before providing any help. In the case of attempted suicide by hanging, this includes using pepper spray before cutting any materials they used to hang themselves and dislodging them. Residents express overwhelming dislike for this policy, claiming that being sprayed after suicide attempt or suicide further diminishes resident's humanity, and not only does it dehumanize the resident but it traumatizes the onlookers beyond the impact of the suicide itself.

Resident Abel reports: "The COs mace people when they hang themselves.... The COs mace them first before checking if they're OK. Then, they cut them down."

Some residents have trouble understanding how residents' deaths, whether by suicide or otherwise, are handled by correctional staff. Resident Dana reports: "I saw my boy Kimmer [pseudonym] die and no one fuckin' cared—it took the CO twenty minutes to realize he died. Then they sprayed him to double-check. That shit is inhumane!" Resident Loftus had a similar experience: "I seen it with my own eyes. An inmate died and was left for a few hours. Until trays [meals] came around."

In recounting these events, residents offer a powerful narrative about grief, shame, humiliation, and fear. They express a strong dislike for RHU policies that they find harmful and dehumanizing, and they fault COs for following these policies in ways that hurt not only individual residents but all of them (if only through observing harm happening to others). Relationships between residents and correctional staff are largely avoided, because residents do not have confidence that the mistreatment of others will not one day become mistreatment of themselves. Lack of trust and confidence in the staff who are the only link to their ability to eat, remain safe, shower, and eventually exit the RHU represents yet another form of masked malignancy, where following policy hides the constant and perpetual harm it may inflict in RHUs.

For other residents, the lack of trust of and relationships with correctional staff comes from asking for things and being denied. Resident Yolo says he asked for psych services after witnessing three suicides, but COs denied his request. This is a common tale among residents. Other residents report asking for but never receiving a meal (sometimes several in a row), medical services (including X-rays and medication), and access to a shower after being pepper-sprayed. These incidents torment residents as they ponder how to cope and survive within the RHU. They breed distrust of correctional staff, particularly COs, and yield a hostile, us-versus-them environment where residents believe their lives do not matter to their caretakers and keepers.

The third most common way residents discuss severed or challenged relationships with COs emerges from incidents with COs that disrespect residents' human dignity. Many of these stem from pepper-spray events, but there are also other notable instances where dignity is challenged, weakened, and denied to residents.

Resident Alexander recalls feeling particularly demeaned in an interaction with a psychological staff member and a CO:

> The COs are terrible. It's not all guards, but the majority. . . . All got a real prejudice against prisoners. Seems like they hate you. [Once] the psych woman came to see me. She tried to call me Mr. Alexander. The CO yelled at her, "You don't talk to him like that! What's wrong with you?" [meaning that she should not refer to him as Mr. and should not use his last name]. [I thought] I am a human being, older than both of you.

Residents also describe RHU policies and practices that make them feel further dehumanized. "You can't even shake their hand," says resident Narrow. "The dynamic is the same as that of a cop to a criminal. You are locked in a cell all night waiting for it to open. You have to stay ready and always be cautions because you never know."

In rare cases, residents do express some simple give-and-take relationships with COs, but few seem deep or holistically positive. These good relationships commonly result from actions by the residents themselves as they work to avoid trouble with COs.

Resident Oberton says about COs: "They're all right. [We] don't give them reasons to act crazy. Act like a nut to them, they'll act like a nut to you." Another resident concurs, saying, "They are civil to me; I am civil with them."

These examples and others like them suggest that residents take on much of the weight of establishing and maintaining a peaceful relationship with COs. In these examples, residents point out their emotional labor as they navigate their interactions with COs and other residents. Sociologist Arlie Hochschild coined the term *emotional labor* in her 1983 book *The Managed Heart*.[6] Hochschild defines emotional labor as the ways individuals must "induce or suppress feelings in order to sustain the outward countenance that produces the proper state of mind in others."[7] Within RHUs, residents contend with unknown or misunderstood personalities, relational dynamics, backgrounds, experiences, and various other factors while attempting to find a livable pathway that does not cause them emotional or physical harm. They must hide or suppress many of their emotions or face consequences from staff, including punishment for outbursts of anger, frustration, and sadness. When emotional labor occurs, residents are not forming real or close relationships with correctional staff because they are masking the harm they feel. They take a don't-rock-the-boat approach to dealing with correctional staff that affords relative peace but does not genuinely advance or contribute to their lives in other ways and does not afford the opportunity for authentic and meaningful relationships.

In the rare instances when a resident expresses sincere trust in a CO, it has been built over time with the CO coming through for the resident by providing things the resident needs. Resident O'Donnley has a strong relationship with one CO in his RHU. He says he learned to trust this particular CO via instinct. He says this CO has been to his door "like sixty times. He knows me and my problems and he's always helping me. He checks on me every round. This morning he asked me if I'd seen psych yet. He's all right." O'Donnley did not elaborate with other examples, but he seemed to genuinely trust this particular CO to help him when needed.

Other residents come to trust certain COs who do not make promises but keep their word. Several residents express respect and trust for COs who respond to their requests by saying they will look into it and then they actually follow up. These instances are infrequent but occur nonetheless and make a meaningful difference to the residents who experience them. Regardless of whether the CO can get the item or allow the request, residents find this type of follow-through helps build relationships and trust among residents and COs.

Sometimes though, trusting relationships are built between residents and COs via rule-bending and rule-breaking. Residents respect (and at times admit to manipulating) COs who break the rules in their favor: COs who pass items between cells, COs who bring them extra meal trays or snacks, COs who provide them extra writing paper, and COs who they develop a personal relationship with. In these instances, all interviewed residents did not take this kindness for granted. They were grateful, every one of them. However, several also expressed worry that they would one day "owe" a favor to the CO who had broken or bent RHU rules for them. No resident said whether they would or would not repay that favor, only that the feeling of indebtedness weighed on their minds.

Only one resident in our data suggests an inappropriate sexual relationship with a female staff member while in the RHU. He describes this relationship as hugely beneficial for his mental health:

[Several years ago] in another institution, I met a female CO and we started talking. Some of the lines got blurred, got crossed. We got into a relationship and I knew it was wrong because I didn't want to ruin her career. I was walking around with a broken heart, broken spirit because I have a life sentence. I had been in jail for eighteen years and no one talked to me like she did. But they found out, and they tortured me because I refused to tell them what was going on. They put me in a death cell with only heat and hot water for five months, trying to get me to rat on who she was. I would never rat on her though. You could bury me seven feet underground in a casket with a phone and say you'll let me out when I tell you who she is, and your phone would never ring.

Interviewer: How/why did that make you feel good?

Resident: She brought me back to life.

Residents' relationships with noncustodial staff (not COs) are generally positive, though again, mostly at a surface level and lacking any real interpersonal depth. Very few residents discussed having any relationship with other noncustodial staff. But of those that did, it was overwhelmingly the same story. They see a psychological staff member irregularly, not often enough, and they are afraid of the lack of support and the breach of confidence when psychological staff reveal information about them to COs and other residents. In most interviews where residents discussed lacking psychological services, they expressed empathy and understanding for the lack or inconsistency of these services due to understaffing. With generally only one or two psych staff per RHU, residents are keenly aware they will get little if any treatment. They express gratitude for the limited time they do get and for the medications they receive to help manage their mental health symptoms.

Resident Mack says he talks to the psych staff when they come by, but the conversation is usually quick and to the point, without much time to elaborate. Regarding his relationship with one psych staffer, Mack says it is "not good at all. They are trained to think they know everything. They don't listen to us."

Mack also worries about the lack of privacy, saying, "They'll share your personal information. . . . I always tell him not to mention my release date because I'm getting out soon and I don't want people to know. But he does it anyway." Mack feels this puts him at risk with other residents and staff because sometimes short-timers (those getting out soon) receive additional punishment or become targets for physical or mental violence in an effort to postpone their release date and keep them inside.

Another resident also expresses a concern about privacy: "They are always making jokes about the dude in cell 17 [because he spread feces on his door]. I don't want them to do that to me." And still another resident worries that "if I do talk, everyone can hear us. Guards might tell other people." This, as all residents know, puts them in multiple layers of danger within the RHU, and perhaps worse when they return to the general population and word about them spreads like wildfire.

Residents' Relationships with Family and Friends Outside Prison

Finally, the last category of residents' relationships is with their family and friends outside prison. For RHU residents, particularly those with DC status, visitation is prohibited (except from attorneys), and relationships suffer greatly. Nearly every RHU resident we interviewed speaks of the tremendous pain they feel over the loss of contact with loved ones outside prison. While it is true that even residents in general population units feel the sting of lost or challenged relationships with those not imprisoned, the RHU exacerbates this pain for residents in countless ways.

For many RHU residents, the time spent in the hole is one of the most mentally and physically grueling experiences in their lives. Outside prison, individuals typically turn to loved ones for support, kinship, and friendship during challenging times. But in the RHU, that lifeline is severed nearly entirely for DC residents and significantly curtailed for AC residents.

RHU resident Beck describes the RHU in succinct terms: "It's a nightmare. Distance with relationships. Breakups. No one to lean your weight on. . . . No visits. Can't talk to family. Can't eat. They don't look at [these] trials and tribulations. Certain dudes fight back here." This is a common sentiment among RHU residents. The hurt and longing they feel for family and friends is ever present and gut-wrenching.

Resident Finlay talks about being without visits from his family:

> I write my family for someone to talk to. There is no pain like this pain. It's painful because you're restricted from everything—the outside world.

You have to fight for your life. You can't do nothing. I have to fight to get through twenty more years. I used to get visits every week, but someone was horse-playing on the block [in general population] and they grabbed me. That's why I'm here [in RHU].

While the lack of communication and connection with family and friends weighs heavily on the minds of RHU residents, it is often the move to the RHU that creates the initial, and perhaps the most, stress. When a resident is removed from general population and placed in the RHU, there is no communication with their loved ones. They just disappear. This creates a devastating hurt for RHU residents, who often reveal that they let their family down so many times in life and now—even while incarcerated—they did it again.

RHU resident Tender says: "If you get a misconduct and go to the RHU, how are they [family] going to find out if you can't call them or write them a letter? You get to use the kiosk and phone privileges on AC status, but not DC. [Your family] don't know what's going on." This continues for RHU residents because they often have no property for weeks or months into their RHU stay.

RHU resident Kinks says, "Getting through the first week is the worst time because you don't have your property, your pen and paper, you can't correspond with family or close friends." Even after that initial period, the RHU continues to block or restrict familial relationships.

RHU resident Becket says that he gets "one phone call a month. You can't build relationships that way, and it is very hard."

RHU resident Egert feels the same:

There's no human contact or interaction [in the RHU]. It's really hard for me not being able to visit with my family. I used to see them often, but now, over here, visits are very limited. I also don't want them to see me through glass. I used to call my mom every day. Now, I don't have access to a telephone.

Visits (beyond legal personnel and clergy) for RHU residents on DC status are nonexistent, and for AC-status residents, very limited. Even when visits are possible though, the location of many prisons in the United States limit visits for many residents in both the general population and RHUs.[8] RHU residents consistently note that the distance between them and their family and friends and the economic hardships a visit involves prevent many from visiting, who would, if they could.

RHU resident Bono reports:

> They've never been here. My mom is old—she's seventy—and it's an eight-hour drive for a six-hour visit, and if something happened to her on the drive, I would never forgive myself. Losing her would be hard. 2008 [eleven years ago] was our last visit. It's rough. [My family] helps me more than it hurts though. It's good to have contact, phone and mail, but it's not the same as physical touch.

Resident Donohue notes: "Most of my family is dying and I have nobody by my side. I talk to my mom, my lawyer, and my girl [when I'm in general population], but everybody else has disappeared."

RHU resident Meeks adds: "It costs $900 for them to get here. For one day."

The weight of these facts rests heavily on the residents. They hang their heads and speak sorrowfully as they share their feelings. It is difficult to listen to them—you can actually feel their ache. It gets harder when they express one of the deeper pains they feel while in the RHU: the thought that their family is sentenced too. Resident Cullen nearly cries when he remarks: "Down here, I don't really get to see my family. . . . I feel like they are being punished too." Resident Yuka adds: "My family is more affected than me."

While the depth of relationships with family, friends, and loved ones is obvious in conversations with residents, it is also a source of immense pain because these relationships are largely severed and definitely hindered during RHU time. What was a lifeline for residents when they were in general population becomes an immovable cement block tied to their ankles while they reside in the RHU. Residents, like free folk, depend on family and loved ones to lift them up, keep them connected, and make them feel whole. Without these opportunities—surrounded only by cellies, neighboring residents, and correctional staff they mostly do not trust—the horror of the RHU exacerbates the constant and gut-wrenching pain that becomes an ever-present sorrow, a reminder of what is lost and what may never be again.

Staff on Relationships

Staff members maintain a challenging relationship with residents as a result of the nature of their work in the RHU. While their primary job involves the trilogy of care, custody, and control, at varying points during any shift, one of these goals may take precedence and obliterate one or both of the others. Although many tout the benefits of forging positive or harmonious relationships with residents, very few residents suggest such staff-resident relationships are common, and even fewer staff mention formative or deeply connected relationships with RHU residents. Most often, staff tell stories regarding the darkest side of humanity—the dangers they face working in the depths of an RHU. Perhaps the residents living there are, as they say, "the worst of the worst." Perhaps the residents living there are experiencing one of the most difficult situations of their life, and their behavior in this temporal locale represents not who they are as people but who they are in those moments, living in a literal and figurative hole. Either way, staff face exceptionally difficult days working among RHU residents, and those days do not end when they punch out and leave the institutional complex. What staff see, hear, and do within the RHU haunts them long after quitting time. The memories infect like a disease and linger long and feverishly for hours, days, weeks, months, or years. In many regards, they alter the staff in untold (perhaps masked) ways, with too many consequences to identify, diagnose, or comprehend. Staff relationships with residents, coworkers, the DOC, and their family and loved ones outside the carceral setting are all strained, troubling, and are often defeating. Almost without exception, staff too feel immense pain from the lack of trusting, positive, and nurturing interpersonal relationships while working in RHUs.

Staff Relationships with RHU Residents

Staff relationships with RHU residents generally consist of the assigned and all-too-familiar roles of the keeper and the kept. Staff regularly describe residents as children, bad seeds, troubled, and monsters. The most common staff sentiment about RHU residents is some form of "You never know what they [the residents] are capable of." While there are noteworthy reasons for this feeling, most residents do their RHU time without causing too much trouble for staff. Yet, incidents involving violence and danger ring salient with staff in ways they often have trouble identifying and describing—and even more trouble letting go of.

CO Cashow remembers:

> These guys have killed people and will do it again. The murders we had here—one inmate stomped his cellie's head in. We only noticed it because a CO saw blood coming out of the cell. The inmate was sitting there right next to the flattened head, smoking! These guys can be friends, but then

one thing can set them off. This guy who stomped his cellie's head said his cellie wouldn't turn down the TV volume.

In this narrative and countless others like it, staff relay feelings of fear and worry about what is possible and what they know occurred. In real terms, these experiences paint an enduring picture of just how far relationships with residents can and perhaps should go.

CO Donner explains how working with RHU residents takes a toll on both residents and staff:

> Guys come down here and they get pissed that they can't talk to their family. Really, they need to realize that when they get hole time, they hurt their family. And, when they might be eligible for visits, they don't get them because of their behavior in the unit. You try and deal with them, but at some point, you're just done with it. Then you become irritable and angry. Work for more than a year down here and you deal with a lot of stuff. Anything positive that might happen down here or any positive progress you make with inmates while they are down here is negated or clouded.

CO Michaels adds: "There are some COs here who just hate the inmates. Like, flat out disgust and contempt for them."

CO Verd compares working in the RHU to working in general population: "In GP, you can establish relationships with the inmates. You get to know them, and they know what to expect from you. Some trust is established. [But] I never trust inmates down here."

In these examples, staff discuss the fear and frustration that creates a level of disconnect rendering these "relationships" with RHU residents truly relationless. Most of their interactions consist of daily tasks, practices, and procedures meant to control and contain residents in ways that keep everyone safe. Little or no attention is paid to forming, building, maintaining, or sustaining relationships.

Yet, despite these feelings, some RHU staff deal with these events and involvements rather differently. In some relatively rare instances, RHU staff express having or wanting to have relationships (of a certain and permissible type) with residents. Sometimes these thoughts reflect sentiments similar to those residents expressed earlier in this chapter. For example, CO Malleck states, "I am a person who treats the inmates the way they treat me. I react based off their actions. I feed off them." And CO Jema says, "You get your job done better when you treat the inmates like men and they treat you like men."

There are also a few RHU staff who take their relationships with residents to a slightly deeper level, expressing empathy for resident situations and genuinely trying to help them. In several examples, staff share how attempting to understand residents improves their relationship. CO Zand says, "I empathize with the inmates because many of the guys in the unit have had really bad home lives." CO Allen concurs: "Establishing a rapport with inmates is so important; you have to know the inmates because every situation is unique." Similarly, CO Otessa says,

> If you sit down and talk with these inmates, they're actually pretty good guys. You know, I think there's three things that men can't seem to control themselves around (*he puts up three fingers to count them*): drugs, alcohol, and children. When those three things are taken away, when they're put in an environment without those things, they're pretty good guys.

A couple of COs discuss specific ways they try to help RHU residents improve their lives. One CO discusses forming a group for RHU residents who were military veterans. Even though the program never really got started in the prison where he worked, he felt it was an important step to show his commitment to helping a group of particularly vulnerable residents by connecting staff and residents through a shared experience.

CO Ayen reveals that he feels good about helping RHU residents in multiple ways:

> I also help them to get things like get copies of their birth certificates and credit reports. One of the worst things I have to deal with is trying to get them to fill out forms for things correctly. But it's good practice. If you go to apply for a job, you can't keep asking them for new application because you mess one up! I also try to teach them about health. I ask them what the first things they're going to eat when they get out will be. Usually they tell me something fried and greasy. But I also try to teach them not just about physical health, but healthy relationships.

Staff Relationships with the Department of Corrections and Management

While in most cases, staff stressed that relationships stem from fear of physical harm at the hands of residents, other sentiments reveal additional issues that challenge staff-resident relationships. Numerous staff suggest they feel burdened by the policies and practices in the RHU.

They perceive that these policies regularly interfere with their ability to perform their work.

CO Kopes says: "Honestly, I just play host to these inmates. They get catered to constantly, and my job has really become getting for them what they want, and not about me actually doing my job."

CO Canner expresses dislike for the level of medical treatment and services RHU residents receive. He compares it with what his family receives outside prison and expresses the sting of the perceived discrepancy. Canner says: "I have an elderly family member who had to give up their house to get a medical procedure, and the inmates get the best medical care for $5. I knew a guy on death row who got chemo. Chemo! Imagine that, paying to keep a guy alive just to kill him!"

And CO McGillacutty tells another side of the powerful story residents tell about using chemical spray on a person who attempts suicide. For McGillacutty, this divisive and inhumane policy creates a barrier to relationship-building with residents:

> When we see a guy hanging [in an attempted suicide], we used to just be able to use mace on him to get him down before anything happened and to stop them. Now, with these stupid policies, if we see it, we have to go get help from psych or sergeant, and by the time we return, that person might be dead already. We could have potentially saved someone's life, but instead have to maybe watch someone die.

While McGillacutty's description does not completely align with those of residents regarding procedures for attempted or completed suicides, it does explicitly note that the policy of spraying or getting help before rendering aid runs contrary to what both staff and residents want. Neither group thinks the current policy for dealing with suicides preserves or recognizes the humanity or dignity of residents in their time of need.

Staff concerns, at times, extend beyond the RHU specifically and into the DOC more generally. CO Sloker says:

> There's no more respect or rapport between inmates and guards anymore! We used to rely on the old guys to keep guys in line. If we were having trouble, we'd have an old guy go up and talk to the person we were having trouble with. [Now] we don't get extra staff to supervise extra services like the peer advocates. They keep taking away guards and adding more people [inmates] and work.

Additionally, staff express great strain in their relationships with supervisors, administrators, and the DOC. A common narrative among RHU staff details the lack of support they feel they receive from those above them and the immense pressure this puts on frontline correctional staff.

CO Donovan suggests: "There is constant stress and anxiety [that comes] from the administration. There are too many bosses. No one wants to give a definitive answer [to any problem] because they don't want to be held accountable."

CO Jenkins concurs: "The LT [lieutenant] we have down here today will give the house away to cover his ass."

And CO Comstock reiterates this point by noting a lack of understanding and shared experience:

> The upper management doesn't experience... threats [from residents] because the inmates need something from them [like] half time, phone calls, for example. And almost none of the executive staff members were previously COs. So, that means that even if they don't experience those threats now, they likely didn't experience those threats before they were in upper management, so they think we are antagonizing inmates to be threatened.

Comstock contends that residents threaten and indeed harm COs with or without being antagonized by them. He believes upper management does not and cannot understand this, based on their experience and career trajectory within prisons on the treatment side of the house.

CO Halston adds another layer to these concerns, noting that when COs feel stressed or burned out from working in the RHU, they have nowhere to go. He says telling supervisors means that information will get out to others and may possibly be used against the CO. Halston argues: "It's not confidential; things get shared. So you go in there [to the supervisor's office] and you talk to a white shirt [supervisor], and that person can share it with upper management. They'll consider a guy weak or unfit, and he'll get weeded out" of the unit or the prison.

In these ways, COs and other correctional staff feel disconnected from and occasionally abandoned by their supervisors and the DOC. This makes working in the RHU even harder for correctional staff in many ways and forges a relationship barrier between line-level staff and those working above them.

Noncustodial Staff Relationships with Residents

Outside of correctional officers, other RHU staff seem committed to building relationships with residents, even though residents' comments do not indicate that these relationships form in any tangible way. For example, correctional counselor Tunney suggests his relationship with RHU residents comes from a level of mutual respect:

> It really is a joy to do this work. I've even received letters from inmates' families thanking me for the work that I've done with their family members. There are five stages of change, and I try and work [these] with the guys in here and on my block to move through them before they are released. I really love doing this work, and my two bosses and the psych staff down here are also really great.

Likewise, Lieutenant Walker notes:

> They keep me down here because I can calm down the inmates. Guys [residents] don't misbehave on my shift. I don't have the problems that some of the staff have. I tell the inmates, "How do you expect me to hold my guys [COs] accountable, if I don't hold you accountable?"

For noncustodial staff, the job entails less emphasis on custody and control and more emphasis on care for residents. Their noncustodial role yields a much different set of tasks and goals for working in the RHU. This comes through in the way noncustodial staff discuss their interactions and relationships with residents. It is difficult to tell though if these relationships are reciprocal or if residents feel the same.

Staff Relationships with Other RHU Staff

Staff regularly discussed relationships (or the lack of them) with residents and relationships with management and the DOC. In relatively rare instances, they also discussed their relationships with other RHU staff. In these narratives, staff generally relay either very close or exceptionally distant relationships—with almost no relationships in between. On the one hand, a few staff described other RHU staff as family or as a team.

CO Tate says, "It's more of a family down here, a team. You depend on each other more than any other part of the jail and it grows on you." And several other COs comment that the RHU staff is like a "second or other family."

However, staff more regularly report nonexistent or troubled relationships with other RHU staff. "I don't associate with people from work," CO Nader reports. "I don't want to be around people talking about this place." CO Yule agrees but suggests that staff relationships within the entire prison are a bit more complicated than what Nader outlines:

> I think the jail is a big community, with lots of smaller communities, where people spend a lot of their time together. There are lots of sports leagues that staff play on, like softball and bowling. People hang out a lot together. I think people here are always nice, but I'm not going to invite everyone to my house for a BBQ (and I do a lot of BBQs at my house). I only invited one person from this jail to my second wedding. I'm just not that close with people here. I don't want to be.

This is perhaps a surprising comment given what we know about the blue line in law enforcement where police and other security professionals, like COs, consider others in their profession a brotherhood (or sisterhood) and look out for and protect each other. It may just be that correctional staff we interviewed did not organically bring up these relationships, yet they exist. It may also be that there is a definite difference between having someone's back and truly cherishing a relationship or friendship with them. In the conversations presented here, COs may also be using distance as a coping mechanism—not wanting to spend time with fellow staff outside of work in an effort to spend their nonworking hours devoid of conversations about and reminders of RHU work.

Staff Relationships with Family and Friends Outside Prison

Perhaps relationships with family are the most important interpersonal connections for correctional staff, and for good reason. Many workers in all types of industry feel this way, and corrections is no different. RHU staff talk about these relationships—for better or for worse—most often and with a level of passion and heart not present in their conversations about residents, staff, supervisors, and the DOC. In their conversations about family and friends outside work, staff were largely animated and their words exuded care and concern for these important people in their lives.

Despite that positivity, working in the RHU presents unique challenges to familial and home life for many staff. As they did regarding risk, staff talk about the mental and physical harms they endure working in the RHU (many of which are masked or hidden) and the myriad of ways this work interferes with their ability to operate as a parent, partner, community member, or friend. For most staff we interviewed, the idea of talking to their spouse or family about their work day is uncomfortable at best and implausible at worst.

CO Lovett relays this reluctance: "I told my wife, 'Don't ask me questions.' She doesn't understand what I do. She's never been in a prison. It would be a long day if everyone walked around pissed off. I've seen all kinds of bad things. If I told you all the things I've seen, you'd probably cry."

CO Ecks adds: "My family actually had an intervention for me. They think I've lost my patience with them. I treat them like inmates, I guess. I don't drink as much, but I think that's because I aged out of drinking, not because of this place."

CO O'Malley recalls: "The last sergeant down here ended up divorced. He made it one year. He said he'd been so upset leaving here that he'd go home and take it out on his kids, and his wife would end up getting mad at him. He told me once that there were times when he would just go home and cry."

Many correctional staff, in fact, were not the first to notice that they changed after working in the RHU. In numerous cases, it was family members—particularly spouses—who realized their loved one was behaving differently at home. This happens in prison in general, but RHU staff said the unit compounds these effects. While some correctional staff are grateful for this vantage point, others voice concern regarding how the RHU environment is affecting their home life and the risks it poses to their relationships.

Echoing CO Ecks, CO Thompson, a former Marine, notes: "My wife said that I sometimes treat her like an inmate."

CO Ubek says: "I didn't notice any changes about myself originally, when I first came here [to the RHU] to work. But I hit a rough patch a few months ago. My wife talked to me about it. It was a real check. She said I was becoming really irritable."

CO LaClair had a similar experience: "Before, when I first got down here [to the RHU], I would take the day out on my wife. She had a talk with me about it. I've since learned to separate work and home."

These are the "good" examples of where correctional families intervened in ways that helped their loved one come to terms with RHU work life and begin to detach from work when they punch out at the end of a shift.

However, for others, the RHU may cause additional harm to family relationships. CO Burnard notes: "There's a lot of guys that work down here that end up being divorced or having substance abuse problems."

CO Forney adds: "Other people said I have an anger problem. It might be a bit worse after [working in] the RHU."

CO Garcia details a struggling home life: "I get irritated quickly. It's mentally exhausting—not physically. And, then you go home and someone nags you, you tell them to shut up."

CO Beeker says: "There's more divorce and family discord [when you work in the RHU]. High blood pressure and anxiety. There is a reason why our retirement age is 50."

CO Teller reflects on his current marital situation, "My wife and I are talking about separating. . . . My callousness goes home. I don't show emotion here [in the RHU], don't show emotion at home. I go in the extra room and shut down."

CO Bittner sounds both angry and frustrated when he says:

> We get spit at, kicked, bodily fluids thrown at us. An inmate recently threw a mixture of spit, urine, and feces at me, and I don't know if I have HIV, so now I have to cover up [wear a condom] with my wife in the bedroom if you know what I mean. And I shouldn't have to do that. [We] aren't allowed to know if they [the residents] have anything [diseases or infections]. So, I have to "cover up" when I do things that married people do in the bedroom because I don't want to risk infecting my wife with something I got here. It takes six months before I can be sure I haven't got anything. Do you know what that's like? Can you imagine?

In these examples, COs express a sense of emotional labor similar to that which residents described. Their narratives suggest that they hide or subdue their true feelings while at work, but once they get home, many of these feelings come out in ways that are harmful to their families. Alternatively, they continue to subdue their feelings at home by shutting out or creating intentional distance between themselves and their loved ones.

Maintaining a family under these circumstances is a formidable burden for COs. While CO Auburn suggests his marriage of over twenty-five years is intact, he traces the legacy of many correctional staff divorces to working in prisons generally and RHUs specifically:

> I've seen lots of changes in other people who work in the RHU. Their blood pressure goes up, they go through multiple divorces. It's hard to

work in such a stressful environment and try to maintain a family. When someone throws shit and piss at you, it's hard to get over that. People end up having a difficult time hanging on to their family. Like me, I have a [long] marriage, but most people don't have that. They just don't deal with the stress and burnout well.

Some COs have found or are trying to find ways of coping with the stress of working in the RHU so that it does not affect with their family life. Many COs express their emotional labor via their growing ability to avoid bringing their work home with them.

CO Umbra describes his strategy for coping: "I live twenty miles from the prison, and I drive thirty-five miles an hour all the way home. By the time I get home, I can forget about work and focus on my family."

CO Limmer adds: "I keep work at work. I sit in my driveway. My wife knows if I pull in and don't immediately come in the house, that's been a bad day."

Aside from the risk of physical and emotional harm, COs often face mandated overtime or double shifts. Many COs relish this chance to earn extra money, but it definitely takes a toll on family relationships. COs often explain their shift choice is purposeful so that they can have time with their children and family, but those relationships suffer when COs work sixteen-hour shifts.

CO Dubes says:

> Overtime means I work 6 a.m. to 2 p.m. and then 2 p.m. to 10 p.m. and then I have to be back at 6 a.m. Since I live an hour and a half away, I wouldn't get home until midnight and I'd have to be up at 3 a.m. So when I work overtime, I sleep in my car, in the parking lot of the prison. As long as you get to work the next day, they [the administrators] don't care. My kids gave me a big blanket just for that [for when it gets cold].

CO Teller, who regularly works the 6-to-2 shift, notes: "I coach a little league team. When I work the 2 [p.m.] to 10 [p.m.] shift, I can't do that. I never get to see my family when I'm on the 2 to 10."

These instances of working a second shift in the same day are far from uncommon. Countless COs discuss working double shifts. It is a bittersweet experience because the shift often provides extra money to care for their family, but this money is for the same family they rarely see when working so much. COs describe this as a form of masked malignancy:

a harm that does not seem to hurt much at first but, over time, takes a dangerous toll on family life.

In spite of all these negative effects of RHU work on friends, family members, and loved ones, a few COs also mention some positive consequences. CO Lamont feels his ability to empathize has improved. He says: "I even bring what I learned [working with RHU residents] into my life outside work. I'm a football coach, and I use the empathy I learned here to help the guys on my team and with my kids [at home.]."

CO Meckner suggests he realized just how stressful working in the RHU can be and he has tried to improve the situation:

> I took some time off and did a lot of fishing and spent time with my kids. While I was away, I realized just how much stress I have from my job that I didn't even realize until I had left the place for a while. It comes home with you and you don't even realize it. It was impacting my family life. I needed a reset.

Resets are a common goal for RHU staff. They achieve this in several ways, including taking time off or driving slowly home or sitting in their driveway after work before going into their home. Some correctional staff admit to using the mental health services available via the DOC. These include SEAP (State Employee Assistance Program, which is for all state employees, not just DOC folks) and a relatively new idea in many prisons called the Cover Room, where correctional staff may go to talk to someone about how the job is affecting them. Other COs simply talk to their supervisors during a particularly rough shift and ask to go to the control room ("the bubble") away from residents for a while to regroup.

In taking these options, COs discuss the practicality of "resetting" but also note the potential stigma and aftermath. For many in this hypermasculine environment, seeking help equates with weakness. In their 2006 work on sexuality and masculinity among firefighters and COs, scholars Sarah Tracy and Clifton Scott find that because prison work is seen as a relatively low-prestige occupation akin to babysitting in some regards, COs work to overcome this negative perception. Tracy and Scott conclude: "To manage these threats, officers distance themselves from the work, blame the inmates and/or refocus on more pleasant, oftentimes peripheral, perks of the job."[9] This point is not lost on COs. They even have a term for needing or using mental health services: "mentaling out." It is a point of some contention among correctional staff. On the one hand, asking for help is a strength and certainly may provide some relief from stress, frustration, and aggravation. However, when other staff—or worse, residents—get wind of a staff member mentaling out or taking time off for mental health reasons, it may be used against the staff in various ways. RHU staff mention receiving taunts from fellow staffers, being moved or transferred from the RHU, or having residents play on that weakness by further agitating them to see if they can get them in trouble or removed from the unit. For correctional staff, seeking and finding help may further challenge relationships with supervisors, peers, families, and residents in ways that exacerbate, not remedy, their difficulties.

RHU Relational Ambiguity and Absence

In the bowels of prison, the RHU holds and contains both staff and residents in a world unlike most others. Without physical touch, meaningful interaction, and trust both staff and residents endure endless hours of a grinding and worrisome existence veiled by fear, apprehension, and loneliness. While relationships among free folk bring everyday people out of dark places, provide support and comfort, and calm a troubled soul, the RHU affords none of these luxuries. RHU residents are alone (except for cellies) with their thoughts, alone with their past, and alone to fight the demons they face. Likewise, RHU staff are part of a team of workers assigned to the unit, but they are policy-regulated to avoid most meaningful contact and relationships with both residents and coworkers (while at work). This employment circumstance takes its toll on individual staff while they are at work and follows them home and into their family and community lives. The many tragic impacts of working within the RHU harm not just staff, but everyone they know and interact with.

Relationships matter. They matter for the genuine connection one feels with another human, for the place to seek comfort at the end of a long and grueling day, and for the knowledge and solace that comes from knowing you are not alone. Many things in life may hinder and cripple relationship building, including distance, anger, anxiety, and fear of rejection. In prison generally and in the RHU specifically, relationships are infinitely stressed or missing. The unit is designed, at its very core, to isolate. It is a *restricted* housing unit. It is a place where people live and work, and it is foreboding, limiting, and purposefully away from everything and everyone else. RHUs are a heightened or intensified form of incapacitation. For residents who live there, some of this is their own doing—or at least that is what prison policy and staff often contend. When residents cannot or do not follow rules in general population units, one option most prisons have available for dealing with or correcting this behavior is to remove them from general population and its somewhat public life and put them into an RHU for disciplinary reasons (DC status). But a lot of residents in the RHU are on AC status and did not commit any disciplinary action or misconduct in general population. They are there for their own protection or for the protection of others, or they are there because of their sexuality or because their preferred/professed gender does not match their biological, physical parts. In addition, there are the more complicated cases where mental health caused or contributed to misconduct or where mental health is so limiting that removing them from the general population may seem like a good option for the safety and well-being of everyone—that is, until they can pull themselves together and learn to live among others. However, what happens in RHU spaces is *not* rehabilitative, and it is *not* corrective unless the purported deterrent effect is assumed to be corrective. It is simply like a grown-up time-out, but one that is overly draconian. Residents who are placed in the RHU are exponentially limited in their ability to build and heal from relationships.

In modern RHUs, residents live a decidedly un-solitary life. Many residents are housed with a cellmate. However, even though they are not alone, they will not necessarily form and maintain any real relationship with their cellmate—or any other person. In fact, the cellie relationship may be physically and mentally harmful. Residents may also talk through vents and toilets to each other and try to maintain a modicum of normalcy regarding human interactions, but these conversations are not confidential and are often against the rules, and the chance of seeing the person you are talking to and having a legitimate conversation face-to-face is limited, at best.

There are also staff all around. But many staff adhere to policy and informal cultural norms and rarely talk to residents about anything other than logistics: stand for shower, stand for count, put your hands through the open wicket while standing backward to be handcuffed for your transport to wherever you are going (which really includes only shower and yard), take or return your meal tray. Of course, there are staff members who do go by the door to talk to residents. There are some staff members, as detailed in this chapter, who do have conversations with residents, try to help them, try to impart wisdom to them, or perhaps do them a favor here or there. But largely absent from these discussions with residents is any real and genuine connection. There are some staff whom residents trust more than others; there are some they can get things from; and there are some that discuss more than just logistics with them. However, no resident in this study suggested they have a good, genuine, deep, and interpersonal relationship with any RHU staff member. And no staff member suggested this type of relationship with residents either.

Maybe this is not surprising. Maybe readers will think, "Well, they committed a crime. They should be treated as criminals." But should they not also be treated as human beings? As human beings who will one day reenter society after having lived for months or years without any real human interaction? Will they know how to make or rebuild a connection, any connection, once they are released? Will they trust anyone? Do we want folks who have lost the ability to trust others released back into our communities? While we have them in captivity, is there no way to make that experience one where they find and learn to maintain and perhaps even cherish human relationships?

Now, it may seem as if staff are the bad guys here, but that is simply not holistically true. Staff also are incarcerated in an RHU. It is restricted; they are locked into the unit; and although they are not in cells, their confinement is, in many ways, similar to that of the residents. Like residents, staff do not get much daylight; they eat prison food (although from a staff menu instead of a resident menu, but it is not much better); they are fearful, worried, angry, frustrated; and if they follow policy, they do not reveal anything personal about themselves to anyone, including other staff, residents, or supervisors. Although they likely will not spend their entire correctional career working in an RHU, they will spend a good number of years working there. During this time, they are restricted too, with very little outlet for coping or dealing with the feelings that come from working in this desolate place. Staff narratives reveal they mostly do not feel close to each other; they do not trust residents (nor should they according to policy); they express a distinct lack of confidence in their supervisors and management; and they feel largely uncomfortable and shunned if and when they decide to use mental health services. What outlet is there for staff to deal with their mental and physical health needs, if not relationships? And these are suffering. And it does not stop when they go home.

One difference between staff and residents is that staff end a shift in eight or sixteen hours and are able to leave the institution and go home.

Some of them go home to an empty house or a house with roommates; some go home to family or they live with friends; and at least one regularly sleeps in his car in the prison parking lot after double shifts. However, a vast number of staff suggest that their home relationships are strained by their workplace environment. While they often try to leave that pain and anguish—the ancillary effects of their work—at work, they find this challenging. They regularly express having no one to talk to about it. Their relationships at home are strained because they bring with them the tension of their work. While numerous scholars examine stress and burnout among COs, few, if any, consider noncustodial staff's mental and physical health or specifically examine home and personal interactions outside of work. Currently, our collective understanding of these complex processes are in their relative infancy. While we have staff "in captivity" at work, is there no way to make that experience one where they find and learn to maintain and perhaps even cherish human relationships?

Without deep, meaningful, and fulfilling relationships, both RHU staff and residents must find other avenues for survival; ways of coping with the effects of this often anomic and regularly dangerous temporal locale. And try as they might, many do not succeed. Instead, both groups bear the scars of trying and of failing indefinitely and in ways that affect every aspect of their and their loved ones' lives. However, despite systemic and cultural odds inside RHUs, residents and staff regularly behave in ways that preserve and protect the knowledge that relationships indeed matter.

CHAPTER 4

Rules

THE STORY ABOUT RULES, procedures, and policies within RHUs in many ways unfolds the way you might expect. The RHU is a tightly disciplined, highly controlled, heavily routinized unit within a broader prison where rules and policies seemingly guide every staff decision and provide secure and structured living quarters for residents and working spaces for staff. Within the RHU, every minute of every day, of every week, of every month, of every year is spent focused on rules, and the majority of those rules are dictated by time: how much time an individual has to spend living or working in prison and how much time an individual has to spend living or working in a RHU.

For residents, time-related concerns cumulatively constitute many of the "rules" of RHU living. Time, as a rule, primarily centers on basic needs. How much time until they feed me again? How much time until I get to see my children? How much time away from my spouse or significant other is too much, and they will leave me? How much time will I spend in this RHU? How much time will go by between the moment I push this button on my wall begging for help until someone comes to help me? For staff, basic concerns also abound. How many days will this unit go without a death or injury to a resident or staff member? How long until a resident accuses me of a misconduct? Will I live through this eight- or sixteen-hour shift and get to see my family for dinner and bedtime?

Within RHU environments. time is a rule; it is a restriction; it is a policy; it is something every resident and every staff member lives by. Time is a crucial feature of RHUs, and the timing of each day literally operates like clockwork. But for all that formality and rigidity, the rules and timing in the RHU are also ambiguous, misunderstood, unclear, and interpreted in vastly different ways. Both formal and informal rules guide the behavior of RHU staff and residents; both groups bend and sometimes break these rules; and both groups regularly try to abide by them, even when they are uncertain how to do so. The narrative of the RHU rules story weaves together a tangled interplay between knowing and not-knowing, accepting and resisting; and the thread that holds the whole tale together—in a seemingly consistent and orderly place that functions on strict rules and timing—is perhaps oddly, inconsistent.

Official rules and policies for RHUs come from a variety of sources. First, there is case law regarding the treatment of individuals housed in prison, although few cases specifically concern those living or working within RHUs. In several notable cases, courts have favored institutional needs for safety and security over residents' needs for mental and physical health and hygiene standards (among other concerns). Much of this work stems from courts loosely clarifying what may constitute cruel and unusual punishment in prison settings. In these cases, residents alone or groups sue a correctional staff member or members, an institution, or the entire DOC for violating their Fourteenth (due process) and Eighth Amendment (cruel and unusual punishment) rights under Section 1983 (which is used to enforce civil rights that a plaintiff claims were violated by state government employees) of the US Constitution.

A key ruling is *Weems v. United States* (1910), where the court noted, "What constitutes cruel and unusual punishment has not exactly been decided." Although the *Weems* case was not specifically concerned with RHUs, it is often cited in other cases for its lack of clarity on when, if, or how a prison might be cruelly or unusually punishing residents. In the subsequent *Wilson v. Seiter* (1991) case, the US Supreme Court somewhat clarified Eighth Amendment rights in carceral settings by establishing the "deliberate indifference" standard for prison conditions. Under this standard, Justice Scalia, writing for the majority, wrote that Eighth Amendment claims in prisons require *both* an objective and a subjective component, where plaintiffs must show that prison conditions are objectively cruel and unusual *and* are the result of prison officials' "deliberate indifference." The ruling also noted that courts should not question the constitutionality of all conditions in their "totality" unless they "have a mutually enforcing effect that produces the deprivation of a single, identifiable human need." Moreover, Justices White, Marshall, Blackmun, and Stevens concurred but wrote their own opinion, adding, "No static test can exist by which courts determine whether conditions of confinement are cruel and unusual." The Eighth Amendment "must draw its meaning from the evolving standards of decency that mark the progress of a maturing society."

Wilson v. Seiter sets the bar fairly high for prison residents' Eighth Amendment cases by creating two specific hoops that plaintiffs have to jump through. First, they must effectively demonstrate prison staff *knowingly* refused to respond to residents' needs with disregard for health and safety. It is a higher standard than negligence and requires reckless disregard that creates substantial harm. Second, plaintiffs must also specifically show how one of their basic human needs was unmet. This ruling is perhaps best demonstrated in *Quintanilla v. Bryson* (2018), where the court notes, "Conditions that fall below minimal constitutional standards of decency do not alone amount to a violation of the Eighth Amendment, however, because Quintanilla must show that the defendants were deliberately indifferent to the risk the conditions posed to his health or safety."

Before and after *Wilson v. Seiter*, courts ruled favorably for correctional institutions in Eighth Amendment cases, including the following:

- *protective custody residents were receiving adequate food, sanitation, security, lighting, and outside-the-cell time, and it was outside its jurisdiction to decide how best to house secured custody residents (O'Brien v. Moriarty, 1974);*
- the Eight Amendment prohibits "inflictions of pain . . . that are totally without penological justification" (*Rhodes v. Chapman*, 1981) but allows them when justification exists such as for lockdowns or security needs;
- the plaintiff did not specifically show that correctional staff acted with deliberate indifference regarding his claims about lack of food, heat, clothing, and sanitation (*Gillis v. Litscher*, 2006);
- "administrative segregation and solitary confinement do not, in and of themselves, constitute cruel and unusual punishment (*Sheley v. Dugger*, 1987); and

- courts should not designate the specific number of hours of exercise residents should get in order to meet a constitutional minimum (*Delaney v. DeTella*, 2000–1).

In select other cases, residents advanced their Eighth or Fourteenth Amendment rights within the US Constitution by winning or settling court cases related to their conditions of confinement while living in restricted housing, including the following:

- *a settlement to increase out-of-cell-time and increase programming and services (P.D. v. Middlesex County, 2015);*
- a settlement that capped solitary confinement sentences at ninety days for most first-time serious disciplinary violations and thirty days for most first-time nonviolent violations, and included a step-down (gradual, earned release) program to exit RHUs and the release of nearly 1,100 individuals from this institution's RHU (*Peoples v. Fischer*, 2015); and
- a settlement that granted a resident (plaintiff) a minimum of four hours outside of cell each weekday; access to a tablet with games, books, and educational materials; and some access to the same food, hygiene items, laundry, and barbering as the general prison population (*Gumm v. Jacobs*, 2015).

Institutional policies and rules originating within DOCs or individual institutions presumably adhere to current case law. Each prison in this study, and many throughout the United States, has an official general inmate handbook. New institutional residents typically receive this resource at intake or shortly thereafter. These fifty-or-so-page printed booklets contain information for residents regarding the grievance and misconduct policies and procedures, financial accounts, mail services, identification cards, visitation, telephone calls, legal procedures, work assignments, transfers, medical services, property regulations (including commissary), request slips, search procedures, the Prison Rape Elimination Act (PREA), cell assignments, programming, food services, religious activities, and other such information regarding daily living. Within the general inmate handbook at the prisons of study is a short, specialized section on administrative custody (AC status within RHUs). However, the general handbook's only mention of disciplinary custody (DC status) within the RHU is in the misconduct sanctions section, where RHU placement, for a period of no more than ninety days, is one of the possible sanctions for a guilty misconduct decision.

Upon intake into the RHU, residents are also supposed to receive another handbook—an RHU inmate handbook—for the institution they are in. This is a more detailed document outlining the rules and policies for the RHU. By official DOC policy, each institution is responsible for maintaining adequate copies of all inmate handbooks and making copies available on the unit (in general population) and in the law library (in both general population and specialty units, like the RHU). Additionally, residents may purchase a copy of the RHU handbook if they desire. Each of the prisons in this study has an RHU handbook (as do many US carceral institutions). This twenty-or-so-page document covers much of the same information found in the general inmate handbook, but it is specifically tailored for the RHU. It begins with definitions of both AC and DC RHU status and continues with an overall rule indicating that residents must follow all orders or they face disciplinary action. It notes that if residents receive orders from staff not mentioned in the handbook, they are to follow those too. In the general rules and regulations, residents are forbidden from (1) using abusive language toward staff; (2) using cell call buttons except in emergency situations; (3) talking loudly; (4) altering any item in their possession; (5) passing items between cells; (6) throwing any item out of a cell; and (7) placing anything on their cell doors, windows, walls, or lights. There are also general rules prohibiting smoking or tobacco products and using a blanket, linen, or piece of clothing for anything other than what it is intended for. In addition, residents must stand for count and turn their cell light on whenever standing or being handcuffed or whenever their wicket (slot in the cell door) is opened by a staff member. Other rules in the RHU handbook cover procedures for exiting the cell, using the staff chain of command for requests, mealtimes, daily routines, shower and shaving, mail, property, special services (such as commissary, telephone, barber, laundry, library, visiting, television, tablets), cell searches and inspection, requests and grievances, and PREA.

In many states, staff learn about RHU policies on the job after they begin working in the unit. In the state of our study, the DOC provides a forty-hour week of training to all staff working in the RHU. The training is offered a few times a year at a centralized location, where staff stay at local motels, away from their family. The RHU School (as it is called) is classroom training with two main instructors and a couple of guest lecturers. Ideally, staff would attend RHU School prior to beginning work in the unit; however, it is offered too infrequently, so that timing does not work out and many RHU staff work in the RHU for some time before attending RHU School, if they ever attend it.

During RHU School, the correctional staff members receive a binder (which they call the rule or policy book) to use during the training, but they cannot take it home or back to their workplace. The class content includes daily lectures consisting mostly of scenarios or situationally based examples, short video clips, lectures, role plays, and small group discussions about events likely to occur in an RHU environment. At the start of the RHU School we attended, the instructor announced that the materials were "last updated in 2010" (it was currently 2019). He also noted, "We will be skipping over a lot of stuff" and "We are missing videos, so the training is dry." There were also not enough training manuals or binders for everyone, so several correctional staff at each table looked at one book. There is no formal test or evaluation for RHU School attendees. Rather, attendance is taken every day, and perfect attendance equaled completion of the course.

The RHU operates with an elaborate series of rules, policies, and guidelines. These rules are provided to residents (some of the time) via the RHU Handbook and to staff (most of the time) via formal training. After that though, the rules are learned via daily trial and error in the RHU. Residents and staff learn from each other and by finding out what works and does not. Staff discretion to interpret the rules is plentiful as situations vary and formal policy is ambiguous at best. The most accurate description of RHU rules is that they are inconsistently understood and inconsistently applied and experienced.

Residents on Rules

Nearly every resident tells a version of the same story regarding rules. It goes something like this. Residents do not know the official rules; they learn about many of them as they go. They express that this is challenging because the formal and informal rules change constantly (via various interpretations and institutional needs) and very few staff know exactly what rules anyone is supposed to be abiding by.

Resident Cutter describes the situation in this way: "No one will say this is what you gotta do. Some might. I don't have an inmate (rule) book . . .

[so we're] walking around violating rules without even knowing. I would enjoy having one [a rule book] to avoid asking questions and getting burnt [denied opportunities by staff]." Resident Snipes concurs, adding: "They don't follow the law [RHU rules]; they introduce new rules as they go."

But there is a deeper story here. Residents do not just misunderstand the rules; they often quite literally do not know what they are. This occurs for three primary reasons: (1) residents do not always or regularly receive a copy of the RHU inmate handbook that outlines the rules and policies of the unit; (2) residents come to understand some of the formal and informal RHU rules by learning them as they go, but staff do not implement them consistently, so this is tricky; and (3) both staff and residents continually break or bend RHU rules, but the residents feel staff mostly get away with doing so and residents frequently do not.

A major concern for residents in the RHUs stems from not knowing the rules. They may not know them because of misunderstandings or staff discretion, but a larger reason is that many residents do not receive a copy of the RHU inmate handbook upon entry. Numerous residents reported never receiving a copy of the handbook, and several commented that even when they asked for one, they never received it. Several staff noted that either they had run out of copies and had not made more or that residents had received a copy upon entry. Additionally, some RHU residents are unable to read or write or unable to do so at a level that would allow them to understand the RHU inmate handbook's many rules and regulations. For RHU residents who are experiencing symptoms associated with mental illness or acclimating to new medication, understanding the RHU rules may also be challenging.

Although not every RHU resident complained about not having or receiving an RHU handbook, many did, and for them it was a point of worry and frustration. Without a rulebook, residents felt like they were living in a state of anomie or rulelessness. While they likely understand the rules and policies in general population (or a good number of them) either because they did receive a copy of its inmate handbook or they lived there long enough to learn the rules and policies via experience, the RHU is a wholly different space. Time does not work the same way in the RHU as it works in general population.

In general population, for example, residents mostly move without chains or shackles to medical, programming, employment, showers, yard, religious services, and meals once they are released from their cell, with a correctional staff escort or with correctional staff watching from posts, towers, or cameras. However, in the RHU there is no movement without a strip search, two to three correctional staff supervising, handcuffs, leg irons, belly chains, and a tethered waist belt (leash). The RHU cells are locked nearly every minute of every day, and a cell opens only when a correctional staff member specifically opens it for a designated purpose.

Additionally, RHU movements occur only if residents follow the pre-movement protocols for each task. For RHU residents without a rule book or without the ability to understand the rules, pre-movement protocols are elusive and confusing. To shower, for example, the procedure in the formal written rules might include signing up for a shower when a CO passes by the cell around 6:30 a.m. on shower day (which varies from institution to institution). To sign up, the cell light must be on, and the resident must be standing at the door. Then at shower time, nearly four hours later, around 10:30 a.m., the resident again must be standing with the cell light on when a CO comes by to escort the resident to the shower. In some institutions, there may be an intermediate step, where a second CO confirms sign-ups in the interim between sign-ups and actual showers. A resident who does not reconfirm the shower request may lose shower privileges for failure to abide by the pre-shower protocols. Once it is time for showers, the escort opens the wicket so that the resident can back up to it and place his hands through it to be handcuffed. In some RHUs for men, the shower policy also involves a resident wearing only boxer shorts and shower shoes and having a towel folded and hung over his shoulder and a dollop of shampoo on his head. If all these pre-shower rules are not followed, the resident risks not receiving a shower that day (and perhaps subsequent days as informal punishment for insubordination).

Learning the rules, even just the shower rules, is difficult without a rule book, but not impossible. Some residents learn through trial and error when they miss showers for not following protocol on a few days and then figure it out by piecing information together. Other residents praise cellmates and neighboring RHU residents for clueing them in on these rules by yelling across cells or talking through vents or toilets where sound carries through the pipes.

Resident McMichael notes: "I leaned on my cellie to teach me the rules here. He told me what to do until I got the hang of things."

Resident Carmine agrees, noting: "When I'm sleeping and it's time to sign up for shower or yard, my neighbor bangs on the wall [between our cells] and wakes me up so I don't miss it."

However, as friendly and empathetic as this system seems, it is not failure-proof. Some residents are not well-liked; some do not have cellies or competent neighbors; some may be deaf or hearing impaired; some take medicine impairing their ability to wake up easily, and so on. In these situations, residents often report going days or longer without simple, basic services such as showers or yard, and many even describe missing multiple meals. Sometimes, residents lose access to showers, yard, or meals for not following the pre-task protocols (standing, light on, signing up, etc.), or they may not receive items (e.g., unit TV on, paper, pens, blankets) or opportunities as punishment for breaking other rules.[1]

Numerous residents realize breaking rules while in the RHU may lead to losing opportunities for basic services even when they are following the rules to get them. For instance, resident Deets notes: "I didn't get fed because I didn't know the rules. One inmate got 'burned' [the word residents and staff use for blocked opportunities for items such as yard, showers, and meals] for a full twenty-four hours because he had clothes hung up [on a makeshift line in his cell] and then he said something [negative] to the CO." The RHU inmate handbook prohibits hanging anything, including clothing, on the walls, windows, or doors of one's cell. Another resident, Neddle, adds that often residents burn themselves. He says: "I usually clean myself in my cell. If you break the rules, you're burned for a shower. Inmates here burn themselves. All you have to do is have your light on, ready to go. They [the residents] just don't follow policy." In these examples, residents take ownership for violating rules even if they are unknown or misunderstood.

Often, residents lose opportunities for shower, yard, and meals as punishment for poor behavioral choices in the preceding hours or days. In these cases, burning as punishment tightly resembles retaliation (a negative act in return for a perceived negative act). Burning is so common in the RHU that the word *burn* emerges in resident conversations almost more than any other word. Residents describe burning as an act by a correctional staff that significantly bothers them, but one they can do very little to prevent or overcome. Sometimes, residents say they have no idea why they were burned.

For example, resident Omar notes: "Don't know about laundry, stand for count. CO will say, 'You wasn't ready,' and burn you for food." Likewise, resident Karp says:

The RHU is stressful. You don't really know anything about when trays [food] come around, and they'll burn you for shower. We get to shower on Monday, Wednesday, and Friday, but they'll burn you for that if they want. The COs here make their own rules.

In these instances, residents Omar and Kemp seem unclear about if, or how, they did anything that contributed to their burning because the implementation of rules seems haphazard to them.

Other residents know when and how they break rules and know there will be consequences. Resident Angles notes: "If I go to the hole [RHU] for the right reasons, I am OK with being here. If I break rules, I know I deserve to be here." Resident Looker adds: "I have a smart mouth and I've been asleep when trays are passed. I get burned for them. It's an unwritten policy for being asleep."

That it is "unwritten" is decidedly true, but with some ambiguity. Although residents have a federally litigated right to meals and both DOC and institutional policy clearly delineate this right, the general inmate handbook notes specifically that three meals will be offered during each twenty-four-hour period with no more than fourteen hours between the evening meal and breakfast. It also specifically states: "The Department will not use food as a disciplinary measure." However, the RHU inmate handbook states that the procedure for opening the wicket must be followed in order for residents to receive a meal (or anything through their wicket). It also states: "Failure to follow this procedure will result in you not receiving or passing any items to staff." So, according to the general rules, residents get three meals every twenty-four hours, and meals may not be taken away for disciplinary reasons. However, in the RHU rules, failure to follow wicket policy may lead to residents not receiving anything through their wicket—which is where food trays are passed.

The vagueness and contradictory nature of this policy (and others) often results in correctional staff using discretion to interpret formal rules. What results is an informal policy regarding meals and other services such as yard and shower that may loosely follow one set of guidelines or a combination of sets of guidelines while violating others. Staff members differ, though, in their interpretations. For example, what a CO on the day shift does may dramatically differ from what a CO on the night shift might do. Additionally, the circumstances of the day, the particular resident, or other factors may mean that these discretionary decisions are not even consistent from a particular correctional staff member from day to day or cell to cell. For residents, this is exceptionally confusing. They feel burned, mistreated, hurt, and angry without known recourse or remedy.

Perhaps it is the inconsistency of rule application that most aggrieves RHU residents. Sometimes this takes the form of staff members disparately interpreting policy; other times it is retaliation for resident actions via burning or additional punishment. In both types of inconsistent rule application, correctional staff use their discretion to interpret a rule or policy as it fits a particular situation, individual, or context but in ways that may not be consistent with their or other staff's past actions for a particular RHU resident or residents. In theory, both the general and RHU handbooks allow for this inconsistency in their language about policies and rules shifting to *meet institutional needs*. But in their lived form, institutional needs sometimes preclude residents from receiving their most basic needs.

Resident Barker describes it like this: "You never know. One day they're [correctional staff] one way, and then the next day they're another."

Resident Daha agrees, noting: "The rules are different here [in the RHU]. They don't follow policy. I mean, they break policy. So, I don't really know policy because they always be doing what they want."

Resident Yaks retells a similar story:

> I got burned for yard because my cellie had paper on the window, which gets me mad at the CO. A lot of things are left to CO discretion. It confuses us. You let us get away with something one day and then don't the next day, so we get confused. Some COs will do a 180, like letting you get away with something one day and then write you up for it the next.

For Yaks, his cellie broke a rule clearly outlined in both the general and RHU inmate handbooks regarding hanging anything on a window. The challenge for Yaks though, was that for one CO on one day, this was allowable (or forgivable), but for another CO on another day, it was not.

The inconsistency of rule and policy application is both puzzling and exasperating for residents. In another example, resident Piper tells this story about correctional staff not following policy:

> I'm supposed to get a haircut every week, but I haven't had one in months. When I see myself in the mirror or a reflection in the glass, I see how long my hair is and how long my beard is. I look like a fucking Muslim. They tell us the barbers are in the hole for smoking weed. So what? There's a staff barber who can come around. But they tell us that he's backed up. Policy

says I can a have a haircut. But, you know around here, just because you're allowed to have something, per policy, doesn't mean you're going to get it.

Officially, the RHU inmate handbook states that a resident barber will be escorted to the unit from the general population to provide haircuts to RHU residents. The pre-haircut policy notes that residents must request a haircut from the 6-a.m.-to-2-p.m. unit block sergeant. Normally, haircuts are done on weekends. No specialty haircuts are allowed. Residents are permitted one haircut every thirty days, but this is subject to change for *institutional needs*—a common phrasing within both the general and RHU inmate handbooks. So, in Piper's example of policy inconsistency, if it has been "months" since his last haircut, that is a violation of policy, but there is one exception. If the resident barbers are not available because they are themselves housed in the RHU for a misconduct, the RHU is policy-compliant because the rules are "subject to change for institutional needs." This caveat appears in multiple places within the RHU inmate handbook. Although it may make good sense from a managerial perspective, it is easy to see how residents—who likely do not know or understand the workings of the entire prison—find any deviation from the stated rule bothersome and may deem it rule-breaking (or burning) on the part of correctional staff. Something as minor as a missed haircut or two may breed mistrust and frustration among residents and have long-standing consequences for residents' mood, manner, behavior, and actions.

There are many examples like this where residents seemingly understand a policy, but correctional staff, for a variety of reasons, do not or cannot follow it. "Being in the RHU gives you a cell without hope," says resident Aguliar. "When I got in here, they put me in a hard cell. This is a cell without a mattress and desk. Usually they restrict hard cells for punishment of RHU inmates who misbehave, but I was put in here right when I got here." The RHU handbook does not provide a specific rule on when or how correctional staff will use hard cells.[2] In fact, there is no mention of hard cells at all. The RHU inmate handbook has one related rule, but nothing specific on hard cells: "Cell assignments will be based on the staff's evaluation of your previous behavior in a facility." Perhaps Aguliar's prior behavior convinced staff to place him in a hard cell, or perhaps that was the only cell available when Aguliar arrived at the RHU. The point is that Aguliar did not understand why he received a hard cell; no one explained it to him. This, again, creates frustration and mistrust for residents.

Resident Baskin provides another example of rule and policy inconsistency: "I'm on AC status, and I'm in a cell with someone on DC status. The policy states that people on these two statuses shouldn't be in the same cell."

Resident Ricardo also cited an example of policy inconsistency:

> A CO asked me if I wanted a cellie, and I said no. They wrote me up for a misconduct. I got a misconduct for replying no to a CO's question. It wasn't a demand. Gave me seven days without yard or shower, cell restriction. [I] caught a write up. [I'd] tell you the same thing. Would you like a cellie? No. They give you another misconduct. It's the little things . . . unwarranted.

In fact, neither the general or the RHU inmate handbooks provide any rules regarding celling residents of different custody statuses together, but the general inmate handbook notes: "Cell assignments will not be made based solely on race. It is your responsibility to inform the staff of any preferences you have about your cell assignment. A preference filed by you will be assessed by staff, but not necessarily granted." In the list of misconducts in the general inmate handbook, there is no mention of refusing a cellie. However, misconduct charges are possible for "refusing to obey an order," which, depending on the exact language the CO used with resident Ricardo, may have been cause for the write-up in his case.

Many residents express a desire for consistency above and beyond the need for rule clarity and any preferred rule changes. Residents generally do not like preferential or differential treatment within the RHU. For example, resident Bartlett says: "Side deals are made between COs and inmates. Because the COs don't care for the lady who helps us [a psychiatric counselor], they'll give inmates extra trays to be disrespectful toward the lady, to scare her." This makes him irritated and angry. For Ricardo, it is less about the mistreatment of the female staff member and more about the inconsistency of giving some residents extra trays, but not others.

Resident Likos would rectify such disparate treatment: "If you violate rules, you should get the same kind of sanction. I understand punishment. I believe everyone who commits the same misconduct should get the same punishment."

Resident Thayer agrees: "I think it doesn't really matter what policy is, right? Just pick what it is and then be consistent about it."

So does resident Tunstall: "One guy just got here and asked if he could have a visit. He got one . . . on Thanksgiving! The staff should just follow the rules; no special treatment."

Resident Buzak connects the inconsistency to the goals of RHU:

> Do I think the RHU achieves the goals of punishment? I think it would if they followed the policy and stayed consistent. Treat everyone the same and keep the treatment the same day-to-day. They need to just stick to the policy—not go beyond it or do anything less than it. If they stick to the policy, I think the RHU would be a good deterrent.

Resident Spear adds:

> I'd like to stop COs from using manipulation as a system. They say *we* manipulate the system, but *they* are the best manipulators. I also want the process to be more understandable. They can haul you down here and put you under investigation. and you're not even sentenced to the RHU. Then, thirty days later, you're still here, and you're still [*uses finger quotes*] "under investigation." It doesn't take a month to figure that out. How much investigating are they doing? There are rules in place for a reason, but don't manipulate it. It further punishes me. . . . I'd say it's really used as a form of torture.

In these examples, and many more like them, residents express a strong desire, perhaps a need, for consistency within the RHU. Residents seem to understand the usefulness of tough policies, stringent rules, and protocols that purport to keep everyone safe. They actually prefer it that way. What they cannot understand or tolerate is the rule bending that comes from widespread discretion and policy interpretation by correctional staff. This anomic environment creates a strain for residents. with potentially harmful consequences for them personally and potentially harmful consequences for staff within the RHU as well. In a unit that already severely restricts movement, autonomy, privacy, and basic freedoms, rule inconsistency piles on another layer of hindrance for residents.

As one resident talks about rules, his eyes begin to fill with tears and his voice becomes shaky: "Today, people are cold and hungry. It's torture. This should not be the law. I am not a terrorist. No trust in the guards. It's not safe because anytime they [COs] defend their duty, they will retaliate. When I press the [emergency] button [in my cell], they will not respond on time. I do not feel safe." This sentiment echoes throughout resident interviews and highlights the inconsistency residents feel and the way that inconsistency ties to risk.

In the RHU, the penal locale with a reputation firmly rooted in rules, policies, and procedures regarding punishment and control, residents overwhelmingly feel most punished by and most fearful of the inconsistent application or implementation of rules. Not knowing what will happen or result from any action or inaction on their part leaves them in a continual state of worry, loathing, and concern. Perhaps most egregious, however, is the effect inconsistency has on their mental state—which by all accounts is fragile, lacking confidence, and in many ways, desperate.

Staff on Rules

The narratives staff tell about RHU rules are similar to those told by residents in several important ways. First, like residents, staff typically do not understand or do not know all or many of the official and formal RHU rules and policies. They often argue that policy does not exist and that policies are perhaps more flexible than they are designed to be. Second, RHU staff tell a bifurcated narrative revealing two competing stories. Many RHU staff believe the unit's rules and policies have meaning and help keep order by maintaining unit control and safety. Alternatively, many staff believe the RHU rules and policies hurt or hinder them personally or their work within the unit. To edge around rules as hindrances, staff admittedly rely on discretion as a navigational tool. For staff, this interplay between rules as facilitators of safety and control and rules as barriers to safety and control weaves a multifaceted account of working in the RHU.

Sergeant Rolls describes the contradiction: "You want to get stuff done, but you still have to follow the rules. If you followed *all* the rules, you'd *never* get anything done." CO Tanks expresses a similar sentiment: "There's no consistency in the DOC. Everything is a gray line. The name if the game is cover-your-ass ... stick with policy.... They [the residents and administration] can't get you on policy. They can [though] screw you, sue you." These correctional staff succinctly sum up staff views of rules, but without any exacting knowledge that instructs on how best to work within the unit. In fact, discretion seems officially baked in to RHU policies, and while helpful in some regards, this ability to interpret and re-interpret rules also leaves both staff and residents feeling confused and unsettled.

The most common accounts of staff not knowing or understanding policy stem from two areas that only indirectly affect RHU residents. The first concerns how long a CO can work in the RHU. Many staff believe there is a rule that disallows RHU COs from working in the unit for more than two years. Others believe this is true but add that a psychological assessment is required after the first year to determine if a CO can stay working in an RHU for a second year. Still others believe that you may work in the RHU as long as you have annual psychological assessments. However, many of the staff who claim you need a psychological assessment to work in the RHU for any period of time admit they have not had one. No staff member was able to produce or directly cite the official version of this rule. In one conversation, a member of the senior management team, Ekko, said his understanding of the policy is that after one year, staff are required to get a psychological evaluation by a prison psychologist. If they are determined "OK to maintain," they are eligible to work in the RHU for another year. Most people rotate out of the RHU to a post in general population after two years working in the RHU. They can rotate back to the RHU after a minimum of a year (largely because posts are one-year appointments). Ekko also notes that some supervisory staff including lieutenants occasionally work more than two years consecutively in the RHU and often without any psychological exams or assessments.

This policy misunderstanding was also apparent in an RHU School class session when one instructor noted: "You can work down here as long as you want, unless you have a bid." A bid is a position staff put their name in for and get on a particular shift at a particular post in the prison.

RHU Lieutenant Smithers describes the process this way:

> We will assess each officer after a year of working in the unit. Then they can volunteer for a second year if they are cleared to continue working down here. After two years, they are supposed to take a break. However, there shouldn't be a time limit because it's a hard and specific unit to work in and that means while a good guy is taking a break, you have to transition someone in. Guys should be able to work down here as long as they want, as long as they aren't burning out.

In a CO discussion of a work time limit for the RHU, CO Roche states: "I don't think there's a limit. Maybe two years in the RHU? . . . It should all be volunteer. But if you told them you needed a break, they would give you one." CO Tunder's interpretation of this rule varies slightly: "You can only work down here for two years. Policy says that after one year, you have to get a psych evaluation." CO Zeb adds: "I'm not really sure if there are any rules about how long we can stay up here." While these different interpretations may seem relatively benign as a point of rule unknowingness, they reveal a deeper and more complex issue in RHUs: the staff working there do not understand the rules that apply directly to them, let alone the rules that apply to residents.

The second policy staff is muddled about is female staff working in male RHU units. This example offers a deeper dive into a larger issue of work-related stressors that tug at COs in ways that may interfere with their work. In this case, the stressor is that many male correctional staff in the RHU do not want women working in the RHU with them. They worry about what it would do to their ability to get the job done and how it might increase their workload. Lieutenant Chambers and COs Bills and Anker, speaking separately and confidentially and in a couple different institutions, offered their thoughts on women as RHU staff.

> Lt. Chambers: I haven't seen any women working down here. At the moment, women *can* work down here. There's no policy saying they can't. Management would be too scared of an EEO complaint. [But] it would be bad if women worked down here. . . . They would be harassed by the inmates. . . . According to the executive deputy secretary, there are no gender posts. By policy we could have an RHU full of women, but even one woman would be a hindrance to the team. It would be like an officer down.

> CO Bills: It would be bad for me to work with a woman. I think there's a policy against women working in the RHU because she can't work the bubble [control room], she can't strip [search residents], so it's like being a person down.

> CO Anker: There was a woman down here working a few years ago as a CO. She requested to work down here as part of her training because she was interested in knowing all positions. I don't really know how it went, but it's not in policy that women can't work here. I don't really care if there's a female on this unit. To be honest, there are several women who I'd trust to be in here all day, every day. They work hard, make good decisions and are real tough. Plus, honestly, there would probably be less problems if there were females on the unit because they are typically

better communicators—and are better at negotiating with inmates. We do a lot of that down here, and they'd be excellent at that. Help keep the peace. Sure, it does mean the guys would have more work to do because a female CO couldn't do movement or intake because of the strips, but they could be in the bubble and do other tasks.

These different views about women COs working in the RHU highlight how rule and policy misunderstandings abound. In each case, the correctional staff member misunderstands some information and makes conclusions using that misinformation about work and workload. Without an official DOC policy on women working in the RHU, the policies most apt to help explain opposition to women working in the RHU are those on strip searches and the Prison Rape Elimination Act (PREA). The general inmate handbook notes: "Unless it is an emergency, a staff member of your gender will conduct the strip search."[3] The PREA policy in the general inmate handbook notes that "voyeurism by a staff member . . . means an invasion of privacy of an inmate by staff for reasons unrelated to official duties." Neither of these policies prevent women from working in RHUs in any capacity—whether in the control room (the bubble) or in any other role or duty. If an entire RHU were staffed with female COs and it was not an emergency, a male CO or staff member would need to conduct strip searches, but unless a female CO in the control room was watching men in the cells in a way that constitutes voyeurism and not in the performance of her duty as a CO, there is no reason a female CO should be prohibited from working there—at least in accordance with these policies. Women working in the RHU is not a topic covered in RHU School training.

Regarding correctional staff interpretation or implementation of rules that directly concern residents, there are many similar stories about misunderstandings or discretion. For example, correctional staff largely concur with residents regarding the main issue residents noted, burning. For staff, burning occurs when residents do not follow the rules. It is an informal punishment for nonconformity.

Lieutenant Rogers spends a long time outlining the situation regarding which things residents automatically get (with some inconsistency) and which are discretionary and may lead to burning:

> Shower and yard are things they [the residents] get automatically down here. So the shower list goes around at 6:00 a.m. I don't think that's in the handbook. They find that out real soon after they are burned a few

times. The inmates need to be up on their door, lights on, window uncovered. They can't have a clothesline up or paper on their back window either. If they don't follow those rules, they'll get burnt for sign-up. Trays go out between 6:30 and 7:00, depending on when the kitchen is able to get them down here. The yard list then goes around at 9:00. Lunch trays go out around 10:30–11:00—again, depending on the kitchen. The library list goes out on Sunday. So that list is a list for approved books the inmates can have while they are back here. On Tuesday of each week, they get the books they requested on Sunday. There's also law library. Every inmate can submit a request to go to the law library. However, you can only have one request submitted at a time. This is something another prison came up with, not how it's always done. But the inmate puts his name down and essentially gets in line. When his name reaches the top, he goes to the law library. We don't let them put in multiple requests at a time because we don't want one inmate to monopolize the space. Once they visit, they can immediately put in a new request to visit. There's no waiting period or anything—they just can't have their name in the queue multiple times. I don't know if yard, shower, and law library would be considered rights because we can restrict them. I guess in that sense it's a privilege, but there's a lot of paperwork if we're going to take them away. Well, food is a right, and access to medical care. If a guy skips nine meals in a row, not nine days, yes he goes to medical to the POC [psychiatric observation cell] cell for observation. However, how the food is given to them is not a right. For example, just this morning we had a guy hold his tray. Now, he'll only get the bag meals because he's indicated to us that he can't behave with the tray.

This represents how the Lieutenant views the policies and rules regarding what and when residents receive and specifically what items and services residents are entitled to.

Only on day four (of five) was there any discussion in the RHU School regarding burning resident for meals. One instructor noted: "Officers can't refuse meals . . . but I don't say anything [to residents] about going to the bathroom, having a drink, or being fed unless they [the residents] bring it up." The other instructor added (in jest): "You're not withholding it; you're saving it for later."

On day five (the last day) of the RHU School, a discussion regarding general restrictions of residents occurred. When discussing an example of a resident refusing to give a broken meal tray back to officers, one instructor tells the trainees they have multiple options including restriction (burning), issuing a misconduct if the resident is making threats, bagged food [a meal delivered in a paper bag instead of on a tray], or having a staff member the resident has rapport with talk to them. Of these choices, the instructor notes that if the resident has a weapon and makes threats toward the staff member or their family, "I'd restrict the shit out of them." He continues: "Does this warrant an [cell] extraction? I'd say you're goin' in! . . . I would spray and spray and spray [OC] and let them sit in there." About restriction and extraction, he says:

> I can't tell you what to do or not do during an extraction, but remember you have to talk about it [report to supervisors or DOC]. . . . Remember, you get to go home. They have to be caged like an animal. You know, I get to go home, take my kids out to eat, go to the golf course. You [the resident] get to stand in a cell and yell profanities for the next twenty-three hours and maybe pass out because you're retarded.

These RHU examples specifically illustrate how correctional staff may interpret policy to use it as informal punishment. In addition to on-the-job training, this message is part of their training course for working in the unit.

The narrative of the COs we spoke with largely concurs. CO Wilkes reports: "There are times when they don't get these things [yard, shower, meals]. It happens when we burn them. I know I've burned guys, but I'm only burning guys by policy." And CO Pells offers an example:

> Earlier, I yelled, "Shower!" He [*pointing to a cell*] was sleeping. I go by policy. I announced showers. He didn't come to the door. He thinks we should be his mom and dad and that we should knock on his door. We don't have time to wait for you. Maybe if we had more officers. We always follow policy, but we still get in trouble. What are we supposed to do?

The issue of burning weighs heavily on both residents and staff. It falls in the gray area between a written policy and the informal implementation of it based on particular institutional needs. For both Wilkes and Pells, burning occurs when residents do not specifically follow the pre-item policy by not coming to their door. But Pells takes his explanation a bit further, noting the need to meet institutional needs, such as the need to do things efficiently without an appropriate number of staff on duty.

However, an examination of the specific RHU handbook rules shows that neither Wilkes or Pells (or the dozens of other correctional staff we interviewed) are directly following the written word. The RHU policy for receiving meal trays instructs residents to adhere to the wicket-opening procedures. Those state that residents must "step back from their door with your palms up so the officer can observe you.... Once you are away from your door, the officer will open the wicket." The policy further specifies that when residents are receiving something from a CO (such as a meal tray), the resident will step away from the cell door, the officer will place the item on the wicket, and the CO will step back and then give resident permission to approach the wicket to retrieve the item.

This information was laboriously provided during the RHU School we attended. One instructor specifically noted that COs should "make inmates step back and show their hands." However, even knowing the policy did not stop this instructor from using his discretion to add a new, informal layer. He said, "I always make inmates turn around and get on their knees and put their hands behind their back. I get a lot of shit from inmates because I make them get on their knees, but I don't care." In this way, the instructor is adding an additional layer of rules to the policy that does not exist in writing. In doing so, he believes it enhances security. Yet, the DOC and RHU policies had been written with safety procedures as a primary goal. While the policy states residents must step back from the door, both Wilkes and Pells (and countless other COs) specifically note they require residents to be *at* or *on* the door, while the RHU School instructor asks residents to get on their knees—in seeming direct violation of the written RHU policy and in a way that may decrease safety. While the policy language is somewhat clear, if a resident were to specifically follow the policy, based on the comments of Wilkes, Pells, and the RHU School instructor, they might be in violation of the application of this policy and forfeit a meal (or other item or service) due to insubordination.

Another common discussion from correctional staff regarding policies and rules is about how policy hinders their work. In these instances, staff believe they understand the rule or policy and respond in one of two ways: they move around it or ignore it, or they perform the policy begrudgingly. There are many examples of policies as hindrances to correctional staff. In perhaps the most compelling example (which also appears in an earlier chapter) CO McGillacutty describes a situation where policy gets in the way of COs' potential life-saving activities:

> When we see a guy hanging [suicide attempt], we used to just be able to use mace on him to get him down before anything happened and to stop them. Now, with these stupid policies, if we see it, we have to go get help from psych or sergeant, and by the time we return, that person might be dead already. We could have potentially saved someone's life, but instead have to maybe watch someone die.

In this example, CO McGillacutty feels some level of concern regarding his inability to administer aid to a resident who attempts suicide by hanging. While there is nothing in either the general or RHU inmate handbook about attempted suicides nor the aid or procedures staff should use in dealing with these events, McGillacutty describes a mace (OC/pepper spray) policy and the need for additional correctional staff present when cutting a hanging resident down. His description of a "stupid policy" suggests his frustration and denotes his dislike of the rules regarding suicides in the RHU.

The RHU School does not cover the OC/pepper spray policy, with the exception of a few comments by instructors, such as the following:

> OC is for *your* protection. If you're spraying someone to get out of the shower, the DOC will not like it. When inmates are just refusing, it's best not to spray That's not why OC was given to us. It could be restricted or taken. We have to watch what we do; we need to be ready to justify that.

In subsequent training days at RHU School, OC again comes up in the lecture on use of force. One instructor states: "Too many times people are using OC when an inmate is just breaking a rule. . . . Intent is a key word in justifying use of force. . . . You have to *justify* use of force." The instructor also tells the trainees that force [which includes OC] is used to "regain control, not for punishment" and describes the use-of-force continuum from show of force to control techniques, to chemical munitions (OC), then active countermeasures, and finally firearms. He also tells the class that "OC can be mixed with smoke, which make it harder to breathe. OC and smoke used together can be lethal, and that's why special teams use it." The instructors also point the class to particular sections of the rule book to learn more, but they do not specifically cover these sections in the RHU School.

A senior management staff member, Ully, discusses the OC (pepper spray) policy as officially present only in the use-of-force policy. He says the rule is "to only use OC after verbal de-escalation fails to prevent harm to property or others. We use OC before we lay hands on an inmate, typically to break up a fight or stop self-harm." He adds: "The only guideline I know of is that we are supposed to use one spray in a one-to-three-second burst. Then, we can follow with a second one-to-three-second burst if necessary." He also warns that when OC is used, the oils and vapors "get everywhere." The staff can relieve each other and step outside to get some fresh air if needed and may also ask for decontamination. This includes a trip to medical to shower and change clothes. The resident who is sprayed is supposed to immediately be transported to medical for decontamination, but they may refuse. The cellies and other residents in the unit are undoubtedly affected by the spray particles, but they are not treated.

Ully also specifically discusses the OC practices regarding residents who hang themselves:

> We do not have a new directive [for OC during suicide attempts], but if we go by current policy, we would verbally address the hanging inmate. If he does not respond, we spray him. Lots of staff are upset about this, and there is some talk about the fact that if the guy is actually killing himself, not faking, spraying him could cause him to jerk around and put more pressure on the ligature. So, now we are trying to look to see if he is standing on a seat or if he's really hanging. If he's really hanging and we don't think he's faking just to lure staff into his cell to hurt them, we don't spray. It's not policy yet; it's more like a directive. I think we got a memo about it at some point. It may become [official] policy, but that always takes a long time.

The confusion about when, how much, and why to use OC is concerning on many levels. It is a powerful tool, and one of the few tangible tools (save handcuffs, chains, cells) that correctional staff can use because firearms are not present inside most institutions. Staff receive OC as a tool to help them maintain control, and while it may do its job, it also may have long-term control-limiting effects via the loss of trust, rapport, and legitimacy that erupts between staff and residents when it is dispersed. The spray is made from an oil known as oleoresin capsicum that comes primarily from chili peppers. On the Scoville heat units (SHU) scale, which measures the "heat" of peppers. OC scores very high. For example, a bell pepper measures 0 SHU; a jalapeño pepper scores around 2,500 to 5000 SHUs; and OC scores between 500,000 to 2 million, with some brands measuring as high as 5.3 million SHUs. Although severely discomforting and not generally life-threatening, the effects of OC spray on some individuals with chronic lung disease or asthma may be more intense, even if they are not directly sprayed. Generally, the spray's effect wears off after roughly thirty minutes, with some lingering effects possible for several hours or as much as a week.

Another example of rules as hindrance comes from CO Tova's description of a policy he feels specifically puts RHU officers at physical risk:

> We are really understaffed, which makes a huge officer safety risk. I'm up here by myself [in the bubble], and it's policy to never have only one CO moving inmates. But if we need to stretch, and there's only one CO with an inmate and then the inmate starts attacking him, I can't leave here. I can only open doors and call for more officers and watch everything happen. We need more staff down here. And we're always moving inmates down here too. We have to move inmates at least once every sixty days, but we prefer to move them every thirty days. So, we're moving inmates a lot and don't have enough staff to do it.

Tova feels he is hindered by the policy that he cannot leave the control room to render aid to a fellow officer who is under physical attack from a resident. The policy may be acceptable when the unit is fully staffed, but as Tova notes, when the RHU is shorthanded, that policy means if another CO is being harmed, all he can do is watch and call for others to help. This makes him uncomfortable and makes him feel as if he is not doing his job to his best ability. Interestingly, institutional needs do not seem to afford Tova the approval to intervene to help a fellow officer in the same way that institutional needs intervene to prevent residents from receiving goods and services. In examples like Tova's, competing policies require staff to decide between following one rule instead of another but will not allow them to follow both explicitly or equally. Tova and other correctional staff find situations like this troubling, and the impact of their decisions—which they know may mean life or death—weigh heavily on them.

In a related example in the RHU School, the trainees were having group discussions about how to get all their work done under tight timelines. The scenario they discussed was what the instructor described as a "typical day in the RHU where there are ten things going on and it all needs to be done in an hour and a half." In a five-person RHU team, they need to get the showers cleaned by residents under direct supervision (each shower takes fifteen minutes to clean), process two new intakes, deal with a chaplain who was arriving in ten minutes to notify a resident that his spouse had passed away and that he can speak to a counselor, distribute meals and supplies, and figure out what (if anything) to do with an unreliable resident's comments that a resident in a neighboring cell is planning to throw feces and urine to flood the shower.

The trainee group from Institution C provides their solution first: "We'd tell the chaplain to chill and wait until all the inmates are secured. Who cares about showers? Who cares when they get cleaned? Meals take priority. And another day, more piss and shit."

Another assigned scenario included a resident not standing at the door to go to yard. Again, Institution C's response greatly differs from formal policy and recommends an informal (non-policy) sanction: burning. "Here's how we'd handle it: 'I don't care. I don't care. We don't care. You're not going to yard.'" They provide the resident's response: "Then, fine, I'm going to hang myself." To which they answer: "10–4, fuck face. I'll see ya in a half hour."

In both cases, there was no discussion by the instructors about the solution except some verbal and nonverbal (head nodding) agreement from other groups. Instead, the instructors moved on to a new topic, leaving much about the trainees' responses undiscussed and for other trainees to interpret as they like. In these examples and similar others, the RHU training reinforces (in this case through complacency and nonspecificity) inconsistent rule application and implementation, without discussion and without a focus on specific rules and policies. Trainees are left with a possible solution (which does not adhere to policy) and other examples (only some of which adhere to policy), but without any real direction, instruction, discussion, understanding, or thorough, policy-driven answers. Throughout the RHU School, these and other issues like them were never discussed again.

Regarding cell assignments, COs and management staff, including lieutenants (who are ultimately responsible for all cell assignments), worry about the implications for them if they make the wrong choice. Diller, a senior member of the institutional management staff, notes that it is not a guarantee that a resident will get a misconduct for refusing a cellie. He says that staff have some discretion regarding this. For example, if the cellie is fearful and that fear is justified, the lieutenant may decide not to make a particular cellie match and not give a misconduct to the resident who refused. Diller describes this action as "cover your ass." He tells a story of a resident who recently refused many cellies over several months and eventually committed suicide. Diller says: "He was able to kill himself because he was alone in his cell, without a cellie, so we have to be very careful about cellie refusals as it may be for another reason." In this case, the lieutenant was investigated for not giving this resident a cellmate. Diller's comments reiterate the fear and worry staff have regarding interpreting policy in ways that will not get them into trouble later on. He notes they document everything and do thorough investigations into any allegations residents make regarding being in danger. They do this to protect themselves from current and future liability.

Other COs describe rules and policy as a hindrance at work and for their home life. For example, CO Turcot says the PREA policy impacts him in numerous ways. As the property manager, Turcot's job is to confiscate residents' property when they are transferred from general population to the RHU. He then has to document everything the residents brought with them and allow them to keep only the allotted items in their cells during their RHU stay (which is considerably more for AC residents than for DC residents). CO Thompson notes:

> When I enforce the rules here, there are repercussions on me. It's putting my reputation and potentially my family life on the line because of me trying to do my job. Because I do property a lot, I get PREA'd a lot [having allegations or grievances filed by residents for PREA violations] because I really enforce the property rules. The worst part is that it affects my personal life. Their [residents'] goal is ultimately to get COs thrown off the block and get a lazy officer assigned instead.

In this example (which also appeared in an earlier chapter), Thompson reveals that he believes residents who do not like the way he enforces the property rules regularly file PREA complaints against him as retaliation. This affects his family life because his spouse and children may learn that there are sexual allegations against him at work. He believes that residents hope he will get moved out of the RHU and an officer who enforces property rules more leniently will be assigned instead. The property rules for the RHU are detailed in the RHU inmate handbook. It states that RHU residents are "allowed personal property that will fit in one records-sized box. This will consist of toiletry items, written materials, authorized prescribed medications, and allowable commissary according to your status (AC/DC)." It goes on to note that excess and unallowable (i.e., tobacco, illegal drugs) personal property will be confiscated. Moreover, there are request slips available to residents to ask for additional legal materials as property. Turcot notes he receives PREA violation allegations and grievances when he enforces property rules by making residents throw out or mail home excess property. Turcot and numerous other correctional staff note a PREA violation may, in fact, be frivolous, but it is often difficult for a CO to explain to his family why a resident filed a grievance of a sexual nature against him. For Thompson, the rule is less the hindrance than the consequences of implementing it.

In their lectures, the RHU School instructors provide a couple of examples of breaking or bending policies when they are perceived as a hindrance. One instructor notes: "Sometimes we deviate from policy and give inmates tablets [electronic devices like iPads], TVs, and radios. It has a lot of benefit for us because they aren't bothering us." In a second example (not officially policy yet, but a directive), an instructor notes that his institution does not double-cell residents when they come to the RHU. He says, "We have room, and it causes more problems." These examples provide fertile ground for policy inconsistency once trainees leave the RHU School and go to (or return to) work within the units. On the one hand, policy is policy. It should be followed. Consistency is key. But on the other hand, breaking or bending policy as it suits your or your unit's needs is also appropriate, common, and easily done when the policy interferes with what staff perceive as their work. In many of these examples, correctional staff break policy for what they perceive as the greater good. For example, if their mandate is care, custody, and control of residents, and breaking or bending policy meets that end in that it keeps the peace, correctional staff may justify their actions as aligned with broader institutional goals. However, when correctional staff interpret policy beyond what a policy actually says, it leaves residents wondering what the rules are. It breeds inconsistency and the feelings that come with not knowing what the rules are and if, when, or how they apply to you.

Although COs commonly explain that they strictly enforce rules within the RHU, there are numerous instances where COs and other correctional staff admit to bending or breaking RHU rules via discretion, as the RHU School examples indicate. In these examples, rigid and formal policies become flexible, informal, and, in fact, inconsistent. CO Turcot notes that he strictly enforces property policies and does not like the PREA allegations he receives as a result. However, in the same conversation, he also notes, "A lot of times though, I always make some kind of exception. Let them keep one more thing than they should, or let them take more to their cell. One on one, we'll figure something out that we can both agree on." Other COs describe changing the pod's television channel away from institutional programming and to a sporting event or other program to keep the residents happy, or giving residents they like extra meal trays or longer time to shower. They also describe conducting yard, shower, and meal sign-ups more loudly or quietly depending on how many residents they want to be signed up and providing extra paper, pens, or other materials (like an extra blanket or pillow) to residents who behave or ask nicely. All of these examples operate at the margins of policy, some bending, some breaking, and only ever for a particular set of residents, never all of them equally.

To dig a bit deeper into the evolution of policies, a member of the psychological staff, Ms. Anders, explains where the policy to house residents with cellmates for their first seventy-two hours in the RHU originated. She says it first emerged as a directive and will later be formalized into policy if results show it works. She describes the process:

> We found in our analysis that many of the suicides occurring in the RHU were occurring within the first three days of being sent to the unit. As a result, we now have them live with a cellie to help mitigate this concern. It's possible that some inmates might actually ask for lockup down here to complete their suicide attempts because there's a greater opportunity for less intervention from others.

In response to our question of whether the double-bunk policy is working to curb suicides, she answers:

> It may be too soon to see administrative changes since we just implemented it. Some of the beginning data may not be entirely accurate because some units may have started abiding by the policy later than others. However, we will be trying to reflect on that data shortly. We currently share recommendations in a monthly meeting with the secretary and the superintendents to improve the follow-up that jails are double bunking for the first seventy-two hours. It started as a directive before we were able to write it in policy, so it's possible we are not just seeing complete compliance across institutions.

We ask her to explain the difference between policy and directives. She answers:

> Well, a directive is a policy, and a policy is a directive. The language difference has more to do with the timing or process of formalization. So, in this example, Central Office sends a directive via email to all the jails saying we want to see double-bunking in the RHU for the first seventy-two hours. As soon as Central Office decides it's something they want to carry out, it's a directive that's sent immediately. It is what it sounds like, a direct order for how to do something. However, the formalization of it in policy takes a bit longer. If we were to wait until it was formalized into policy, then there would be no action between the time when we submit it for a policy amendment and when it becomes a policy. With a directive, we can expedite the speed in which jails must change a process. It also allows us time to get feedback from the field that may be necessary to make it a sound policy amendment. Then, we can submit a more final and tested version for a policy update. We have to put an inmate in a cell with a cellie for the first seventy-two hours. There's a directive in place. But it's not easy to do because of restrictions.

The unit manager (UM), Yates, was sitting in on this conversation (with the approval of Ms. Anders) and responds to this last comment, saying, "I haven't seen a policy." Then, the two began talking about a resident who is suicidal who will most likely hurt or kill someone or himself. Ms. Anders comments, "Sometimes we care about suicide. Sometimes we don't."

This directive-to-policy conversation between Ms. Anders and UM Yates reveals how institutional policy changes may occur. However, neither Anders nor Yates spells out whether this information was provided to residents. In our interviews with residents, several described the seventy-two-hour double-bunking policy. The overwhelming consensus from residents was that they could see the value in this action, but they felt wholly uncomfortable monitoring a potentially suicidal resident without any training or assistance. Many residents felt this was not their job, and they should not be asked to do this. UM Yates's comment about not having seen a policy suggests that either a formal policy is not in place yet or Yates has not received communication about it. Perhaps it is still only a directive. When Ms. Anders, as a member of the psychological team, notes, "Sometimes we care about suicides, sometimes we don't," this chilling statement suggests that although the suicide watch policy may have a basis in good intentions, it is troubling that potential suicides may not always be a priority for policy decisions within the broader institution or the RHU.

The policy about residents being notified of new or revised policies is spelled out in the general inmate handbook:

> When DOC policies are changed you will be given notice of the change(s) and the most current policy will become effective, regardless of what information is in this handbook.... When a rule change is made, you will be given a memo that outlines the change and/or a notice will be posted on the housing unit. All notices and signs prepared by DOC officials are considered policy and must be followed. Copies of policies and procedures that contain rules that directly affect you are available on the housing unit and in the facility library.

No information about notification regarding policy changes or directives is provided in the RHU inmate handbook, but information about accessing the RHU law library is outlined (as previously discussed in this chapter). A senior member of the management team, Hooder, specifically describes how staff receive policies and directives:

> We get all policies and directives via email. But we get so many of these it's hard to keep up. The directives come in the form of a memo. They used to summarize the major changes in the email, but now you have to open the document and read the whole thing. So, I might read the whole thing and discover they changed one word. What happens instead is we spend a lot of time sitting around with guys saying, "Didn't we get a directive on that?" And no one seems to remember when we got it or what exactly it said.

For correctional staff working the RHU, rules and policies are often as elusive as they are for residents. Staff readily admit they do not always know particular policies, and sometimes they do not know what they do not know. They also frequently and openly discuss the multitude of ways they maneuver around policies and rules that they do not like or that they feel hurt or hinder them in some way. For staff as for residents, inconsistency abounds and both the manifest and latent effects of non-adherence or discretionary use of policy and rules reverberates in the walls and halls of the RHU, ricocheting from resident to staff and back again in countless ways, creating uncertainty, fear, confusion, and undeniable harm.

Ambiguous, Inconsistent, Confusing
How can the most restrictive unit in a prison also be the most inconsistent? After all, the RHU is where the perceived "worst of the worst" are housed—the residents who could not stay in general population for any number of reasons. It is the place where residents remain locked in their cells up to twenty-three hours a day, seven days a week and are only removed for shower, yard, time in the unit's law library, or a rare non-contact visit. It is also the place where staff must receive extra training to be prepared for the specific and intensive work involved here. And yet, for both residents and staff, inconsistency abounds.

The simple answer involves the complexity of the human condition. Each day in the RHU presents new challenges, and each must be met with some degree of creativity. Creativity begets inconsistency. For residents, this involves learning to live in a small cage with limited movement and activity and no real contact with the outside or even the inside world. In doing so, residents sometimes push the boundaries—perhaps trying to find a small piece of privacy or autonomy, or trying to find new ways of coping with the reality of the RHU. This may entail rule breaking, rule bending, or an attempt (often in vain) to figure out exactly what the rules are, how they are interpreted, and by whom. For staff, this involves learning to work in a prison within a prison, locking up human beings in small cages where their mental and physical health suffers and they manifestly or latently beg for relief from the suffering. In doing so, staff members sometimes push the boundaries—perhaps trying to claim or reclaim their dignity or power or to gain or regain control. As for residents, this may entail rule breaking, rule bending, or an attempt (often in vain) to figure out exactly what the rules are, how to interpret them, and how they interpret them compared to staff and other residents. Depending on the specific scenario, these boundary pushes may appear as peaceful ways of coping, such as residents sleeping all the time or staff providing an occasional extra tray of food to a resident. Or they may appear as forceful or angry protests, such as residents harming themselves or refusing orders or staff burning residents or calling them names. No matter the perception, cause, or consequence, inconsistency in rule interpretation and adherence is perhaps the only consistent aspect of RHU life. It is a pain and a blessing for both residents and staff. This inconsistency becomes all that each knows and what they perhaps depend on most in the institutional bowels beyond view behind walls and bars that both bind and suffocate residents and staff in unimaginable ways.

CHAPTER 5

Reentry

REENTRY IS EXACTLY what it sounds like: going back to somewhere and being able to get back in. In the world of corrections, *reentry* is a common term used to describe the process involved when an individual exits a prison or jail and returns to the community. They have been away and are now *reentering* or returning to a different life—one that contains their families, friends, and neighborhoods outside of carceral walls, bars, and doors. However, reentry does not mean freedom for many individuals as they will carry their criminal history and their experiences within penal institutions with them. Additionally, many reentrants will also have other forms of supervision once released from custody, including probation or parole, or both.

Prior to the use of the term *reentry*, correctional scholars did not pay much attention to life after prison. One of the first uses of the term *reentry* occurred in 2000 when Dr. Jeremy Travis, then director of the Urban Institute, and his colleague Dr. Joan Petersilia, then at the University of California, Irvine, co-hosted the first Reentry Roundtable, bringing together scholars and practitioners from around the United States to discuss the challenges involved when prisoners return home. At this meeting, an impressive team of folks discussed everything from recidivism (rearrest, reconviction, and reincarceration), to employment, housing, and programming for returning individuals, and even to the effects reentry has on families, children, and communities. From there, reentry, along with the related concept of reintegration, worked its way into scholarship and is now a large and seemingly ever-growing area of correctional focus and research.

In prison research in general, reentry is a common concern. Many prisons and jails host a series of reentry planning and preparation opportunities for residents, including courses to prepare for reentry, case management regarding reentry planning, and even movement of some individuals to private or RHU cells in the days or weeks prior to reentry to ensure safety from other residents who may want to harm or prevent a soon-to-be reentrant from leaving custody. Within RHUs though, there is very little conversation or planning around how RHU residents will reenter society (outside prison) or the general population, which is another form of reentry of sorts and one many residents navigate. Time in the RHU is a bit of a time-out from the general population, with only scant RHU attention to reentry. There are some notable exceptions though in specialty RHUs, where specific programming uses a gradual or step-down model. In these programs, such as an RHU designed for those with severe mental health diagnoses, residents often work their way through a program with various classes and tasks to complete while they move from step to step, edging closer to general population reentry.

Additionally, some RHUs incorporate step-down models for RHU residents who have spent considerable time in the RHU and may have forgotten how to live in the general population. For example, residents who have spent ten or more years in the RHU may need a gradual system to help them learn to live among others again. This can include increased time out of cell and being around others, a few hours spent in the general population unit before returning to the RHU, and psychological counseling to prepare them for general population reentry. All in all though, community reentry is a distant dream for many RHU residents, and general population reentry is just a cell transfer without much preparation or planning. Reentry then is just an exit from the RHU, and what comes next is merely a new unit, a new cellie, and a bit more movement, but it comes with a host of new challenges that residents are largely left to navigate on their own.

Residents on Reentry

For the few residents who discuss reentry, it takes on two distinct forms. The first is intra-carceral reentry from the RHU back into the prison's general population. Because the RHU is essentially a prison within a prison, RHU residents sometimes muse about returning to the general population. As a form of reentry, this movement is typically either fraught with fear and concern or eagerly anticipated with hope for a more socially normalized routine.

For most RHU residents, a stay in the RHU is relatively temporary, but many residents continually cycle in and out of the RHU during their prison stay. For some RHU residents, however, their time in the RHU lasts much longer. What may begin as a short sentence can get longer and longer with misconducts and infractions, or it may have started prior to recent changes that disallow indefinite RHU stays. The stays of RHU residents in the prisons of study ranged from thirty days to one resident who had been there over thirty years. Typically though, residents in general population receive a misconduct for a negative behavior (or in some cases request/receive RHU placement for various issues in general population), then go to the RHU on disciplinary (DC) or administrative (AC) status, serve their time, return to general population, and recycle through this process again and again and again. In these cases—which are many—RHU residents are familiar with the reentry-to-general-population merry-go-round. It becomes almost routinized. It is, in fact, a common, even expected, part of the carceral experience. RHU residents often muse about times they spent in RHUs at this or other institutions, comparing them, citing differences or similarities between staff, facilities, and privileges. Just as many say criminal activity and a prison sentence are common components of young Black male life courses, so too is the RHU. For many, it is a normal, standardized, and accepted part of prison living.

The other form of reentry, returning to a community, is less frequently discussed. In the few discussions of post-carceral community reentry, residents long for love and familial relationships and gainful employment, while others express a desire to help themselves or others once they get out of prison. For a few residents, this practice is familiar, common, and somewhat normalized because they have experienced it before. But for others, this is a new form of reentry—one that comes with some level of anxiety and stress. Most RHU residents will return to the general population prior to their release into the community, but there are a few who "max out" (serve their entire sentence or the end of it in the RHU) and reenter their external community directly from the RHU. In both cases, RHU residents sometimes ponder what the world will be like upon their release: Will their family and loved ones welcome and accept them? Will they find a job? Will they be able to stay out of prison? The next sections of this chapter consider both reentry pathways by using resident narratives. The chapter concludes with staff perceptions of reentry and compares both groups.

Intra-carceral Reentry: From the RHU to General Population

For most RHU residents, the RHU represents a temporary locale—one from which they will eventually return to general population. In fact, one resident refers to it as a "big boy time-out." In some cases, residents relish the thought of leaving the RHU and returning to general population. They may look forward to the increased privileges and relatively greater movement that general population provides. Some are excited about getting to see their old friends and acquaintances in general population or pleased that they may be changing to a new general population cell block upon RHU release.

Resident Kalls suggests his mental health will likely improve when he leaves the RHU. He notes he is "better in general population" and cites what he sees as an improvement in his mood and feelings when he is not in the RHU.

Resident Jebs says he looks forward to the social interaction and goings-on in general population as a welcome change from the isolation and drudgery of the RHU: "Last year, I was in the hole [RHU] for six months and then when I got sent back to population, I didn't sleep for two days because I didn't want to miss out on anything like I had been for the past six months."

These responses, though noteworthy, are atypical for RHU residents. Most RHU residents are not looking forward to general population reentry—facing it with some fear or uneasiness instead. Resident Abler worries about his physical safety in general population:

> I'm scared of being in prison. The fight that landed me in solitary was a hit on me [an ordered attempt to try to kill him]. If I had not fought back, I would have been killed. When I leave solitary, I think I will be sent right back to the same cell block where my attackers still live. They are waiting for me to return.

Another resident, Kempo, tells a story about a resident he knew who tried to stay in the RHU out of fear:

In February, a guy came down here and owed over a thousand dollars [to another resident in general population]. So, [to get down here] he threatened a lieutenant. Then he lied on a request to security, so they put him on AC rather than DC status while he waits for a transfer [to another prison].

In fact, numerous residents recall how they or other residents have tried to stay in the RHU on purpose. This suggests a somewhat common diminished or absent desire for general population reentry.

Resident Lawler says: "I wouldn't think someone would choose to live here, but they definitely do. I guess if you run up a drug debt or something. I've seen it here and at other institutions. . . . They refuse to leave the RHU."

Resident Walters adds: "They don't want to go to GP [general population]; they're scared. When it's time to get out of the hole, they act out—thirty to forty arguments, threats. They act out to get more DC time."

While instances of residents trying to get into or stay in the RHU are somewhat common, there is more to this story than just fear. Some residents note that they like the quiet and the alone time of the RHU. For example, when asked if there was anything he would miss about the RHU after returning to general population, resident Victor replies: "Yeah, the solitude. Isn't it crazy that I say it's lonely but that I'm also gonna miss the solitude? I guess it's important to human nature to have time to yourself and with your thoughts."

Resident Klock agrees but links his connection to the RHU to people caring about and listening to him. In response to a question about what he might miss about the RHU, Klock says to the interviewer: "Yeah, talking to you right now. I don't care about being in population or in the RHU. I'm still in prison. Talking to someone who cares about us or does something for us is what I'll miss. This [our interview] made my day for the next six months—*this* is all I needed." For Klock, who also comments that he regularly sees a counselor [psychiatric staff member] in the RHU but does not have regular access to her when he is in general population, the connection to another person—be it an interviewer or a psychiatric staff member—is meaningful and perhaps edges him toward wanting to stay in the RHU.

Notably, though, most residents do not discuss intra-carceral, general population reentry or external, community reentry at all during our interviews. Thoughts generally rest on day-to-day concerns, day-to-day living, and survival (both mental and physical) within the RHU. In the intense mundanity and routine of RHU life, residents keep conversations mostly to topics regarding risk, relationships, and rules. For residents, the RHU is about the here and now—how they must live to keep living.

External Community Reentry: Leaving Prison and Returning Home

For the few residents who talk about leaving prison and reentering external communities, conversations mostly focus on what they miss and what they are looking forward to once they get out. Job plans, family reconnection plans, and staying on a positive path are among the most common themes.

Resident Nelson says: "I do plan to get a job when I get out and go to wherever my kids are."

Resident Raufer says: "I'm going to go to school when I get out."

And resident Bushey simply notes: "I'm not coming back."

In more-telling tales, residents Calcur, Minnich, Smithers, and Abel, in separate interviews, describe their specific familial goals upon reentry.

> Resident Calcur: I've never met my one daughter. She was born the day I got sentenced. I was pissed at my baby momma for not showing up to court, but then I found out she was in labor. They won't bring her to see me. She doesn't even know I'm her dad. As soon as I get out, I'm gonna go meet my daughter.
>
> Resident Minnich: I'm going to continue building a relationship with my son, who will be nine. He was four when I got locked up. I'm also going to get a job. My father owns a company and wants me to work for him. I'm going to maintain it, build a relationship with my family, [and] build my mind.
>
> Resident Smithers: My wife always visits me, calls me, and has stuck by me. Thinking about her keeps me going. When I think about doing something bad, I look at her picture. I asked her a while back, "Do you still want a divorce?" She said "No, why would I?" I just told her I wanted to hear it from her. I thought she didn't, but I wanted to know for sure. She's stuck by me when my brothers and sisters haven't. They don't want anything to do with me, but she's really stood by me. [Before prison] I didn't treat her well, so when I get out of here, I want to make up for that.
>
> Resident Abel: I've been given a lot of time to think. I have a son who will be six when I get released. I feel bad for not being there for him. I don't want him to think, "Where was my dad?" I have my high school

diploma and two college degrees. Now, I don't care about that and want other things. Really. I'm just concerned about other people looking down on me. I don't want my son to see me like this.

But, for all the longing to go home, there is also a pronounced sense that RHU residents feel an overwhelming pain spurred by missed opportunity. That missed opportunity, for most, comes from the lack of available programming in prison in general, but specifically during their time in the RHU. For RHU residents, it seems confusing why if they are the "worst of the worst," they are given no opportunities, while locked up twenty-three hours a day, to better themselves. Resident after resident reported a distinct frustration and sadness regarding the lack of classes, treatment, and preparation they believe they need to be better in the prison and within society.

Resident Lusk sums it up well:

> Where's the rehabilitation? They don't rehabilitate, teach you to be a better citizen. This is nothing but a five-star college to become a better criminal. You don't know how to steal a car? You will when you leave. You don't know how to steal credit card information? You will when you leave here! This is supposed to be the department of corrections. They aren't correcting anything. You're leaving here the same, if not worse.

With similar sentiments, Resident McComb states:

> It's at its lowest here. I'm not used to living like this. There should be classes here or something. They could give us more trades. We leave society and come back with the same problems. You know, like I'm a drug addict, and they could do something for me. But instead, they keep putting me back out [to my external community] with no way to handle myself. So, I can't even get a job because I don't have something to offer anyone.

And Resident Yardley says:

> In the minds of others, you're a criminal, and you're always going to be one. Because of this, they don't give you opportunity to improve while in prison. They use your jacket [prison records] against you, and that is the reason they don't make programs rehabilitative. . . . That label is a form of torture, and the anger builds up [in you]. (*His eyes fill with tears.*)

Resident Tends reports: "Prison doesn't help me prepare for release. Even the judge who sentenced me said so. He only sentenced me to eight to sixteen years because he said that prison isn't going to help me become a better person."

Many residents who discussed their eventual return to home communities expressed an impending feeling of worry about finding their place in their family, home, town, and neighborhood. This worry is coupled with the gut-wrenching sense of inadequate preparation for their new, post-prison life.

Of course, not all residents have positive thoughts about reentry. Several mentioned wanting to commit crimes upon release (including one who noted they would find and kill a CO and his or her family).* But for the most part, the relatively limited number of residents who did talk about reentry wondered aloud if they were ready, if there was actually a way to be ready, and if and how they might remain free? To deal with such doubts, some residents constructed reentry plans for self-improvement. These represent both a form of reentry preparation and a means of coping with their current situation and status.

Coping with Reentry Perils within RHUs

Without adequate programming, if any, RHU residents rely on themselves and sometimes each other, to prepare for intra-carceral and post-prison reentry. They do this, however, mostly without support, training, or adequate resources or tools. This leaves many residents wondering if they are doing the right thing, if they are appropriately prepared, and if there is any way for them to remain out of RHU and out of any kind of custody in the future?

Resident Ziller explains: "Over time you adapt more than you think. But going home is difficult because you realize how much the time in solitary affected you." Ziller says he's been diagnosed with anxiety, claustrophobia, depression, antisocial personality disorder, and bipolar disorder since he began serving time in the RHU. He explains that he needs

---

* As part of our informed consent process with residents, we make sure residents understand that if they threaten to harm themselves or others in real and tangible ways, we must break confidentiality and report these instances to prison authorities. During further in-depth conversations with this resident, we learned that he was exaggerating and did not actually plan to kill anyone. We discussed him with custodial and psychological staff without revealing his name, and given what was said and the context within which it was delivered, they agreed with our assessment. Thus, we did not break confidentiality for this instance.

treatment because "you gotta find something you like to stay sane, or you can lose your mind in the blink of an eye." Ziller is telling an all-too-familiar tale of residents having to meet their own needs within the RHU without the help of professionals or treatment programs. To do this, residents sometimes innovate by finding ways to cope without things they need and even ways of getting them.

Scholar Sydney Ingel and her coauthors write about the strain and gain of RHU life. They detail how blocked opportunities to needed resources and services lead residents to take matters into their own hands at times, making the policies and practices within the RHU that are meant to control considerably less effective.[1]

Numerous residents discuss the lack of programming and options for self-improvement within the RHU. Resident Yonner notes: "I'm trying to position myself to be in a better position when I get out, but it's hard when they really block you."

Residents like Nixon use available resources such as writing, reading, and exercise to cope and find ways of self-improving and preparing for reentry:

> I watch TV and listen to music. I read and use other people's tablets, but that was back in the day [when he was in general population, where tablets are available]. I can't do that anymore. I do some singing, dancing, and my puzzle books. I have a lot of emotions when I don't have that. That's why I got puzzle books. If I don't have anything to do, the emotions just build up.

Resident Balse bemoans the lack of activities and programs:

> They don't even give us classes. No classes or programs to take. When I was in federal [prison], they gave us classes. Trades we could learn. Here, they don't update anything. And they give us nothing to do but fight. They did have carpentry when I first came here. But since, they've gotten rid of it. All these youngsters [younger residents] do is sit here and rap. They need something to do for when they get out. Nothing . . . they don't do nothing here. The youngsters are rotting. I'm old. I don't care. They need something though.

Resident Frank adds that it is not only the lack of programming in the RHU that bothers him, but it is also how going to the RHU affects his opportunities in general population:

The books here are shitty. There are no opportunities for education, and you always lose your prison job when you come here [to RHU]. If you were enrolled in classes in gen pop, you have start them over from the beginning when you get out of the hole.

Residents Mears and Wesby also find ways to do what they can to prepare themselves for reentry to both general population and their home communities. Mears says: "I feel good when I learn something new by reading. There's nothing else I can do besides that. It's monotonous." Resident Wesby prepares himself physically: "I do yoga and meditate every day. That enables me to learn more about myself."

As they plan to eventually leave prison, many residents realize that time in the isolated RHU may cause problems. They try to rectify that by getting any social interaction they can. Some hope to do this through cellies; others through going back to general population. Resident Rocco says:

I'm trying to be more social when I get close to my release. I chat with COs for that too, but not about anything personal. It doesn't really help though; it's frustrating. I'm not social. I worry I will get out and overreact to something normal. The more I open up, the more they press my buttons.

Resident Vandy has other techniques to prepare for reentry: "Sometimes I take naps and work on my calisthenics. It's hard to do in the cell 'cause I don't have much room. . . . I send out for law books [order by writing to outside vendors]."

Resident Sueter goes beyond helping just himself and tries to help others prepare for community reentry: "While you're in here, you have to get your stuff together. We laugh and joke, but we have to get it together. I try to pass on what I can to help others get themselves together so we can all get out and go home."

The RHU Reentry Paradox

For RHU residents, the dream of reentry to general population or their external community is not lost, but it is often a bitter prospect fraught with worry coupled with an acute feeling of missed opportunity. Most RHU residents perceive the RHU as "a big boy time-out," as one resident calls it. In parenting, the use of the time-out is somewhat controversial, with child care experts from medicine, psychology, and other fields touting both the benefits and challenges of forcing a child to idly sit and think about the negative behavior or emotion they previously exhibited.

For children, time-out is typically short, with many experts firmly arguing that parents and caregivers must ensure the child knows they are loved and valued and knows they are in time-out due to an attitude or behavior, not because of who they are as a person, not because of some innate character flaw. The time-out is coupled with a conversation afterward with the parent that ensures the child understands the reason for the time-out and a discussion of how the child's behavior was inappropriate and how not to do it again. Within the RHU though, the time-out is just an exercise in additional incapacitation—further removal from social interactions plus an opportunity to think, but without appropriate guidance about those thoughts and the actions that led to the time-out.

As a society, we seem keenly aware (and science backs us up) that adolescent brains are not fully formed or developed until much later than was previously thought. Most recently, scientists began arguing that the brain is not fully developed until the late twenties for most. Although not all residents enter prison early in life, many do. In criminal justice and psychology, we also understand that many individuals who are criminally involved regularly possess a social history of bad decisions. We are so aware of this tendency toward what we sometimes call "criminal thinking" that we have whole classes and programs designed according to the principles of cognitive behavioral therapy and that are intended to teach individuals involved in the criminal-legal system new ways to think.

Yet, when we put these individuals in RHUs, we offer none of these resources. We leave them alone—alone with their thoughts, the same thoughts that likely brought them to the RHU in the first place. We give them no social interaction; no human contact; very little, if any, psychological counseling; and no access to programs, treatments, therapy groups, or classes. For most RHU residents, there are no intra-reentry classes that, like an appropriately executed parental time-out, help individuals learn what they need to do to succeed when they leave the time-out. Additionally, any resident who maxes out of the RHU and exits prison to return to their home community will likely not have access to post-release reentry classes. Even residents in general population have no guarantee of reentry classes because many prisons do not have these, and those that do offer only limited programs to relatively few residents. Yet, we expect somehow that RHU residents, all by themselves, will learn the error of their ways and emerge better people.

Residents seem to understand this paradox at a visceral level, and their stories and conclusions are not pretty. Their words speak volumes about the pain caused by the RHU and how the system is failing them—even when they know what they need and specifically ask for help. In separate interviews, several residents reflect on the lack of opportunities:

> Resident Kellen: It's the worst time of your life when you're supposed to get out and you can't do nothing.

> Resident Cudder: I came here by myself. I will leave here by myself.

> Resident Nox: There aren't any advantages here. Keeping someone for this long is not going to help them. For example, if you have a dog that bites and you keep the dog in the basement all the time, when you let the dog up, it will still bite. The RHU is creating monsters. Some people are so comfortable, they don't want to leave. Or they don't care. *I care. I want out.* . . . This is violating. I hate this the most.

Staff on Reentry

Perhaps the most telling aspect of staff perceptions of and thoughts about reentry—be it intra-carceral or post-release community reentry—is the near total lack of attention to it. Although we asked staff and residents the same questions and spent similar amounts of time with individuals from each group, only seven of ninety-five staff we talked to had any comments about either type of reentry. It simply is *not* a topic they think about and certainly not one they discuss. Staff narratives in the chapter on relationships suggest that they think about and discuss their own return home—after each shift. However, the same is absolutely not true regarding residents. In fact, of the seven staff members who mentioned reentry, only one offered a positive, substantive reentry-focused comment. The other six staff discussed reentry negatively, noting their dislike for any programs or treatment that do not fit the mission of punishment within the RHU.

Overall, the main concern of the very few staff who discussed reentry was residents not receiving the proper punishment they believe the RHU should dole out. COs Gilmore and McGullicutty in separate interviews discussed their beliefs that the RHU is too soft or lenient on residents. They felt the punitive goals were left unmet.

> CO Gilmore: The amount of freedom the inmates get has increased so much. It's like a fucking day camp in here. It's frustrating because they are supposed to be getting punished, but instead they are getting stuff that they can't even get at home. They don't have to pay for shit. They get a roof over their head, cable, three meals a day, toilet paper, everything provided for them. I know some guys here who were homeless before, but did stuff to end up in prison so that they just wouldn't have to live on the streets anymore. It's crazy.

> CO McGillicutty: This place [the RHU] is not a punishment to be here, but it is a consequence for inmates' actions—they lose privileges by being here. But the inmates are offered a lot more perks here than they were a few years ago. They are allowed to have commissary here now. It's to the point that they have just as much as they did when they were out in population, so they don't really benefit from being up here. For this place to be a punishment, they would have to lose privileges.

CO Mills offers the only comment about intra-carceral reentry in our data. He is upset because the RHU consistently releases residents back to general population because of housing issues:

> We should be running at 90 percent capacity in the RHU. We're at 85 percent now because people are refusing [to accept cellies in the RHU]. We have to release people with sanctions. If you put an inmate in with a cellie who refuses and they hurt them, it comes back on the staff immediately. If something happened, that staff member would be fired.

For Mills, the punitive theme continues in his comments about not wanting to release RHU residents with sanctions that would normally keep them in the unit. Mills criticizes the logistical need for the RHU to release some residents back to general population before serving their full RHU sentence. He reasons that if an RHU resident refuses to accept a cellmate and there is nowhere else to bunk an incoming RHU resident, if COs force the double-celling and one of the residents hurts the other one, the staff member is potentially liable and may perhaps lose their job. While this is not an explicit anti-reentry sentiment, it does link to Mills's desire to keep residents sentenced to the RHU until they are punished according to their sanction and not to release them early for any reason, even for lack of space. For Mills, seeing punishment through its full course outweighs any potential desire to use the RHU for correcting resident behavior.

Mills's comments also signal a larger challenge (perhaps it is the elephant in the room) of correctional work by noting the desire to fill RHUs and keep them full. This aligns with prison-boom findings and the if-you-build-it-they-will-fill-it mentality that so many communities experienced in the 1980s and 1990s in the tough-on-crime years in the United States and still today.[2] By design, RHUs are meant (at least in part) as a last resort (at least in theory) for residents who cannot or will not abide by prison rules. This point is lost on correctional staff like Mills, who wholeheartedly adhere to the need to not only punish residents using the RHU but to do so by keeping the RHU residents for the entire length of their RHU sentence. It also signals a vicious (albeit informal) policy problem in RHUs that stems from an exchange of power among COs and residents. While the informal and generally accepted rule includes "if they will accept a cellie," residents do not have the power to ultimately choose cellmate placement. But years of forced double-bunking in RHUs, without considering resident preferences, has, in fact, led to some violence between cellies when a cellie is forced upon an unwilling celled resident. In these cases, staff perceive they may be held liable or at fault for not taking a resident's wishes seriously (which may constitute a threat). Mills worries about this and blames residents, not the system, for the problems in the RHU's diminished number of residents. It is, perhaps, another example of correctional staff believing and firmly buying into lore about residents as problems, without thinking through the broader contextual and cultural challenges a failing system faces and dishes out.

Not all staff agree, though, on reentry. In fact, one staff member discussed reentry positively and at some length. After describing several treatment programs available to residents in the general population and a special RHU unit for mentally ill, CO Montgomery goes into some detail regarding his feelings about and role in residents' community reentry:

> I think reentry programs are important, and any chance I get, I spout my reentry stuff! It's important to get them to start planning what they're going to do once they get out. In fact, I try to tell them that they need to start planning what they'll do once they get out the day they come in. I also help them to things like get copies of their birth certificates and

credit reports. One of the worst things I have to deal with is trying to get them to fill out forms for things correctly. But it's good practice. If you go to apply for a job, you can't keep asking them for new application because you mess one up! I also try to teach them about health. I ask them what the first things they're going to eat when they get out will be. Usually they tell me something fried and greasy. But I also try to teach them not just about physical health but healthy relationships.... It's really important for them to plan. I tell them you have to get your ducks in a row before two months before you're getting out.

For Montgomery, prison time in general and in the RHU specifically is one stop on a longer life pathway. Montgomery feels preparation is key for residents. He tries to do his part to help residents get out, and stay out, of prison. Through their tone and delivery, Montgomery's comments offer a refreshing and hopeful perspective, particularly when compared to the less optimistic reentry discussions with other staff—or the glaring lack of them.

The Missing Reentry Narrative
All told, the message of this chapter is simple: risk, relationships, and rules are at the heart of daily life for both RHU residents and staff, but reentry (either intra-prison or community) is not a primary focus of nearly anyone's attention. The question is why? What explains how and why residents locked in small cells behind bars and razor wire for twenty-three hours a day—without adequate nutrition, social interaction, or educational and treatment options and with near-constant fear and worry—do not regularly consider a life with more movement and some privileges in general population or a life of autonomy and freedom outside the prison walls? And for staff who work in the intense and complex RHU environment with residents for eight or sixteen hours a day (when they work mandatory double shifts), why is there seemingly little concern for preparing residents to reenter general population where their colleagues work (and they sometimes work) or the communities where former residents will live and work among families and neighbors?

For residents, there are perhaps several plausible explanations for their lack of thinking about reentry of any kind. Many RHU residents have long or lifetime prison sentences, so thoughts about community reentry post-release may be painful reminders of a life they will never again have or never pursue, at least not while they are still relatively young. But

95 percent of all residents, even those with long sentences, will eventually be released from prison. Maybe the deeper answer emerges from the adage "out of sight, out of mind." Thinking about community release when you are facing another twenty or thirty years of custody may be overwhelming in untold ways. It may also be that community life outside of prison is not a priority when day-to-day existing and survival make thoughts about living and thriving outside of prison a luxury that residents do not have the time or energy to pursue.

One way of thinking about this is with the theoretical principles of Overmier and Seligman's psychological theory of learned helplessness.[3] In their research on learned helplessness in organizational life, management scholars Martinko and Gardner define learned helplessness as "the notion that after repeated punishment or failure, persons become passive and remain so even after environmental changes that make success possible."[4] For some residents, life outside prison may have been less than ideal, so the thought of going back to that life does not register as a goal worth pursuing. In fact, it may constitute trading one set of threats for others. For these residents, imagining a non-carceral life may be an exercise in futility if they have never known a positive or safe life. For example, consider what post-prison ideas might look like for youth tried in adult court and sentenced well into their adult years. For residents who entered prison early in life and stayed for a long time or even for residents who just stayed for a long time, it is likely that they do not know what they do not know. They do not understand or comprehend what they are missing on the outside. For residents like this, imagining a world beyond prison may not just be difficult, it may be nearly impossible.

As for residents' lack of concern for intra-prison, general population reentry, there are also several plausible explanations. While life in the RHU is often challenging, many residents also find life in general population difficult too. Some residents, as evidenced in the narratives presented above, actually find some value in the RHU. It is generally safer because residents are locked down and do not mingle with each other, except for their cellie. This is particularly important to residents who may owe general population residents money or favors or may fear violence from other general population residents. It is also generally quieter in the RHU; with fewer residents and more control of movement, residents frequently report some level of calm or at least solitude in RHU living. There are also fewer opportunities to get or use drugs or alcohol. While not all RHU residents find this valuable, for some, the RHU affords time to detox or stop using substances—sometimes in the hope that they may stay substance-free upon return to general population or the external community. Additionally, some residents cycle between general population and the RHU so regularly that a trip to the RHU may become a routine part of their carceral experience. For these residents, there is no need to think about or talk about intra-prison reentry; they have been through it before and understand the ins and outs of this movement. Finally, for RHU residents who have been in the RHU for many years—and perhaps expect to be there for many more years—reentry of either type may be a distant and mostly neglected or avoided dream—a form of tenacious resilience. When hope of reentry is lost, it is not surprising the reentry narrative is also missing.

While any of these explanations may ring true for RHU residents, they place the onus of reentry planning and preparation solely on residents—the reentrants—and do not include any expectation of organizational or systemic assistance or motivation for reentry planning. By expanding our thinking about how and why RHU residents (individuals within the system) rarely discuss community reentry, it is possible to think beyond the individual and to a broader, more formal organizational, agency, or environmental (systems) level.

By not saying much, RHU staff speak volumes regarding their concern for or understanding of their role in reentry. Only one of ninety-five (0.01 percent) interviewed correctional staff within RHUs discussed reentry as an occupational or personal goal. In fact, only seven of ninety-five (0.07 percent) staff interviewed even discussed reentry at all, and six of the seven talked about ways to *prevent* reentry or *further punish* residents instead of focusing on release. In the confines of the RHU, staff are mostly *not* thinking about, talking about, or doing anything to help residents prepare for any kind of reentry, and their unit, institution, and the larger correctional system are also not encouraging them to do so. Instead, the broader correctional system is, in fact, manifestly or latently (depending on the particular system) discouraging it. This is equally true for intra-prison reentry to general population and post-release community reentry.

The punishment goal of rehabilitation is largely absent from correctional institutions today, but perhaps nowhere is this truer than within the RHU. The RHU is not a place where institutions send residents for enhanced therapy, treatment, education, or training. These are not the explicit or implicit goals of the RHU. The RHU is, as has been mentioned, "a big boy time-out"—a place for removal, a place for sanctions, and a place to tuck away residents who the institution does not want to or feels it cannot control in general population settings. While the narratives in this chapter suggest that some RHU residents purposefully try to go to or stay in the RHU, for most residents the RHU is a sanction for misconduct. They may have understood the likely result of their misdoings, but it did not deter their actions because prison culture has both a formal and informal rule book that speaks much louder to many residents than the threat of further incapacitory punishment via the RHU. The RHU's primary goals include incapacitation, deterrence, and retribution, but *not* rehabilitation.

The RHU is specifically designed to punish, with perhaps a sub-goal of improving safety and security for residents and staff by removing certain individuals from general population, even if temporarily. The RHU succeeds at achieving its incapacitation goals. It effectively removes individual residents from general population for punishment or sanction and keeps them confined until the institution decides to send them back to general population or until they max out of their prison sentence and return to their external community. It may also succeed, depending on the perspective, in serving a retributory function. Resident and staff narratives (if only limitedly for staff) suggest no real evidence though of RHUs deterring anyone. Reentry of any kind requires rehabilitation. However, rehabilitation is not a primary concern for most RHU residents and is a concern for only very few RHU staff. Rehabilitation is not a goal or an outcome almost anyone in the RHU finds worth pursuing. The reentry and reintegration narrative is rare at best. In most cases, it is forgotten, abandoned, brushed away, and is, in fact, missing.

CHAPTER 6

Reform

REFORM WITHIN RHUS is just one word residents and staff use to describe change, implementation, improvements, and fixes. For everyone involved, reform may be formal, planned, top-down administrative changes to policy or practice, such as new or revised programs, guidelines for adhering to changes in the law or DOC or institutional policy, or even new food, commissary choices, uniforms, or equipment and supplies within the unit. Reform may also emerge via informal, horizontal, ground-level decisions or changes to policy or practices, including resident movement times, television programs, and library offerings and guidelines for borrowing books. Or in some cases, reform may just be in the hearts and minds of residents and staff—something they want or need but not something they are expecting or experiencing.

In the RHU, each real or tangible change—even the most minute—are noticed because the rhythm of daily RHU living usually has a slow, steady beat. When any change—small or large—interrupts that rhythm, everyone notices the subtleties of the variance. Sometimes, the change, though recognized, does not acutely register as wholly different, and life goes on as usual. However, sometimes change rips through the RHU and causes great stress and strain for residents or staff, or both. Some change is discussed and outwardly resisted, but some manifests as an undercurrent of anger or frustration, and the aftermath may seem difficult to blame on one particular change instead of the RHU circumstances in general.

Additionally, needed change may become conversational fodder. Both residents and staff desire changes (reforms) among their own group and, at times, possess a keen interest in seeing or manifesting improvements.

During interviews with both RHU residents and staff about reform, we focused our questions in two areas: changes that had been made and changes they would like to see. Regarding noticed changes, there was very little to report. Both staff and residents overwhelmingly agree the RHU has changed minimally over the years save its perceived deterioration. There were though, two notable exceptions: the introduction of televisions and the classifying of residents with a severe mental health diagnosis as D-codes (now placed in a specialty RHU unit called the Diversionary Treatment Unit, or DTU).[1] The general consensus among both residents and staff is that the RHU was *never* a good and just place, but it has steadily decreased in quality and substance over time—though residents and staff vary considerably on what constitutes quality and substance. This stems from both residents and staff believing that each has become tougher, angrier, and less humane than they were in prior years. No one discussed any physical or architectural changes within RHUs, though some residents thought RHUs at particular prisons were decidedly better than those at their current institution. This was generally due to perceptions of how staff and residents treat one another and the introduction of televisions to the units several years ago. There is disagreement among residents about the TVs, with most residents liking the distraction they bring, but a small and vocal group thinking the arguments over which shows to watch and the power COs use to determine TV programming and availability create more harm than good. Staff mostly dislike the TVs, arguing they coddle residents in ways that do not fit with their version of punitive RHU goals. Because both residents and staff mostly neglect any discussion about existing reform, the remainder of this chapter focuses primarily on each group's desire for change and their ideas for how to improve the RHU.

Residents on Reform

For RHU residents, reform or change is a day-to-day concern, but most residents do not let reform ideas overtake their thinking. This means that residents regularly engage in thought exercises regarding changes they would like to see in the RHU. They often take those thoughts a step further to consider how or in what ways those changes might improve their RHU, post-RHU, or post-prison lives. However, most residents do not allow reform fantasies to occupy too much of their thoughts, and most residents express hope, but not blind hope, that some of their ideas regarding change or reform will come to fruition. In fact, for many residents the exercise of thinking about possible reforms is as far as they ever believe it will go. They do not regularly express these ideas to anyone, or only to a very few individuals—mostly other residents.

Changes or improvements to staff is by far the most prominent kind of change desired by RHU residents. This theme occurs again and again—so much so that even when other reforms are mentioned, changes involving staff are almost always also present. Residents also privilege several other desired changes including items relating to basic needs (food and hygiene), policies, programming, and resources. There is also a litany of change ideas that include improving healthcare, offering employment options, fixing race relations, and improving access to privacy within RHUs.

The most salient change residents desire involves improvements to RHU staff. These concerns hover around a handful of specific requests—all with the goal of growing the capacity for RHU staff to work with residents in humane, just, effective, and helpful ways.

Resident Richland summarizes this feeling:

> The COs are unprofessional. Like, on a scale of one to ten, they're a two. For example, the humanity is not there. I understand in a situation like prison they have to keep their jobs, but they could have a little humanity. I can see why no CO wants to be in jail. I do see the good in some of them, but others, I don't.

Resident Hinder concurs:

> The inmates who cut themselves really need to see psych. The COs will tell them just to kill themselves. It makes them [the residents] feel awful. If the COs had a good attitude, that would be better. The COs need to be trained. Right now, the COs just react without thinking. One guy hit his call button in his cell, and the CO just told him, "Fuck you!" It was real disrespectful.

Several other residents offer similar statements regarding what they feel are barriers to their future lives and selves and the deficits they face through RHU living.

Ruffs: Not a lot of problems with inmates, but there's drama with staff. . . . We are like animals. . . . They don't have patience. They do whatever they feel. They don't take us that serious. Try to fix everything with medicine, pills, and a lot of punishment. . . . Why don't they try to make me a better person? Give me stuff to keep me busy? [The DOC needs to] teach staff what to do.

Angelson: The culture needs to change here. You can't speak to the lieutenant or anybody. . . . It's not allowed . . . talking to anyone here. If you try to talk to any of them, they lock you up more.

Wenders: I have to self-harm to get help. I beg for help and they [the COs] just laugh. I can't deal with the pain, so I cut myself. They spray me [with OC/pepper spray] before I can ask for what I need.

Other residents put a fine point on their desire for reform, calling out staff for a variety of behaviors and treatments they feel are unnecessary and unjustified.

Resident Halverson notes: "I would change how the COs treat inmates, like how they talk to them. They are super-disrespectful. We are both grown men and I won't get disrespected, even if I'm the one behind bars. They wouldn't say half that stuff to my face if I wasn't in a cage."

Resident Ogger says that living in the RHU "is like wasting your life away. It's a cruel form of punishment. I'm diabetic. My button rings for two hours sometimes when I need something. It's like you're subhuman. I treat my dog better than I get treated down here."

Resident Milano adds a bit more depth to the conversation about needed changes to staff:

[The RHU] sucks. Staff don't take you serious. They judge someone over what they do, even if it's to protect yourself. They don't take suicide seriously. You don't get the same amount of food in population. They say a lot of people are playing around. . . . They think it's a game. The COs were just looking at him when he hung up [hung himself]. My cellie was going through a crisis. He kept pressing the button and telling them. He was trying to hang up. They took him down, but they wanted to spray him. He was stressed out. Since I've been back here for fifteen days, both of my cellies tried to kill themselves and I had to save them. In seven years in prison, I've never seen that. They don't let me talk to someone if I'm traumatized [by seeing inmates kill themselves]. In [another prison], you tell them you need something and they do it. They're more respectable. [Here] they tell us to eat a dick, kill ourselves, call us faggots. If you give back [return insults], you get written up.

For residents, it is not just about the custodial staff, like COs, though. They also have reform ideas regarding psychological staff and speak distinctly to their need and heartfelt desire for change in this area.

Resident Nells says, "They need more psych training. I'm a mirror of people who are in control. If you're positive, I'm positive. . . . They start to act like us."

Resident Fooks adds:

I have spoken to psych a few times here. (*Laughs a lot.*) I don't get the feeling they actually listen to you. They don't look at you and they don't hear a word you say. They seem to hear what they want. I request a meeting with psych if I need something, but I don't see them come by very often. They do a "tour" (*uses air quotes*) if we're locked down, but that's about it. One time during a lockdown, the psych came by, didn't even look in my window, but I heard a voice at my door, "Fooks, you all right?" I said nothing. My cellie said nothing. The psych within a second said, "OK, then you're OK," and walked away. My cellie and I just looked at each other like, "What the hell?" We were shocked. She didn't even know which one of us was Fooks and never looked in the cell.

For Fooks, and numerous other residents, psychological services may be improved with more regular visits, care, and reflective listening. In speaking with him and other residents, this, to them, seems like a simple reform, but one they do not completely understand even needing. Residents seem confused and concerned that the psychological staff who are supposed to listen and help them also seem to find residents a nuisance rather than the reason for their employment. Other residents expressed similar sentiments regarding the need for reform to the psychological staff and their services.

Resident Kelps says:

I wrote psych five times and no one came in fifty days. I was taking anxiety meds in county jail, but I stopped when I got here to GP [general population]. But when I got to the RHU, I felt like the walls were closing down on me, so I kept asking for psych. I needed help. I was having panic attacks, anxiety. I needed—and still need—psych to come talk to me. I may need to get back on my meds. They never come by though.

Resident Adler also sees similar issues with psychological staff: "Currently, the intake interview with psych is a five-minute conversation going over your diagnoses and medicines. They *should* ask you about your feelings, your symptoms, how you're doing, triggers, and try to do an actual treatment plan . . . not just [give you] the cheapest medicines."

Resident Renki adds another challenge and possible reform involving psychological staff: "A problem is that you can't talk to the psych staff at night. At some prisons they have psych staff available around the clock, but not here. They do a round every day here, but there needs to be a night psych staff in case something happens."

The common thread in these resident comments about correctional staff is that they need help and wholeheartedly believe they are not getting it. They feel they are treated inhumanely and that their needs too regularly go unnoticed, untreated, and in fact, no one—not COs or psychological staff—cares at all that they have unmet needs. Reform ideas from residents overwhelming revolve around changes to staff training that would include a new or renewed focus on how to care for and treat the resident RHU population.

In addition to reforming staff, residents also cite the need to reform other aspects of the RHU, including issues related to hygiene, food, policies, phone, programming, and books (listed in order from most to least common). After concerns about staff, residents' second most common item on the needs-reform list relates to hygiene. This category includes showers, sanitation, cleanliness, and self-care.

Resident Kenner says: "We can't groom ourselves here. We can buy cosmetics [toiletry items], but we can only shower for three minutes every other day, excluding the weekends, and the showers are cold."

Resident Zaller concurs about the cold showers: "They need to fix the water. The showers are cold. . . . They need maintenance to fix the water. We put in a grievance. But they keep the showers cold so less inmates sign up."

Resident Naral adds: "I've been in the RHU five days, and I don't have the clothes I'm supposed to. I have no deodorant, no basics, and it's affected me. I want to change my clothes. I've had the same clothes on since I came here."

Resident Knight raises a concern related to hygiene: "Sanitation is an issue here. You can get athlete's feet and then it costs you because you have to pay for medical."

Resident Card says: "It's pretty bad . . . the cells are. The toilets are fucked up, and sometimes they'll go a couple of days full of shit and piss. The cell is good right now though. The linens [bedsheets] aren't changed either, only when the COs feel like it."

And resident McElhone adds:

> The inmate workers need to clean more. Right now, they're only cleaning twice a week. It needs to be a lot cleaner. You're in charge of cleaning your own cell, but they hand you all the supplies through your wicket, which is disgusting. That's where your food comes in, too! So you have a toilet brush touching where your food touches as well. They also don't give you a rag, so you have to use your one rag to clean [your cell] and dry off [after a shower]. It's disgusting.

Although readers may be imagining the dark, dank, dirt-floored hole from the film *Shawshank Redemption*, that is not the case for the RHUs in this study. However, residents' strong desire to be clean, have a hygienic and sanitary place to live, and receive basic toiletry products (such as deodorant) seems too straightforward to overlook. They are not asking for electric razors, hair dryers, and cologne. They are asking for reforms or changes that afford them the basic necessities many of us take for granted. They are asking for someone to notice them, someone to care, someone to look at and treat them as human beings.

Residents also focused their reform suggestions on another basic need: food. This is not surprising given the common lore about prison food (or institutional food in general), but the reform comments coming from RHU residents largely focus around concerns that they are not getting enough food and the food they receive is not helping them maintain or improve their health.

Resident Sullivan says: "We need more to eat. We're so hungry down here. We're hungry all the time. I don't even care if the food tastes like crap. I just want to have enough to eat."

Resident Becks notes that his food tray is often missing an item or two. This is challenging to him when he already believes he is not getting enough to eat: "Today's chicken patty . . . the patty wasn't on my tray and I told the CO. He just didn't give a shit."

Resident Lawson also comments that he wants more to eat: "We need to be fed better. Better food . . . more protein, carbs . . . better taste and quality."

Several residents also complained that the food is cold when it should be served hot. This is a health concern for residents as they wonder if the food is safe to eat after sitting at room temperature for an hour or more before serving.

Resident Clarke says: "Have you seen the trays come in? They come out at 10:55 a.m. and we won't eat until 12:30 p.m. There's no heater at the bottom." He also complains that the amount of food served in the RHU should be more than general-population residents receive because the DC residents cannot order food from commissary and the AC residents' commissary list is restricted. This means they are procedurally forbidden to purchase items to supplement their allotted food.

Resident Macomb and several others offer a possible reform for the RHU food challenges:

> There is not enough to eat down here. Some meals are OK, but if I could change anything, it would be to ask them to give us four pieces of bread with a side of peanut butter and jelly when they give us our last meal of the day. Then we could save that to have a snack later. It's a long time between dinner and breakfast and I'm really hungry. The last time I was down here for 130 days I started at 240 pounds and was down to 204 when I left. We need more protein and calories.

Resident Fuchs concurs, adding that he believes feeding the RHU residents well would greatly improve their mental and physical health: "I'm hungry, every day. Right after I finish breakfast, I'm hungry. [When I am not hungry,] I'm in a good mood, not depressed. It's a bonus. Maybe I'm a little more talkative. The feeling of being hungry is not cool."

For most RHU residents, food—or the lack and quality thereof—is an endless concern. They repeatedly stress their hunger and their belief that the lack of proper diet restricts their ability to think, move, and function. They also admit that hunger may lead to poor temperament and outbursts. They worry continually about the amount of weight they are losing and the way not having enough food affects their bodies and minds. Several residents also note that taking food with their prescribed medicine is important, but with the timing of food and medicine deliveries, this is not always possible. In these thoughts of reform, residents are not asking for steaks, lobsters, and Chinese takeout. In fact, aside from one resident who talked about another institution that occasionally gave residents hoagies and pizza as an incentive for good behavior, no resident mentioned wanting a particular type of food—just wanting more and better food, served hot. This basic need for nourishment resonated throughout the interviews and lays bare the survival needs in the RHU nearly every minute of every day.

Residents had several other ideas for reform, including some closely linked to staff and institutional changes such as the need to amend or alter existing policies and programming. Common reform topics in this vein included reworking the OC/pepper spray policy (discussed in the chapter on risk), policies around phone usage, and the inequitable enforcement of policies in general (discussed in the chapter on rules). Here is a sample of residents' reform thoughts on these topics:

> Resident Carlos: I really don't like how they use OC spray. I haven't read the policy on it and when they are and aren't allowed to use it, but man, I just think it seems wrong what they are doing. For example, there was a guy that was acting out and they used two cans in his cell. Now common sense says that two 20-ounces of OC spray just seems too much.

> Resident Gentry: The COs talk about spraying inmates excitedly. They [the COs] need psych evaluations to make sure they don't do anything inhumane. They are in misery. . . . [They need to put a] psychological hold on *them*.

> Resident Candence: I would like to see improvements in communication. There are times where the COs do not tell me that they are picking up the clothing to be laundered. This bothers me because it takes away an opportunity to keep clean. I would also like to be able to make phone calls. Because I am far away from home and cannot get visitors. I wish they would also stop paying attention to past infractions that I already served time for. This is unfair especially because it contributes to decisions being made now and about my future when I am different than I was previously.

> Resident Radcliffe: You know we have tablets in our cells when we're in GP. We get email, music, etc. I get emails a lot from my attorney about my case. But when we're in RHU, we can't have our tablets. This makes sense to me, but it's a pain that I cannot still get email from my attorneys. I wrote the administration about this, asking if I could just go to the

kiosk once in a while to check the email, just from my attorney. I told them they could block all other email I got from family, etc. They told me no. My request was denied. They said my attorney is supposed to send me mail, through the mail, when I'm in RHU, but I can't tell my attorneys I'm even down here, so how do they know? For all they know, I'm just not responding to their emails. Sure, they'll eventually figure it out, but I've been down here two weeks so far and I haven't gotten one piece of mail from anyone yet. That makes me mad and worried.

Resident Espinoza: We get no phone [in the RHU] and that's hard. I used to talk to my family a lot. Like two times a week. No one writes letters anymore, so without a phone, there is no communication with family. We need to have access to email and phone, even if limitedly. Just to check in. To keep us calm and supported. My family writes if something happens, but that's it. I've been down here seven months so far. . . . I don't feel good about myself when I go to the hole 'cause my family needs me *bad*.

Finally, a popular thought about reform involves RHU programming and incentives. Many RHU residents express a strong desire to improve themselves and use their time in the RHU to do so. But as current RHU policies and practices stand, no programming or incentives are available to RHU residents. Much of this conversation, however, is not about a specific program or service, but about the RHU not providing adequate opportunities for residents to improve themselves.

At a rudimentary level, better access to books would be a good start. Resident Monhollen suggests that one thing they could do to improve the RHU is to "get new books! They could get new books from Books Through Bars. I can get books that way, so they can get books that way. They should make it easier to get them or make it OK for us to pass them [to other residents]. Some COs won't pass them for us."

Resident Kato agrees, adding: "When you're done with your books, you should be able to just return them and get more, not have to wait for the form. In general population, books are in abundance. In the RHU, it's different."

And resident Liston notes: "We need to have a library on the block. It's easier to return them, so you don't get charged for them. And if you go to the library and they don't have the book that you pick, they pick a book from another author. If they don't have one from that author, they'll get you a random one from the genre."

Resident Dennis also wants to see reform to the book-borrowing process. He says that in order to ask for a book, you "need to use the book-list form. But COs never have them. They're always out." Dennis wants better access to the paperwork to request books so that he can get the books he wants to read when he wants them. For residents, books offer a lifeline out of boredom and provide an opportunity for self-improvement and growth. Without books, residents feel even more alone and isolated.

In addition to books, residents sometimes focus on programs more generally, often programs that include incentives. Resident Jacker says "I would like to see a punishment system that works in all levels so that a change in levels would result in changes in privileges."

Resident Monroe is a bit more specific:

> I understand it's DC, but not having stuff to look forward to makes inmates more hostile. Give us something to earn, maybe some commissary, so we can try to do good and earn something. We could earn visits. It's hard to be here for eight months. Even a phone call a week would calm us down 'cause we'd have something to look forward to.

Although Monroe does not lay out a specific incentive plan, he urges reforms that incentivize good behavior within the RHU.

Resident Mince agrees: "What does it [the RHU] do for you when you get out? Nothing. They use the wrong methods to try and change people. The only thing to probably make someone wanna change is visits with their families. Incentives."

In these examples, residents again beg for ways to improve themselves and potentially earn rewards. They want reforms that benefit them in tangible ways for both the present and the future.

Although residents do not offer concrete guidance regarding what types of programming (save book access) they desire or need and what behaviors should be incentivized, they are abundantly clear that they believe these suggested reforms would yield results. Residents overwhelmingly want the RHU to provide pathways to self-improvement and change. Residents want to have agency over their own self-improvement; they strongly desire an opportunity to use their RHU time more constructively.

While residents complain about the inequity of their RHU sentence (number of days received) versus those of other residents, no interviewed residents blatantly argue they are perfect or that some form of punishment for bad behavior is unjustified. Some argue the RHU was never the answer, but most others suggest more equitable sentences make sense. Still others suggest that if the institution wants or needs to use the RHU for behavioral modification, it should fully embrace that goal and make the RHU work toward that end: rehabilitation. This is opposed to relying solely on retributive, deterrent, and incapacitory goals—which residents do not think have either short- or long-term positive effects for individuals or institutions.

Staff on Reform
In large part, RHU staff have one primary goal in mind stemming from the underlying and hugely popular perception that the RHU is meant to punish. This perception is particularly interesting given the historical legacy of solitary confinement as a means to show prison residents pathways toward morality and repentance through silence, bible reading, and time to think. One original corrections goal was to reform and rehabilitate residents, albeit via punitive means. Scholars Ashley Rubin and Keramet Reiter detail this history in their work on solitary confinement (particularly within Eastern State Penitentiary and supermax prisons), noting that despite its failures, solitary confinement persists because of "prison administrators' unflagging belief in solitary confinement as a last-resort tool of control."[2] In fact, Eastern State Penitentiary, according to Rubin, held on to its system of separate confinement far longer than any other prison. In fact, most prisons at that time used the Auburn rather than the Pennsylvania System because it was considered more humane. The Auburn System of congregate confinement afforded residents an opportunity to work together during the daytime. They were held in solitary confinement only overnight. As it was learned that the Pennsylvania System was causing residents to go insane and commit suicide at particularly high rates, Eastern State eventually abandoned the practice of separate confinement, and most science now suggests total deprivation and solitary isolation are intensely harmful, with both short- and long-term negative mental and physical health effects on those who experience this form of punishment.

Despite existing knowledge that the current system, very much like separate confinement in many ways, largely failed because it caused undue harm to residents, many staff believe today's RHUs need reform only to return them to their solitary and incapacitory roots or to become more punitive, or both. Many staff argue the RHU should not embrace rehabilitation of any kind, thinking that is coddling or rewarding residents' bad behavior. While this idea was expressed by the vast majority of staff in this study, there were a smaller number of staff who engage reform thoughts about improving the RHU through attention to staff needs and RHU culture and incentive programs for residents. These staff saw challenges or took issue with current RHU practices and policies and, in some cases, outcomes. They offered suggestions for reforming the RHU in ways they felt would benefit the institution, the staff, the residents, and eventually the external communities where residents will return post-prison.

Staff reform ideas around punishment goals hit on a variety of related topics, including improvements to psychological staff, fewer privileges for residents, and recognizing victims' rights. For example, CO Cooks sums up the situation like this: "It's a jail within a jail. . . . How do you improve it? I don't know how to answer that. They give them everything. They already did it. It's not like Pelican Bay anymore. . . . Inmates might be in a cell 23/7, but they're getting everything." Cooks continues with a variety of additional thoughts along the same lines: "We reward bad behavior, inmates manipulate. I have a problem with someone committing a crime and then getting rewarded [by] watching TV." He continues, "I understand we all have to adapt to inmates, but they're still in the RHU." Then he adds, "90 percent of inmates are in jail because they have no discipline. They come back because they haven't learned."

CO Cooks was not alone in this thinking, though he was a bit more verbose than most. CO Inders notes: "Jail isn't supposed to be *fun*! I blame bad parents who didn't make their kids take responsibility."

CO Rox states: "There's a lot of taxpayer money to babysit these guys . . . I lived in a bunker in Iraq for a year and these guys have a better shitter [toilet] . . . Tablets [like iPads] are terrible because they are one more tool to communicate with people on the outside."

CO Wendels feels similarly: "It's frustrating. The point of corrections isn't punishment [forceful action to deprive and deter] anymore. It's frustrating for staff because it's more talking now."

These CO perceptions highlight some critical goal misalignment within RHUs, at least in theory. Several years ago, in the prisons of study, the state moved from language describing the RHU as "institutional punishment" to language that notes the unit is meant for "corrective action." The meaning of this change appears largely lost on many correctional staff working on the unit today, or perhaps they misunderstand its intention.

For RHU COs, punishment largely equates to incapacitation and deprivation to ensure deterrence and retribution. If the state intended *corrective* to mean forced compliance, the COs' perceptions tightly align with the DOC goal. However, if the state intended *corrective* to mean behavioral change or rehabilitation, the COs' perceptions vastly misalign with the DOC goal.

Additionally, one CO tied his reason for wanting additional and harsher punishment to victim's rights. Although he is the only CO who noted this in this study, his point provides important insight into COs' reform thinking.

CO McMasters says, "There are no victims' rights anymore. Inmates get TVs, tablets, kiosks, email. *Victims get nothing and they don't get their family member back.*" McMasters is arguing *for* punitive RHU measures and *against* RHU privileges to ensure retribution for a crime like murder, which some residents may have committed prior to coming to prison. However, most individuals are in prison for drug and property crimes, not violent crimes like murder. While DC residents do not receive any privileges in the RHU, AC residents may receive some perks such as in-cell televisions and some commissary, and general population residents usually have access to many privileges including tablets, televisions, radios, and increased movement within the general population unit and broader prison. McMasters's statement expresses passion and an immense feeling of injustice or lack of fairness—in his view. He feels the RHU provides too much to undeserving individuals who have taken too much from society already.

Taken together, these CO statements about RHU reform suggest a strong desire by correctional staff within RHUs to return to, or begin, a stringent focus on restrictive punishment with less coddling, even fewer privileges, and no incentives for RHU residents. COs Cooks, Inders, Rox, Wendels, and McMasters represent a host of other correctional and custodial RHU staff in expressing reform ideas with punitive foci. Their statements reveal deeper concerns, too, regarding the fairness and justice of a system that provides, as they see it, so much for residents who are undeserving and have already taken much from society via their past actions. In the staff's concerns, there is some suggested reform, but also a bit of latent exasperation that they feel not much will change. None of the quoted COs offer any specific suggestions for *how* to change the RHU to better meet its perceived punitive goals, but they contend this change is sorely needed.

The perceptions of these and other correctional staff highlight a broader point regarding the individuals serving time in the RHU and the goals or purpose of corrections generally and the RHU specifically. Many residents are in the RHU with an AC status. So, while they committed a crime to get into prison, they did not necessarily commit a crime or an in-prison infraction to get into the RHU. The same is true for many DC residents who are in the RHU for rule-breaking behaviors in general population that are not necessarily "crimes" and are typically nonviolent. These infractions include not locking into their cell when they are supposed to or refusing an order. In many ways, the RHU has become a controlling catchall for residents whom correctional staff cannot or do not want to deal with. It is, as one resident said, "a big boy time-out." Sure, some residents commit crimes, even violent crimes, in prison, but the vast majority do not. These rule-breaking actions may not directly impact prison or community safety, but they may have indirect implications on safety. The RHU is one avenue for dealing with rule-breakers, but it is far from the only available option. In this way, incapacitation philosophy reigns. Residents' punishment is incarceration, and their punishment for rule-breaking is double incarceration within the RHU. However, giving someone a TV, for example, does not change the fact they are incapacitated. In the perceptions of correctional staff, though, the RHU is not only about achieving incapacitation; it is about achieving near or total deprivation.

A few other COs offer reform ideas aligned with punishment thinking, but with a bit more specificity. CO Jewett's reform thoughts focus on improving psychological services in the RHU to better control residents who he believes game the system: "I would have psych do a better job of calling [residents'] bluffs and monitoring [severely mentally ill residents]." This concurs with Inders's thinking above that working in the RHU is not punitive enough, as it "involves more talking now." It also follows similar thinking from CO Nabors, who suggests that the current approach that includes talking to residents and helping them is troubling: "We aren't able to do *our* jobs!" For both Inders and Nabors, their perceived job includes supervision and control via incapacitation, but not rehabilitation and conversational counseling and assistance. They, and numerous others like them, long to return to the days where a CO's job in the RHU involves watching, controlling, supervising, moving, and punishing. To this, CO Villa feels there is hope: "Lots of staff say the pendulum needs to swing back to punishment and discipline.... It's just a matter of incidents ... and it will happen."

The juxtaposition between correctional staff's and residents' reform perceptions is stark. Residents overwhelmingly want the RHU to provide pathways toward self-improvement and change, while correctional staff want residents to be better behaved while in prison and the RHU, but then adamantly want to deny residents tools to achieve behavioral change when they have nothing but time to use these tools to better themselves.

Perhaps the most common RHU reform requested by COs is more staff, or, as CO Leiblor states, "more manpower." Many COs thought one of the largest needs in the RHU, next to the need for increased punitiveness, is to have enough COs for each shift. Too few COs, they claim, leads to overwork and the current staff's inability to keep up with all the resident misbehavior. These COs claim that more staff would dramatically improve control within the RHU, resulting in fewer misconduct incidents and a safer environment.

While the majority of COs favor intensified punitive measures as their preferred reform, several other COs had alternative ideas. These counterviews lean more toward helping RHU residents in rehabilitative ways. CO Mattingly was perhaps the most vocal on this subject. Three times during his interview, Mattingly noted the need for reform and the potential outcomes that a wholly punitive and inhumane RHU environment may have on both individuals and communities. In response to the question "Would you have solitary?" Mattingly answers, "I would, but it wouldn't be in the sense of . . . I mean, a cell, yes, but not locked in twenty-three to twenty-four hours a day . . . just live by yourself." Mattingly suggests another option, adding that in their version of the RHU, residents would spend most of their time out of cell with some additional restrictions. They would also have better contact with their families through telephone calls and perhaps other means.

Both CO Mattingly and another CO, Dobby, also long for a reformed RHU culture. CO Dobby notes, "I want to change the morale of the jail." He adds that this would include improved comradery among staff and would eliminate what he sees as the problem of staff feeling entitled. Mattingly concurs with Dobby's RHU cultural reform idea: "I'm trying to change the culture of corrections. . . . They [management] don't feel like it [loving on the inmates] should be done, but these guys are coming back to our communities." Mattingly expresses a bit more on the topic of reforming RHU culture by providing some insight into the origin of the current cultural challenges:

> The biggest issue is understanding the new CO culture. . . . Young COs are always trying to prove themselves. . . . At the academy, they [trainees] are told to always say no. [But] inmates are people. I don't care what they did. You treat them like humans. If they get out of line, we'll handle it. But if they give you respect, you give them respect. I don't care what they did. It's for God to judge.

In this same regard, CO Bento suggests that the DOC management adds to the RHU cultural problem when they do not "take care" of the staff in these units. He says his reform would include getting rid of the prison superintendent:

> He [the superintendent] will come down here and tell us that we are all the hardest-working guys in the jail. Then three weeks ago, there was no air conditioning in here. There isn't a water fountain down here either. They don't take care of us. There's a real disconnect because the administration doesn't know what we are going through. They like to say they do, but they don't.

Although there are far fewer COs discussing cultural reforms, among those who do, the general consensus is reform is needed. Aligned with this type of reform thinking, several other COs also placed value on reforming the RHU for residents, not just staff. In these conversations, COs discuss the possibility of including more activities and programming for residents and adding incentive programs to help residents earn privileges or earn their way out of the RHU.

CO Dunn suggests: "I think the RHU needs a step-down program so that they [residents] can go into a transitional unit once they are done with their RHU sentence before they go back to general population. . . . [The change] is just too drastic." Dunn thinks this approach would provide a bridge between the heavily restricted carceral life in the RHU and the less-restricted living conditions in general population. He feels this would improve the transition for residents in positive ways that would benefit both residents and staff. Although Dunn does not specify reentry type, his reform ideas would likely affect both intra-carceral reentry and post-prison community reentry.

Sergeant Agare agrees, but with a slightly different idea for particular resident groups:

> Low-level drug users and nonviolent criminals should be given diversionary programming, including the military. For example, offer people

convicted the chance to go into the military, and if they serve three years and are clean, wipe their records. *If you're going to give a guy a clean slate, give him a clean slate.* Prisons should only be for violent offenders, rapists, murderers, and child molesters.

Agare also feels "people with mental health issues should be housed in a psychiatric hospital," not prison or the RHU. In this perception, Agare seems to see RHU residents as varied—not just murderers and rapists, as other COs do. In doing so, a whole other world of possibilities opens up for RHU reform.

Somewhat aligned with this thinking, CO Wexton says:

> I might make every post a bid post [a position in the institution that is relatively permanent]. Management doesn't really like bid posts because they think it breeds complacency, but honestly, I think when you have people assigned to units and blocks, then COs can get to know the inmates.

For Wexton, getting to know the residents is an important change for the RHU, but perhaps more so throughout the prison. While many RHU staff do work on the unit regularly (even if it is not technically a bid post), Wexton's reform idea is to form relationships (albeit professional) with residents to improve communication and compliance. Wexton, as well as others in the chapter on relationships, feel that working with rather than against residents is an important component of efficient and effective RHU work—and one that could use some improving.

The Point of No Reform

It is largely and surprisingly *not* the case that staff working and residents living in RHUs actively and regularly discuss, seek, and advocate for reform. While residents focused a few reform thoughts on improvements to staff that may lead to better treatment, they also spent some time thinking about items and services that may improve their day-to-day lives, such as changes to hygiene procedures and availability (i.e., showers, toiletries) and food. Residents, though, mostly stopped short of asking for any system overhaul that might include disbanding RHUs or dramatically changing them. And for nearly every RHU resident interviewed, reform seemed a distant fantasy rather than an actual possibility. It was almost as though they would engage in a thought exercise to a point. but taking it further to some kind of conclusion was not possible or perceived as fruitful in any way.

Staff do not hope for sweeping reforms either. Instead, they focus on thinking about ways to better match RHU practices to the overall unit goal of, as they perceive it, punishment. Staff offer limited reform thoughts, touting the benefits of increasing staff numbers in the RHU, providing fewer privileges to RHU residents, and focusing on control and security concerns with little, if any, emphasis on communication with or rehabilitation of RHU residents.

What might explain how and why both RHU residents and staff think so little about possible reforms in a place neither group is particularly enamored with? There are perhaps several plausible answers. First, scholars and scientists working in the field of psychology consistently find a significant and disadvantageous link between criticism (real or perceived, verbal or nonverbal) and mental health. This work suggests that criticism affects self-worth and confidence and may lead to or exacerbate depression, fears, and feelings of shame. There is also a growing literature suggesting that criticized individuals may blame their criticizer but may also detrimentally blame themselves (as, for example, survivors of abusive relationships often blame themselves for abuse). This may manifest in anger but often also emerges in the form of self-doubt, anxiety, or submissive behavior. It does not usually include siding with or approving the criticizer, but rather internalizing the put-downs in ways that manifest in uncertainty and self-blame.

For residents living in the RHU, reform thoughts most often take the form of wanting or desiring better treatment. They do not demand it. They simply ponder whether it is possible and at times make the explicit connection to how this change might improve their mood and manner. Remember resident Richland who asked for "a little humanity" from COs, and resident Hinder who said the way the COs talk to residents makes them "feel awful"? Also, resident Ruffs, who asked, "Why don't they [the COs] try to make me a better person?" And resident Ogger, who commented, "I treat my dog better than I get treated down here." And resident Nells, who mused, "I am a mirror of people who are in control. If you're positive, I'm positive."

In these examples and others, residents seem to express disempowerment to change how the staff treat them but desperately want to be treated with respect, dignity, and humanity. Over time, these intended or unintended put-downs and mistreatments may have an effect on any reform that residents allow themselves to imagine or hope for. The near-continual verbal abuse, harsh tone, and mistreatment residents endure from correctional staff perhaps seeps into their psyche (which is likely already shaky due to RHU placement and the conditions in it) and edges them closer toward anxiety, depression, and the dread that they do not matter—even if they think they should. In cases such as these, where hopelessness and despair take root, there is no need to desire or imagine reform. What is, is. And all that's left for residents to do is paddle or sink.

In terms of paddling (aka trying to stay afloat and alive), residents at times discuss a few more specific RHU reforms, including better access to or availability of hygiene opportunities and products and food. These items represent inherently different desired changes for residents. While most residents who discuss the need for these types of changes do not do so with false or overwhelming optimism, there is a small degree of hope present in these reform thoughts. The difference here is that these changes do not require philosophical shifts by COs or goal realignment. Instead, they simply require time and a small degree of effort. A CO can still want to punish RHU residents but may also provide them their legal right to receive a shower and food. Residents seem hesitant to request or desire overhauling these procedures, but instead desire incremental changes to existing rights, such as having warm or hot water for showers and getting all the food on their trays during meal delivery. Nothing more than the basics, but a desire or hope for minimum standards of decency.

A second plausible explanation comes from the organizational behavior literature and its conceptions of help-seeking behavior. In this work, asking for help is broken down into its requisite smaller parts, including requesters identifying what they need help with, finding individuals and resources to fill this request, and initiating contact with the person or persons who may be able to provide help. Within the RHU, all three of the subcomponents of help-seeking are challenging. Residents often do not know what they need help with—though they may believe they need help of some kind. This is common with individuals involved in the criminal-legal system for many reasons, but perhaps most importantly because they often do not have the people or resources helping them pre-incarceration so they often do not know what they do not know. This equates, at times, to not really knowing what it is that they might need. Help-seeking also requires individuals to find individuals to help them and to initiate contact with a potential helper. This also extremely challenging within prisons generally and RHUs specifically.

The thoughts of resident Angelson provides insight into what residents perceive as blocked opportunities to seek help: "The culture needs to change here. You can't speak to the lieutenant or anybody. . . . It's not allowed . . . talking to anyone here. If you try to talk to any of them, they lock you up more."

But there's more. Prisons are hot beds of power struggles between both residents and staff. This is well documented in the scientific literature and popular culture (including media). Incarceration commonly manifests feelings of powerlessness among residents, and for many residents, asking for help may yield feelings of further disempowerment. Asking for help in general, particularly from correctional staff members who residents overwhelmingly feel do not treat them as people, may force residents to acknowledge their own incompetence and dependence on the very people who they complain and worry about. It may also limit residents' ability to maintain or improve their self-image and feelings of worth. Further complicating this situation are other intervening factors including the power dynamics present in gender, status, race/ethnicity, and age that all press up against organizational norms within RHUs and create a holistically hostile situation for help-seeking, or in this case, thinking about and inquiring after reforms and changes to the RHU. In these ways, the costs of asking for help may outweigh any potential benefit. Thus, residents may prefer focusing inward, relying on themselves and in some cases each other (as seen in the relationship chapter), rather than relying on correctional staff for help.

Similar contentions regarding help may explain the lack of correctional staff who engage reform thoughts beyond increased punitiveness. Staff, too, commonly perceive criticism from residents, coworkers, upper management, administration, the DOC, and the broader community. This criticism comes from lack of occupational support, but also from staff feeling neglected or unappreciated. CO Bento's previous comments highlight this feeling among correctional staff. Bento says: "They [the correctional managers/administrators] don't take care of us. There's a real disconnect because the administration doesn't know what we are going through. They like to say they do, but they don't." Over time, this barrage of criticism or put-downs may lead staff toward feelings of anxiety, hopelessness, depression, or self-doubt. Coupled together, the criticism and resulting feelings may suggest a plausible reason for staff to focus on the one reform they have some control over: punishment.

Additionally, the help-seeking argument provides a viable framework for staff not asking for or thinking about reforms beyond those meant to further control and punish residents. Just as with residents, staff would need to identify or define the problem they need help with, search for resources, and initiate contact with someone who could provide help. Within RHUs—isolated from the broader prison environment and the DOC more wholly—this is a tall order. With minimal staff training, if any, focusing on the complexities that residents face before, during, and after incarceration and the overall lack of systemic concern for staff health and well-being, help-seeking may require too much from staff. The knowledge barriers alone are, at present, likely insurmountable. Couple that with the power dynamics previously discussed, including acknowledging incompetence and dependence, and it is not surprising that staff do not think much about RHU reform or change. For many staff, it seems, reform is only something they can personally do on a shift or with a coworker crew, but not something bigger and certainly not something their voices likely would contribute to.

Thinking through the general lack of interest and attention both residents and staff give to reform thoughts leads to a disturbing point. Both RHU residents and staff may sense that they are simply cogs in a much larger and complex system that is disinterested in their views and perceptions. As such, expressing these views and perceptions is really just an experiment in futility and may cause additional pain and anguish for both groups as their pleas for help will likely—in their view—go unanswered.

CHAPTER 7

Reversal and Revision

WHILE LIVING OR WORKING in a literal and figurative hole, residents and correctional staff endure daily challenges largely unmatched in other residential and employment locales. The physical space alone creates nearly insurmountable barriers to growth and advancement, but the climate and cultures once inside—forged by rules, policies, and penal philosophies closely aligned with punitiveness and control—yield intense risk to mental and physical health, relationships, and interpersonal interactions leaving hopes regarding reentry and reform dashed, if even dared to be considered. Additionally, RHUs suffer from goal misunderstanding and misalignment. Both staff and residents seem utterly confused regarding the goals of the unit, and their narratives ebb and flow between stories involving incapacitation, deterrence, and retribution, with little thought of corrective actions via rehabilitation (also a goal of punishment). Reform or change of RHUs is possible through complete abolition or some altering or amending that transforms RHUs into rehabilitative environments where people live and work together to improve each other for their own and the greater good. The masked malignancy of harm that currently cuts through RHUs like a sharp-edged blade may be dulled and sheathed in favor of other weapons of choice: trust, listening, learning, and growth. Then, resilience would become transformational for both staff and residents, and the RHU would move from a hole to a place to become whole.

Not Really a Choice

While common perceptions might suggest that residents suffer as a result of their own actions (i.e., rule-breaking via misconducts), and staff take employment in the correctional field of their own accord, these perceptions are holistically misguided. Both of these arguments imply free choice. but in prison environments, free choice is rarely an option. Instead, correctional systems regularly rely on convenience and history to guide actions that presumably improve safety and control even when these come at the expense the mental and physical health, relationships, and the present and future lives of both residents and staff.

While it is true that some RHU residents receive sentences to the unit based on violent misconducts, the vast majority of others "earn" their place in the RHU for simple, nonviolent, rule-breaking such as refusing to stand for count, making a mess in their cell, or possessing contraband items such as cigarettes, cell phones, or drugs. In prison, rule-breaking is a fairly normative and common occurrence. Residents are not in prison by choice and have virtually no autonomy during their stay. To recoup some level of control or power, residents, at times, do not follow institutional rules. To respond to these infractions, correctional staff possess an immense array of countermeasures to correct or change resident behavior. These range on a continuum from informal responses, such as discussing the incident with the resident, to moderate formal responses, such as restricting privileges for phone calls or visitation, to highly incapacitating formal responses, such as placing a resident in the RHU. By design, the RHU is a last resort; an option for only the most egregious resident misconducts or for an extreme need for protection and safety for the resident or others. Yet, with 20 to 40 percent of the US prison population spending time in RHUs each year, there appears to be widespread RHU overreach and overuse.

Correctional staff come to work in prisons through a variety of avenues, most often resulting from a lack of viable job opportunities in their communities and little or no higher education, advanced training, or relevant background experience. Many US prisons are located in rural and somewhat remote areas of states and predominantly draw their workforce from the local community.[1] Additionally, most correctional staff positions require only a high school diploma or GED, a background check, and no prior law enforcement or correctional experience, and they pay a living, or at least relatively livable, wage. They also typically offer job security, union representation, and post-retirement security though pensions. As such, nearly whole communities may work at a nearby prison out of necessity and function, rather than a free choice among many acceptable options.

Because of the length of time it takes for a background check—which delays hiring for both the candidate and the prison—many former military personnel make good correctional staff hires as they often already possess the required background checks. Former military personnel may also receive some additional points on civil service exams necessary for prison jobs and credit toward retirement for their prior military service. These perks make prisons a good post-military employment option. Again, this may not necessarily constitute a free choice from an open universe of options, but rather a coerced choice. The system may act like a funnel from the local community or former military employment to prison service, making a prison job the best available employment option.

Once correctional staff begin a prison job, the RHU is rarely their first post. Instead, the RHU is generally, but not always, reserved for more seasoned employees. Correctional staff, nearly all men in the prisons of study, are often "invited" to work with the team in the RHU by current RHU staff and supervisors. Sometimes, the move to working in the RHU rather than general population affords a shift change for a correctional staff member (e.g., from the 10-p.m.-to-6-a.m. shift to the 2-p.m.-to-10-p.m. shift), which may make home life more manageable. For COs with children, for example, aligning their prison shift opposite their spouse's shift at the prison or elsewhere means that children always have a caretaker at home. Correctional officers regularly try to do this, and the RHU is one way to accomplish this goal. Additionally, some correctional staff suggest that working in the RHU is an important part of an upward trajectory in correctional work. Much the same as military personnel sometimes seek rotation to combat duty to earn awards and the possibility for promotion, RHU COs regularly discuss the RHU as a stepping stone toward advancement. In both examples—shifts and promotion—the RHU represents a means to an end: a coerced choice made for reasons other than a strong desire to specifically work in the RHU or the prison.

If most residents and staff do not freely choose the RHU, if everyone seems unclear about its goals, and if the RHU environment is harmful in a litany of ways to both groups, why then do US prisons still rely heavily on RHUs? While there are likely any number of answers to this question, the narratives in this book suggest two primary motives over many others: convenience and history.

RHUs as Convenient

Correcting or managing rule-breaking, deviant, maladjusted, or even just plain irritating behaviors and actions is a difficult business. It requires patience, resources, and individualized approaches for services and treatment. None of these are easy in a carceral setting. To understand this, let us consider troublesome behavior in another context: families.[2] In families, when a child acts inappropriately by breaking household or parental rules or norms, parents have many options for how to deal with these indiscretions. One possibility is locking the child in their room or a closet or bathroom and not letting them come out for a certain period of time until they are calm and ready to behave. Sitting them in a corner or in any "time-out" locale is another possibility. Another is to physically harm them into submission. And another option is to take away privileges such as sweets, iPads, computers, or phones or restrict their movement or reduce their out-of-house time by lowering their curfew or prohibiting gathering with friends. When parents are unsure which options to take, they may seek external information. While not every parent will seek outside assistance with these family situations, many rely on other family members, neighbors, friends, parenting help groups, podcasts, websites, and even the vast array of parenting books available today. The advice from these resources for how to handle troublesome behavior in children of any age typically ranges from relatively holistic like parenting with kindness and reason to exceptionally detailed and specific approaches for particular types of children and particular types of parents. For example, there is explicit advice for boys versus girls, for kids with general mental health challenges or with specific disorders such as attention-deficit hyperactivity disorder (ADHD), anxiety, panic attacks, body-image challenges including anorexia and bulimia, and so on. There is also advice for single parents, military parents, religious parents, mixed-race/ethnicity parents, same-gender parents, and the like. In all these resources—though the messages and ideas vary—one underlying theme is parents doing what they feel works best for both themselves (and their parenting style) and their children. The expressed goal of parenting in these books and other resources is not rigid compliance and complete control, but rather, a mutual teaching-learning environment where both parents and children learn from and teach each other to improve their relationships and begin operating in ways that advance them both individually and as a unit. In achieving such a goal, the entire family—as well as perhaps the community and their future selves—benefits.

Some of this parenting advice pushes boundaries of what many currently accept as mainstream and indeed expands our thinking on what may work in our own family with the resources available to us. Rarely do these parenting books promise immediate changes in either parents or children; it is generally an iterative and long-term process that requires patience, but it is presented as one worth undertaking for both present and future benefit to all. And rarely do these parenting books suggest that an approach one family takes will be the exact correct approach for another family. Each uses an individualized approach tailored to best meet the needs of the members of the family. Of course, some of this advice is just that: words of advice. But other guidance is based on sound science achieved through rigorous testing and case results. That is, the data suggests that the recommended approaches or tactics have some documented merit and positive outcomes. In learning more, parents may develop beyond what they know to discover and adapt new ways of parenting that expand both theirs and their children's lives for the better. Presumably, these kids will grow up to become happier, more well-rounded, increasingly productive community members who may one day raise their own children in similar ways, if they chose to parent. Everyone wins!

On the whole, parenting is analogous in many ways to working with RHU residents. Yes, children do not often kill other children, and parents ideally possess a level of love and support for their kids beyond what any correctional staff member may feel for prison residents, so this example is a bit overstated. However, it serves as a gentle reminder that most individuals within the RHU also have not killed anyone. Just because residents are in the prison locale purportedly reserved for the "worst of the worst" does not mean they are, in fact, the worst. Remember, many—even most—RHU residents end up in the RHU for rule-breaking behaviors (or a history of them) that do not involve violence of any kind, including murder, but instead, they are likely there for something else, such as drug use or any number of mental health challenges that existed pre-prison or are new or exacerbated by incarceration. Additionally, remember that most (some 95 percent) of US prisoners will eventually be released back into their community (just as children grow up and join communities as adults).

Despite the similarities between parenting and RHUing, patience, resources, and individualized care, treatment, and services are extremely uncommon in prison. It is far more convenient when managing disruptive or troublesome individuals to use a one-size-fits-all approach (such as sending a child to their room or sending a resident to the RHU for misbehavior). This requires significantly less preparation, oversight, and upkeep. Also, prisons, unlike families, are typically managing 1,400 individuals simultaneously. Without resources that would yield patience, such as advanced and long-term training for RHU staff and appropriate numbers of correctional staff of all classifications (custodial, psychological, medical, etc.) and without individualized practices, such as treatment options for producing behavioral change and an approach that sees each RHU resident as a human being with unique needs, RHUs overwhelmingly and nearly entirely miss a vital opportunity to provide critical services to a population that is in desperate need of, and literally begging for, help.

The explanation of convenience does not end here though. RHU residents are not the only ones begging for help. In the narratives in this book, it may be difficult for readers to hear RHU staff asking for resources, treatment, services, patience, and individualized approaches, but do not be fooled. Staff do not commonly ask for these things directly, but in the stories they tell about the pain and anguish they feel and in their retelling of experiences with their own mental and physical health—particularly related to fear, risk, and family life—they are asking for them, even if without precise words. Some of the staff's need for help stems from US carceral systems' lack of goal clarity or contradictory goals. Plus, US prisons are not systemically designed for this level of attention to individualized detail. With historic overcrowding, tight budgets, inadequately trained and educated staff, inadequate numbers of staff, outdated or antiquated buildings and equipment, and a pronounced focus on custody and control over care, RHUs' primary goal is not treating, helping, assisting, or reforming. RHUs do not see or treat residents housed in them as individuals, but rather as a group or an underclass of "problemed" individuals in need of strict reinforcement of rules and a healthy dose of incapacitory punishment to instill deterrence for any future misguided behaviors they may consider or attempt and retribution for the ones they already committed. RHUs are perceived as the easiest road toward achieving control. RHUs are a convenient solution to an incredibly complex problem.

RHUs as Repeated History

Closely akin to the explanation of convenience, the historical explanation is embodied in a common saying in correctional environments, "We've always done it like this." With over two hundred years of history in the American carceral context, RHUs solidified their place as a preferred tool for wrangling and subduing unruly prison residents. Using the consolidation model, where disobedient and disruptive prison residents are relocated to a restricted setting or unit within a larger prison or where the entire prison operates as a highly restricted institution (commonly called a supermax), RHUs provide intensified security and control via segregation that occurs in a setting largely devoid of movement, activity, treatment, and human interaction.

Although all RHU goals are not well-established and vary widely among institutions,[3] several primary goals associated with the RHU rest in the three common statuses assigned to residents: disciplinary (for punishment), administrative (for control), and protective (for safety) custody. In these goals, care and need fulfillment via rehabilitative behavioral modification are overtly absent. Instead, prisons in general and RHUs specifically rely on a long history that includes segregation as a form of control for managing difficult individuals. That is, RHUs rely on the limited prospects garnered through incapacitory, retributive, and deterrent strategies to manifest positive changes in resident behavior.

Think back on the parenting example from the previous section of this chapter. In bygone years, parents did regularly, or perhaps often, send their children to their rooms or to "the corner" or even evoke corporal punishment as a reaction to bad behavior. It was not only common, but believed to be a mechanism of appropriate and good parenting. Strong discipline via physical punishment was, at one time, commonly thought to help children learn right from wrong and remember that lesson going forward. While there are still some purveyors and believers of this thinking, the science of parenting largely shifted to a positive discipline approach made famous by Dr. Benjamin Spock in the mid-twentieth century and later by Dr. William Sears.[4] Dr. Spock's initial, controversial approach asked parents to trust their own instincts and offer care, love, and support to guide and mold children's behavior toward better choices. Dr. Sears's series of books exudes the benefits of attachment parenting through touch, bonding, empathy, and love.

The point here is simple. Over many decades, parenting practices evolved. Although they are far from perfect, the scientific literatures in medicine, public health, education, social work, and psychology have learned, grown, and adapted their advice and recommendations for modern parents for the benefit of both the parents and children—in fact, for the entire family and broader community. However, despite sound science exposing the many pitfalls of inhumane treatment of adults, the years of research claiming spending time in RHUs takes a tremendous mental and physical toll on individuals,[5] and the empirical and theoretical work that considers how adults may change their behaviors,[6] prisons and correctional systems remain largely unchanged.

Additionally, the same strategies and tools are being employed despite changes in the population of residents. This is true in not only RHUs but in prisons generally. In US prisons and RHUs, we lock up not just the worst of the worst. Increasingly, prisons incarcerate poor people, individuals with nonviolent offenses, and those with mental illness and substance use or misuse issues. So, not only has the carceral approach remained the same, but it is being applied to a population that looks much different from prior decades. This static state continues to harm residents, staff, families, and communities in unfathomable ways. The choice to continue the current course without reliance on research and science to guide individual, organizational, and systemic reforms within prisons creates a predictable predicament with great costs and even greater harm to literally everyone.

RHU Reversal or Reduction
Reforming RHUs holds promise, but the answers are extremely complex and implementation of any or all of them requires intense goal-driven focus that keeps humans, humanity, and dignity as its crucial center. One possible way out of the current predicament is to reverse course and completely stop using RHUs within prisons and jails. In organizational theory, the abolition of the RHU represents a second-order change, a change that includes a discontinuous, often radical, shift that alters and upends the fundamental properties of a system.[7] Within carceral

contexts, this might include disusing prisons altogether. This is not impossible, but it is largely improbable given the role of carceral systems throughout history and the deeply ingrained beliefs and attitudes about the rule of law and what to do with lawbreakers. A modified second-order change might include discontinuation of RHUs, but not necessarily prisons overall. Although a worthy and important goal, at this writing there is very little evidence of this occurring in many prison or jail systems in the world, so believing that this is a possible is an invaluable exercise, but whether it might work is yet largely unknown.

Short of ending all reliance on prisons, jails, or RHUs, there are at least two other possible reforms that entail limiting or overhauling RHUs in real and substantive ways. These are first-order changes, or incremental changes in a stable organizational system that leave the system itself largely unchanged. Both of these reforms focus the correctional goal on *correcting behavior* via rehabilitative means to achieve both short- and long-term safety goals within prisons and specifically within RHUs and beyond prison. First, carceral systems could dramatically change RHU practices by halting RHU use for especially vulnerable individuals, such as those with mental health diagnoses and youth, and by setting a maximum on the number of days an individual could spend in an RHU. Prisons and jails could, instead, rely on other mechanisms of instilling control and care to change behavior. Second, at a minimum, if RHUs continue in their present form, reform must include changes that improve the humanity and dignity of the experience for both residents and staff by creating pathways to immediate and future behavioral changes that yield immediate and future benefits to prison residents and staff as well as external communities.

RHU Revision: Limiting Time, Limiting Residents

First-order changes in RHUs are becoming increasingly common due to many factors, including legal work and social activism promoting an end to solitary confinement.[*] Perhaps one of the most prominent drivers of solitary confinement reform emerges from the United Nations Standard Minimum Rule (SMR) for the Treatment of Prisoners (1955/1957/2015)

---

[*] Although the term *RHU* is preferable, many of the reforms in this section of the book refer to the practice as *solitary confinement* despite that term's limited application. Because most of the world uses *solitary confinement*, this section uses *RHU* and *solitary confinement* interchangeably.

(also called the Nelson Mandela Rules). These guidelines state, among other standards, that solitary confinement should be used only in extreme cases as a last resort and for no more than fifteen consecutive days. They also posit that individuals with mental or physical disability or illness and youth should never be held in solitary confinement. The United States has not committed to the SMR, although some movement toward these standards is taking root.

In 2016, President Barack Obama called for solitary confinement reform, noting that solitary confinement is "an affront to our common humanity."[8] At that time, he ordered the US Justice Department to investigate solitary confinement and then implement reforms in US prisons, including some in RHUs. These recommendations included ceasing to use solitary confinement with youth and for low-level infractions in federal prisons. While symbolically important, the federal system houses less than 10 percent of the nation's total prison population, so unless the symbolism directly persuades state systems to also change, the effects of this reform may be somewhat limited.

Also in 2016, the Cook County (Chicago) sheriff, Tom Dart, ended the solitary confinement practices in his jail, opting instead for a rehabilitation unit called the Special Management Unit (SMU).[9] Dart notes this new unit houses mostly residents who have assaulted correctional staff or other residents. The SMU residents receive increased out-of-cell time, programming, and time to interact with other SMU residents, but do so while remaining chained to stationary tables. The Cook County SMU chains residents to ensure the safety of staff and residents. In an interview in the *Chicago Reporter* in 2019, one SMU resident observes, "Solitary versus SMU is not a big difference," because of the great discomfort of wearing chains and shackles.[10] In the Cook County SMU, out-of-cell time increased from one to four hours a day, and residents may earn a transition to other SMU pods where shackling is not necessary. Since this reform, the Cook County Jail reports a significant decrease in resident assaults on other residents and in staff use of force. While the jail staff are now some of the SMU's biggest supporters and advocates, residents still claim inhumane handling abounds, including poor-quality food and mistreatment by correctional staff. Under current definitions of solitary confinement, the SMU no longer officially fits the bill. However, with just four hours a day out of cell and limited opportunities for development and engagement, the SMU still looks very much like an RHU. That fact is not lost on residents.

As of 2019, twenty-eight states introduced legislation to abolish or severely restrict solitary confinement. Of these, twelve passed reforms: Arkansas, Connecticut, Georgia, Maryland, Minnesota, Montana, Nebraska, New Jersey, New Mexico, Texas, Washington, and Virginia. Additionally, New York State governor Andrew M. Cuomo adopted some parts of the Nelson Mandela Rules when he signed a 2021 bill into law that prevents prisons and jails from holding people in solitary condiment for more than fifteen days and bars the practice entirely for youth, the elderly, pregnant women, and individuals with disabilities.[11] Likewise, Colorado State prison director Rich Raemisch implemented statewide reforms to lower the number of individuals in RHUs and limit residents' time served in them to no more than fifteen consecutive days. Raemisch notes that solitary confinement "has not solved any problems; at best it has maintained them."[12] In 2021, Colorado also introduced a bill to end the use of solitary confinement in jails. That bill is currently tabled.[13]

In 2019, New Mexico implemented some sweeping changes within RHUs. After a series of lawsuits, the state legislature banned solitary for pregnant women, children, and individuals with serious mental illness. It also mandated jails and prisons to report their use of solitary confinement to the state government as an oversight mechanism. The New Mexico Correctional Department also created separate housing units for individuals with sex offense convictions and former law enforcement officers, making solitary confinement unnecessary for these groups.[14]

New Jersey also limited their use of solitary confinement in 2019, with the signing of reform legislation that restricts solitary confinement stays to twenty consecutive days or thirty days total over each sixty-day period.[15] Like New Mexico's legislation, the New Jersey bill also requires documentation and reporting of solitary confinement use to an oversight body.

In 2015, prior to these reforms, in a court settlement, California agreed to stop holding classified gang members in solitary confinement indefinitely, reserving RHUs for gang members with serious infractions or crimes for no more than five years. This case also created a new RHU for residents with rule violations while in the RHU who are not ready for general population. They are housed in non-solitary high-security units, which affords them some visits and programming. In 2016, with Senate Bill 1143, California banned the use of solitary confinement units for youth for the purposes of punishment, retaliation, or coercion.[16]

North Dakota also reformed its use of solitary confinement in 2015, changing the name from Administrative Segregation to the Behavioral Intervention Unit (BIU) and dramatically decreasing the number of residents sent there. It also increased out-of-cell time to four or five hours per day, added group sessions three times a week, and added new programmatic and recreational activities. Staff also now "write up" individuals for positive behaviors and focus on skill and rapport building with residents.[17]

Recently, RHU reform made its way into the US House of Representatives as the Solitary Confinement Study and Reform Act of 2019.[18] This legislation seeks to establish a national committee to examine solitary confinement and make recommendations for national standards that would significantly decrease its use. As of September 2019, this bill remains within the Subcommittee on Crime, Terrorism, and Homeland Security. If institutional isomorphism (a theory within organizational studies that explains how organizations and structures wind up looking similar) holds,[19] as more and more states and jurisdictions limit their use of RHUs to particular resident groups and limit the number of days a resident will stay in the RHU, the normative, coercive, and mimetic mechanisms of isomorphism should lead more prisons and jails to follow suit.

The efforts at reform and changes in RHU policy by various US states and the federal government mark solid and salient movement away from years of overuse and misuse of RHUs in prisons and jails. They also represent a conscious effort to bound the use of RHUs by limiting the number of consecutive or total days individuals may spend in RHUs and limit RHUs' scope by prohibiting their use with vulnerable individuals such as people with mental health diagnoses or youth. With the exception of just a few changes like the Cook County Jail's SMU, which allows out-of-cell time—albeit chained—for RHU residents, the current reforms do little to change day-to-day living in RHUs for those still confined there for any number of days.

A second group of first-order changes involves incremental changes to daily RHU environments intended to improve the humanity and dignity for those living and working in these intensely harmful environments while also working to change behavior and assist residents and staff with self-improvement. Scholars and activists have not been not quiet on these reforms, but with markedly less success thus far.

RHU Revision: Improving Humans, Including Humanity

Sometimes, seemingly small or gradual changes make a world of difference. In terms of RHU reform, there are numerous alterations that correctional systems might consider to improve RHU living for residents and working environments for staff. Some of these are more complex and possibly more resource dependent than others, but the human improvements and cost savings may yield benefits to perceptions of risk, forming or repairing relationships, understanding rules, and preparing for reentry beyond what is currently imagined. Assessing if there are any positive behavioral changes and safety outcomes from these proposed reforms yields a litany of crucial questions for future research, which are definitely worth pursuing. The reforms considered here are not fully vetted, examined, tested, or, in fact, proven. However, they represent vast expertise and humane suggestions toward a better pathway forward. At the very least, they provide hope that RHUs can do better.

Reforms to Lower Perceptions of Risk and Develop and Improve Relationships

Lowering perceptions of risk in the RHU for both residents and staff may sound like a tall order, but perhaps this is possible. The design, the sounds, the smell, and the monotony of being in the RHU scream risk. Locking human beings in tiny cells without natural light, without any real contact with family and loved ones (save mail), and with very little to do except think, write, read, and pace means in many ways we have placed individuals ostensibly in need of the most assistance, programming, and treatment in a place where none of these things occur. And we have placed staff in a situation with few if any resources to help or teach behavioral change. In doing so, we created a situation that stretches human capacity to its far-reaching limits.

RHU residents perceive risk primarily stemming from mistreatment by correctional staff and a little from other residents, although their contact and interaction is exceptionally limited in the RHU. Residents continually cite worry regarding their physical and mental health and relationships and the way they feel while inside the RHU worsens all of these. RHU staff primarily perceive risk of physical harm from residents but also believe their own physical and mental health and relationships are at risk working in the RHU. United Kingdom prison scholar Alison Liebling's vast work suggests that what really matters most for achieving a "good prison" is to create a safe, nonthreatening environment where residents are reasonably treated, staff are approachable, and the processes are predictable and perceived as fair. When this occurs, both staff and resident time is freed from worry and fear, and people are able to work to engage in their own and others' self-betterment. Liebling also finds, with some limited exceptions, that culture is what matters most in prison, and it exceeds other common interacting variables like race or ethnicity and gender. According to Liebling, a positive, trusting, clear-sighted, and transparent culture is the single most important predictor of a positive, successful prison.[20]

Changing prison culture, norms, practices, and policies in the United States to adhere to a more humane approach may prove quite difficult, but it is doable. Charles Glisson, of the Children's Mental Health Services Research Center in Knoxville, Tennessee, researches this type of change in social service agencies. His work suggests that "organizations establish the social context for services, organizational social context that directly affects service quality and outcomes, and organizational social context may be changed with planned organizational interventions."[21] Glisson suggests using the sociotechnical model of organizational effectiveness. In this model, effectiveness depends, in large part, on the fit between the social context (culture and climate) and the core technology (goals and outcomes and the means of achieving them). Glisson notes that often organizations adapt their technology to fit their organization's social context rather than changing the social context to fit and support the core technology. In prisons, this means that when a reform or change that may affect organizational culture enters the carceral space and staff perceive a misfit or misalignment between the new innovation and their existing culture, rather than adapt their culture to align with the reform, they instead adapt the reform to fit within their existing culture. This leaves the reform hindered and basically set up to fail from the outset.

For Glisson, effective implementation of reform must first begin with understanding and addressing the social contexts (cultures) so that the technologies (reform) have a legitimate chance to succeed with fidelity (work according to their design). While this model is fairly technical and includes specific focus on three primary domains—the consumer domain (residents), the organizational domain (prisons/units/staff), and the technical domain (reforms, programs, practices)—it suggests a need for first assessing organizational social contexts, examining the dimensions of organizational social context that may interfere with reform and then focusing on delivering reformed programs and practices into the organization and its social context (as it is understood) in ways that will fit, align, and support the effectiveness of the reforms. This does not just mean pulling a reform off the shelf and quickly training prison staff to implement it. Instead, it requires thoughtful attention to the social context or organizational culture long before reform implementation. In prisons, this would also require a thorough overhaul of key carceral goals. Without this pre-implementation, prisons will continue current cultures, and new reform will never advance change, but rather they will simply be redefined and reformed within the existing, dominant prison culture.

One popular option for improving the culture of US prisons, and specifically RHUs, relies on a program sponsored by groups such as Amend: Changing Correctional Culture. Amend is a California-based nonprofit directed by Brie Williams that funds and organizes trips for American prison directors and staff to tour Norwegian prisons and for Norwegian prison officials to travel to US prisons to train American correctional staff. Norwegian prisons tout just a 20 percent recidivism rate for residents released as compared to 50–75 percent recidivism for residents released from US prisons. Programs such as Amend's begin to address some of Glissen's pre-implementation model domains, but they may not go far enough toward really addressing existing organizational social contexts. To date, however, the Norway model has impacted some US state prison systems in positive-leaning ways.

Norway has, in many regards, taken a different approach to incarceration, which American prison management and staff from states like Oregon and North Dakota find enlightening.[22] Using a system Norway calls "dynamic security," prison staff rely on advanced communication techniques to interact and build relationships with residents. They favor rapport over segregation, discipline, and additional forms of punishment and have seen marked success in many regards. Norwegian scholars including Ellen Anvig and colleagues conducted focus groups with residents in a Norwegian prison and found that residents readily discussed their carceral experience and reentry preparation positively.[23] Perhaps most importantly, residents felt they receive humane treatment and expressed feelings of trust, equality, and respect in their relationships with correctional staff. Additionally, residents felt they developed autonomy and the ability to use their own agency to improve their reentry chances post-release. In turn, staff regularly report minimal incidents of violence or misconduct among residents, which improves overall prison safety and security.

After these trips, states like Oregon and North Dakota implemented versions of the Norwegian system in their state prison systems, and thus far, the results are positive. The former director of Corrections and Rehabilitation in North Dakota notes: "There is such an overemphasis on punishment and punitiveness [in the American prison system].... You know Norway talks about punishment that works ... to actually make society safer by getting people to be law-abiding individuals and desist from future offending."[24] While North Dakota and other states have experienced some staff resistance to the imported Norwegian model's components, over time, the benefits seem to outweigh the downsides. When staff see reduced violence, misconducts, and infractions and instead experience improved resident behavior, they often come around to these humane and proactive reforms in ways that overcome old leanings toward punitiveness. In fact, in a 2019 *Detroit News* article,[25] Cyrus Ahalt, Amend's associate director, notes that participating staff in Oregon's DOC "called it the most rewarding experience of their careers and a turning point in their professional lives."

Prisons in other countries are possible models for American reform, but there is some reason for skepticism. Scholars Keramet Reiter, Lori Sexton, and Jennifer Sumner study Danish prisons and have found that despite the more humanizing approach to incarceration in Denmark, residents still regularly report feeling isolated, with a distinct lack of autonomy from the power wielded by the broader prison system and its staff.[26] While the Norwegian and Danish systems are far from perfect, there are valuable lessons in these exchanges and the subsequent innovation and reform initiated in American prison systems. One important point is that American correctional staff and managers see and acknowledge a different approach, one that intensifies and privileges humanity and dignity. It is too early to tell with much confidence if these programs will last and are producing improved outcomes (such as recidivism reduction), but breaking away from punitive ideologies and cultures in the broader prison system and within RHUs is certainly a step toward a reform that may eventually take hold more widely in the United States.

Beyond complete cultural overhaul all at once, incremental changes may begin to move the needle in American RHUs to improve their cultures and make room for alignment in the future between more advanced reforms and existing culture. Both the incremental and future reforms carry the goals of RHU closure, restricted use, and improvements during use. In moving toward positive prisons and positive RHUs, there are perhaps dozens of possible reforms that might chip away at the risks residents and staff perceive. We present four below.

Fixing the Food

First, to improve physical and mental health, to reduce healthcare costs, to potentially decrease irritability, anger, and aggression, and to instill healthy habits for life beyond bars, the food situation in the RHU requires immediate and holistic reform. The World Health Organization (WHO) concurs, noting that prison food "not only affects physical and mental health"[27] but also impacts future reentry and reintegration postrelease. In countless interviews within RHUs, residents describe weight loss and hunger and the effect each has on their mental and physical health. Science verifies these findings in many ways because food is linked to the risk, prevention, and treatment of noncommunicable diseases such as cancer, heart disease, hypertension, and diabetes—all common and disproportionate among US prison residents.[28] While the institutional food options in general populations in prisons are generally no better, the RHU eliminates commissary food purchases for DC-status residents, leaving them with no means of supplementing their diets with additional calories or alternative meal items. This is not to say that prison commissaries generally provide healthy food options, but for hungry residents, anything is better than nothing.

A possible option is considering food service contractors that prioritize macronutrient-rich meals for delivery and commissary. Current success within public school districts, with similar financial and organizational constraints, show promise for introducing healthy meal options. For example, in San Antonio Texas, one school system increased its fresh fruit, vegetable, and whole-grain offerings for students and found it actually *cost less* to feed students this way.[29] In prisons, fixing the food is not wholly new territory. For example, the Victor Valley Prison in California offered and studied the New Start program by inviting the prison's five hundred young adult residents to begin a series of classes and workshops combined with a healthy, vegan diet. Some 85 percent of residents agreed and to date, the data shows no fighting and more cooperation among the New Start group than those eating regular prison fare. In fact, within ten days, New

Start participants expressed improved feelings overall. Additionally, in the seven years of the program, recidivism among participants decreased 2 percent overall.[30] Likewise, in England, 231 young adult male prison residents participated in study that gave them either a multivitamin and a fatty-acid supplement or a placebo. After 142 days, the vitamin group showed a 35 percent reduction in disciplinary incidents and a 37 percent reduction in violent behavior as compared to 6.7 percent and 10.1 percent respectively in the placebo group.[31] Finally, in a Maryland female prison, the state devised a plan to reduce weight gain and improve chronic conditions such as diabetes and heart disease, citing improper diets as a major contributor to these health challenges. First, the plan recognized that the dietary needs of women differ from men. Next, it cut calories and replaced wheat for white bread, added a variety of fish and fresh fruits and vegetables to the menu, reduced or eliminated sugary drinks, and added low-fat yogurt and cottage cheese to increase women's calcium intake. Preliminary results indicate increased morale among women residents, and the benefits of this program are expected to extend beyond prison as the women take their new nutritional knowledge home with them post-release.[32]

Framed by the initial positive results of these innovative models, RHUs may reform their food programs to include healthier options like fresh fruits and vegetables (aligned with institutional policies regarding these products because prisons often worry residents will use them to make homemade alcoholic beverages, which are contraband). RHUs may also work to increase whole grains in RHU meals by replacing white with wheat bread and adding additional whole-grain foods. Providing RHU residents, particularly DC-status residents, with the opportunity to purchase healthy snacks from the commissary list would enable them to quell hunger healthfully and would supplement prison-supplied food. Because prisons generally take a financial share of commissary sales, allowing a limited commissary list with health food options for DC residents could offset any increased costs from improving the nutritional quality of prison-served meals. Ideally, healthier eating would also contribute to better overall mental and physical health in residents, thus reducing medical and psychiatric care costs for prisons. RHUs may also consider, as California has implemented, a vegetarian/vegan option for all prison residents as a way of improving their overall physical and mental health. If costs are a factor influencing these decisions, prisons may use existing science to identify foods with good nutrient-to-cost ratios. For example, some work finds approximately thirty fruits and vegetables that have a good cost-nutrient ratio, including fresh oranges and carrots and canned vegetables like tomatoes and green peas.[33]

While these recommendations may seem to be only for residents, that is decidedly not the case. Staff working in correctional institutions generally eat from the same menu as residents—though typically in separate dining halls with some additional items on their menu (such as a salad bar). They do this for security reasons—so they do not have to leave the prison grounds once they are cleared to enter for a shift and because mealtime is limited and prison food is free. As such, staff are suffering right alongside residents by eating meals for many years without appropriate nutrient density. Refining institutional food options would contribute to the staff's overall health, including fewer sick days, fewer mental health concerns, increased mortality, and reduced reliance on health insurance. Fixing prison and RHU food is imperative and offers cost savings and health improvement for everyone living and working inside.

Incentivizing Appropriate and Prosocial Behavior

Another reform to improve resident and staff perceptions of risk and staff-resident relationships is to build behavioral incentive programs into RHUs to encourage residents and staff to earn privileges, rewards, and other perks. Contingency Management (CM) is an evidenced-based practice used extensively to induce behavioral changes with clients in alcohol and drug treatment, but also within some criminal-legal settings. Built on an operant-conditioning framework, CM provides a structure for desired behavioral change by working with participants to identify goals, break them into achievable subgoals toward a larger goal, and issue rewards for each achievement. Not all CM programs are quite as detailed as this, but scholars Maxine Stitzer and Faye Taxman's work suggests a formal and comprehensive behavioral contract (a written agreement) that clearly lists expectations and associated rewards. This contract adds real and tangible value for both participants and purveyors of CM programs.[34]

Numerous studies suggest the merit of a CM approach. In a meta-analysis of CM in prison settings, prominent scholar Paul Gendreau and colleagues consider the results of twenty-nine CM studies and note the following:

Of all the treatment interventions available to correctional authorities, CM programs are the best fit with the general thrust of accountability-type policies and the use of incentives to promote discipline and structure, and to motivate inmates to earn the right to receive more privileges leading up to early release. Based on the meta-analytic evidence produced to date, there is no question they can be useful motivators of prisoners' behavior.[35]

While some prison programs already use a variation of CM in their step-down, earned-release, and gradual-rewards programs within therapeutic communities and specialty units for residents with mental health diagnoses, these are rarely used with in RHUs. However, changing behaviors that could reduce violence, suicide, self-harm, anger, and other misconducts among RHU residents is precisely what should happen to better prepare RHU residents for intra-carceral reentry back to the general population or community reentry post-release. And changing behaviors among correctional staff within RHUs could reduce resident mistreatment and improve staff overall well-being.

CM offers a pathway toward reducing risk of physical and mental harm through behavioral improvements. This increases both immediate carceral and eventual community safety in untold ways. Additionally, because CM programs would be administered by correctional staff with residents and by correctional managers with staff within RHUs, they help solve the "no carrot and no stick" problem. Contingency Management approaches provide a carrot (incentive) for staff to improve both their own and residents' behaviors. RHUs are so restrictive that staff find it excessively difficult to amend or mold residents' behaviors, and their own behaviors often suffer. When a prison resident acts out, staff possess a litany of tools for approaching that behavior ranging in severity, as noted previously, from informal to formal sanctions. However, in the RHU—the most restricted area of any prison—staff often feel bound to a punishment-and-control model. RHU residents, particularly those with DC status, already have no privileges, so threatening to remove nonexistent perks is a moot point (no stick). And RHUs have few, if any, incentives to offer (no carrots). This leaves RHU staff feeling some degree of powerlessness and residents believing they can act out or misbehave and only really risk physical harm or receiving more RHU time. A CM program incentivizes prosocial behavior for RHU residents and staff. It also affords an opportunity for staff and residents to work together and interact.

In 2012, scholars Francis Cullen, Cheryl Lero Jonson, and John E. Eck discussed incentives (though not specifically tied to CM) in their article "The Accountable Prison."[36] In this work, the authors challenge common conventions that do not hold anyone accountable for post-release recidivism. In their theoretical model, when correctional staff are only responsible and accountable for maintaining in-prison control and order, there is no incentive for them to develop any methods or practices to improve residents during their carceral stay. For Cullen and colleagues, the accountable prison prioritizes recidivism reduction as a primary goal. While not ignoring the need for control in prisons, the authors argue for adding features to custodial supervision that include helping staff understand, and really know, the evidence-based literature in corrections. When their explicit and incentivized goals include recidivism reduction, correctional staff will, the authors argue, work much more proactively and diligently toward that end. A developed reward system would include encouragement and capacity building for staff, but would also include plenty of staff input regarding how and in what ways they would prefer to receive rewards. Cullen and colleagues also suggest a gradual implementation of any accountability system with volunteering prisons. Where better to start than within the RHU, where reentry can be either intra-carceral or community reentry—both of which involve potential recidivism? Further, prisons generally and RHUs specifically may also consider additional success measures as steps toward recidivism reduction or as positive outcomes regardless of recidivism. In the RHU, success measures for residents might include days without misconducts or active participation in therapeutic groups or individualized therapy. Or there might be systemic success measures within prisons, such as having no more than x percent of residents in the RHU at any time or limiting RHU stays to an average of x days. The reward system could also extend beyond custodial staff to include psychiatric and programmatic staff, who could work in tandem with custodial staff toward achieving positive outcomes.

Both CM systems and the accountable prison model provide incentives toward achieving goals for both staff and residents. Residents learn that behavioral modification earns them positive rewards, and staff get to work in a place where residents are actively trying to improve their behavior while staff are actively assisting them and trying to improve their own behaviors. This puts residents and staff at considerably less risk for mental and physical harm and lessens the RHU burden on both groups.

Both may also have positive and important outcomes which provide both cost savings and improved familial and community lives.

Increasing Care and Improving Access to Development Options

The third reform, both decreasing risk and improving relationships of all kinds within RHUs and between RHU residents and staff and their families and loved ones, requires intense focus and redesign. RHU residents overwhelmingly feel they are not receiving the physical and mental health care, interactional contact, and training, education, and programming that they need to improve themselves while housed in the RHU. The narratives from the current study suggest rehabilitation is not a goal (or not a prominent goal) RHUs embrace.

While many staff suggest RHUs need to return to their even more punitive and incapacitory roots, neither staff nor residents are served by the lack of available treatment and educational offerings. If "idle time is the devil's work," the RHU is the devil's laboratory. The RHU is not only a place where tedium leads to havoc; it is also a place where havoc is designed and developed. Staff—not just the RHU staff, but the broader prison staff as well—also suffer when residents have nothing but time on their hands. When RHU residents serve time in the RHU and receive no treatment, education, or programming and few, if any, mental or physical health supports and have little to no contact with anyone, especially family and friends, they often begin to experience or decline further into the depths of worry, anger, and sadness. Couple this with DC residents completely and AC residents nearly completely cut off from their in- and outside-prison connections and relationships, and the situation worsens. And if that is not enough, RHU residents also experience lockdown nearly twenty-three hours a day with no natural light, few reading materials, few, if any, interactions with others, and a distinct lack of hygiene products and services (i.e., limited shower time, few self-care products, and infrequent, if any, haircuts). The results should not be surprising to anyone. Countless scholars, psychologists, and scientists discuss the detrimental effects of living in a solitary confinement setting for any length of time. But instead of idle captive time, why not take advantage of a captive and excessively bored audience?

The profound impact positive social interactions have on individuals is remarkably well-documented in the scholarly literature. However, this is true not only for interactions with friends and family; it is also true within organizational environments. Scholars Heaphy and Dutton detail how "social interactions at work, whether brief connections or enduring relationships, have physiological correlates and effects." Physiological effects may occur within cardiovascular, immune, and neuroendocrine systems. Although their research is just a starting point for digging deeper into this important question, Heaphy and Dutton posit that "physiological resourcefulness" is "a form of positive health in which the body can build, maintain, and repair itself during times of reset and can more easily deal with challenges when they occur."[37] In RHUs, the distinct lack of strong, or any, positive relationships between staff and residents, residents and residents, and residents and staff and the at-times strained relationships between staff and residents and their external prison contacts such as family and friends point to the importance of improving physiological health through positive interactions. Interactional improvements to RHU living and working may contribute to better mental and physical health outcomes for both staff and residents and may improve post-release outcomes as well.

To reduce idle time, improve relationships, and incorporate productive learning and development time, RHUs could provide opportunities for residents to contact family and friends. To accommodate security concerns, this could be accomplished via in-cell tablets. These devices work like iPads without internet but with limited reading, audio, music, and educational content and the ability to email via a secured system and call family and loved ones or even use FaceTime (in some facilities). In this way, residents could stay connected, experience love and support, and reduce feelings of loneliness or feelings that they abandoned their loved ones. Additionally, tablets would provide RHU residents the opportunity to do legal research, continue any eLearning or distance-learning educational courses they started prior to coming to the RHU, or start a new course while there. They could listen to music, send emails, and even watch some tablet programming (which might ease the stress regarding shared televisions in the RHU pods). All of these options with tablets reduce idle time and enhance prosocial behaviors.

While it is possible that all these options in RHUs may encourage residents to choose the RHU for quiet or protection if they feel unsafe in the general population, that would provide two benefits for prisons. First, it would highlight flaws in the current system so that prisons could increase the focus on safety in general population. Second, if the purpose of the RHU shifts from incapacitation, deterrence, and retribution to rehabilitation, the RHU punishment becomes treatment for the safety of all.

RHUs could also add group therapy, treatment, programming, activities, and social time between RHU residents by using the empty dayrooms in each pod if they are available, and the psychiatric rooms or cages or interactions via tablet if these physical space options are not available. With proper supervision, RHU residents would not have to be chained and shackled to tables (as in the Cook County Jail), but that option remains possible for RHUs where resident-on-resident or resident-on-staff violence is a concern. All prison tables meant for residents are already bolted the floor and RHUs already possess numerous chains, cuffs, and shackles. In the prisons we visited, such programming and activities exist in a mental health RHU, where resident behavior is even more uncertain and erratic, with few violent incidents—although the quality of these activities and programs is untested.

RHUs might consider improving their staff by adding staff with expertise in particular issues. Despite resource scarcity, this is absolutely possible and could be a win-win for communities, correctional institutions, residents, and staff. With some carefully crafted legal agreements and contracts, RHUs within prisons could partner with local universities, for example, to bring in unpaid interns to work with residents and staff to improve mental and physical health offerings, programming, treatment, educational, and other needed services. Many US prisons rely heavily on volunteers to supplement their training and educational offerings without having to pay for these services. The RHU is a perfect place to expand volunteer opportunities. Additionally, medical residents and psychiatric apprentices often need sites for practical experience toward degree completion. While these individuals would have to be carefully vetted and extensively trained in prison rules and procedures, it is clear from our data that no RHUs we studied have enough staff to appropriately supervise and also work with RHU residents in meaningful ways.

RHUs may also want to consider working with academic partners to further investigate what is needed to improve RHUs. For example, ceiling caps for rotation tenures for RHU staff need to be studied. Currently, prisons often operate with a formal maximum on the number of years one can work in an RHU before mandatory transfer to another prison unit. Across prisons, this seems to be inconsistently enforced and widely misunderstood. Prison systems may consider using quantitative methods (like the Koper curve)[38] to consider the most productive and meaningful tipping point for staff rotation. This also holds for psychiatric and other RHU staff who experience intense stress and burnout. Other studies might go beyond staff burnout and stress (common in the academic literature) to include physical health and wellness in other ways. Studies of RHU residents also need advancing beyond the typical (though crucially important) psychological battery of questions regarding suicidal ideation and mental deterioration while in RHUs. Studies of RHU residents need to be undertaken on identity, empathy, relationships, risk, procedural justice, and punishment, like some our research team has completed. Knowing more about both RHU staff and residents is integral to reforming and improving RHUs for future residents and staff and the communities where they both reside.

Staff overwhelmingly express their feelings of ill-preparedness for dealing with, understanding, and handling residents with mental health concerns, including those who came to RHUs with diagnoses and those who develop mental health diagnoses while inside RHUs. Many staff feel they do not have adequate training or understanding to best meet residents' needs and as a result, they feel they may be contributing to residents' worsening conditions. Staff also regularly report feeling a deterioration in their own mental and physical health and personal relationships when they are working in RHUs (and prison in general). This is not new, but it is so common that it deserves attention here.

RHUs should continue further educating and training all staff about issues related to mental health (via mental health first-aid courses) and de-escalation and communication (crisis intervention training). However, RHUs can go further in this regard with a holistic and ongoing approach to staff wellness. They may consider other strategies to provide ongoing interpersonal and mental health training for RHU staff, such as booster trainings with more in-depth information about themes of other trainings. They may also add staff sensitivity training, particularly as related to gender identity of residents. Further, adding incentives for mental and physical health coaching or meeting health benchmarks would improve staff's overall health. Additionally, to improve staff behavior, enhancements to training and education are always a starting place, but training a correctional staff member via printed materials and PowerPoint in a classroom—as is relatively standard for most prison staff training about the complexities in carceral environments regarding human interaction, mental and physical health, and social control—is lackluster at best. Staff may greatly benefit from continued training, live coaching, and more interactive training approaches for both learning more about mental health and wellness, but also for a whole litany of correctional issues and challenges including implementing directives, policies, and practices within RHUs.

The key to these reforms, though, may be the cultural shift that must happen within prisons to make these changes normative, not exclusionary. The highly masculinized prison environment does not currently allow much space for staff mental and physical health discussions, trainings, and incentive plans. Having any problem may make staff look or feel weak, a trait no one values in carceral environments. A new culture characterized by healthy eating, healthy habits, and healthy thinking will take some time and effort, but the outcomes will overwhelmingly surpass expectations and provide lasting and life-saving results.

In the RHUs we studied, staff sometimes report using mental health programs, including complimentary counseling sessions, mental health days, and other related services that broker mental health resources. However, our data suggests wide discrepancy regarding those who participate and the reasons that others do not use or do not feel comfortable using counseling, calm rooms, or other programs regularly or at all. Nonuse may significantly contribute to diminishing mental and physical health among RHU staff. RHUs may consider programs that incentivize staff to participate in health-focused initiatives. Incentives may include days off, being excused from a mandatory shift, or extra days of bringing in outside food for personal consumption during meals and breaks. These are incentives for participating in a wide variety of health-focused actions, including reaching a specific number of steps, utilizing the cover room or another private locale for mediation or calming, participating in community intramural sports, or attending local gyms or fitness studios. Similar incentivized health programs operate in private organizations and show that it is possible to systematically capture activity information to reward staff for taking steps to improve their overall health and wellness.

RHU Rules Reform: Increasing Understanding, Transparency, and Accountability

The most common theme in both the resident and staff narratives regarding RHU policies and procedures is that no one knows or understands all of the rules in the RHU. As a high-security, highly restricted carceral unit designed to achieve strict control and behavioral consistency, the RHU fails on almost every level. Both residents and staff repeatedly report misunderstanding, misuse, overuse, and confusion around the specific rules each group is supposed to follow. This informational abyss creates an unpredictable environment for both residents and staff and leaves both groups feeling unsure and unsafe in an anomic tomb.

A substantial overhaul of RHU policies and a fully developed plan for sharing and explaining RHU rules and training both residents and staff on them are crucial for improving the humanity and dignity of both residents and staff. For starters, every RHU should consider consolidating its resident handbook into translatable forms for RHU residents with varying language, comprehension, cultural, and educational backgrounds. Putting these rules into a simple, easy-to-understand format would go a long way toward helping RHU residents understand their rights and the rules of the RHU. Ideally, these would be on the cover page of each RHU handbook; each cell should have its own copy; and each tablet should have a tab where residents could access the handbook instantly. RHUs could even paint the rules on cell walls![39] There is good literature to support the importance of appropriate signage in assisting behavioral change.[40] For example, ample empirical work finds that putting signs in close proximity to a requested behavior that is relatively convenient increases the likelihood that individuals will perform the requested behavior.[41]

Additionally, the handbook should be regularly updated, and if RHUs want to improve resident compliance, a council of RHU members should have input into RHU rules and translations for each edition of the rulebook. Providing some agency and voice to the seemingly powerless and voiceless would enhance the RHU experience for residents, give them a stake in the outcome, and likely improve overall compliance. Additionally, the RHU handbook needs to be available for individuals in their language and meet ADA requirements for individuals with mental or physical disabilities. The RHU should never run out of copies of the rulebook; residents should never have to purchase copies; and residents should be rewarded for knowing the rules and for following them—not only punished when they do not know them or break them.

Staff should receive more than just RHU School or academy training on working in prisons in general to help them understand the intricacies and differences between working in general population units and RHUs.

This requires formal and ongoing (continuous) training and coaching from professionals in psychology, social work, education, health and medicine, conflict resolution, anger management, and other such fields and disciplines to help RHU staff not only know the rules, but to truly understand them. Where do the rules come from? Why do we do it that way? What other things have we tried and to what end? RHU staff should be encouraged to contribute to RHU policy revisions as needed and at least annually, to encourage compliance and uptake. RHU staff should also receive rewards or incentives for knowing the rules and upholding them.

Additionally, RHU residents and staff should demand more from their DOC regarding rules, policies, and procedures. While it is understandable that the DOC rules are often written in loose and vague language to avoid legal entanglements and allow for localization, unclear DOC rules usually mean unclear rules in individual prisons. When this occurs, discretion regarding what the rules mean, who they apply to, under what circumstances they apply, and if there is any wiggle room is left to individual staff.

Rules that too loosely guide day-to-day behavior can put everyone at risk. Take, for example, meal delivery. In most RHUs we visited for this project, the federal or state law notes the need for adequate food and nutrition to sustain life. The DOC policy might get a little more specific, noting that residents have the "opportunity" to receive three meals a day. And finally a particular prison's RHU policy might note that a resident must be standing in their cell with the light on when meals are delivered and be ready to accept the tray through the wicket. Although all the prisons in this study have slightly different RHU meal policies, this example is indicative of the rules governing meal delivery in RHUs in general.

A resident could interpret the meal-delivery rules (if they even have a rulebook) as meaning that they will receive three meals a day as long as they are standing with the light on in their cell when meals are delivered. However, a staff member may have a different interpretation and understand the rules to mean that residents must receive the "opportunity" for three meals but do not necessarily have the *right* to three meals. See how it gets dicey? A resident may believe that as long as they are visible to the staff and able to accept the tray through the wicket, they will get a meal, but one staff member may demand that they be standing with the light on, another staff member may be OK with just the light on if the resident is getting out of bed and moving toward the door when the staff comes by with the meal tray. What if the resident is doing push-ups and quickly stands up? Is that "standing"? What if the resident flips the light on right as the staff member gets to the door? Is that "light on"? Some staff do not mind calling out to a resident who is still asleep to awaken them for mealtime, but other staff may note that the RHU policy makes no mention of this and thus it is not required.

If simple meal delivery is laden with confusion, anxiety, and lack of clarity, imagine an entire day in an RHU. How do residents get paper, showers, recreational yard time, access to legal materials, or anything else they may need? How do they request medical or psychiatric assistance? If the process to provide or receive food has this many interpretations and discretionary choices, would you not eventually get angry, frustrated, violent, or just go mad? Posting the rules in clear, easy-to-understand language in various places and for all to see could eliminate a lot of confusion and make RHU living and working easier for residents and staff.

If rewriting policies and rules to make them clearer and more translatable for residents and staff requires more than prisons or DOCs will do, prisons should consider introducing alternative measures to make sure, at a minimum, all residents receive basic access to life necessities such as showers, meals, and recreation time in the yard. One possibility here is to simplify the existing rules and move away from, for example, requiring residents to sign up for yard and shower (sometimes more than once) or be standing with the light on to receive these services. RHUs could instead operate from the assumption that every RHU resident wants these things when they are provided, not just offered according to RHU activity schedules. Knowing this, staff will be able to plan accordingly. This would potentially save time because RHU staff would have to travel through each RHU pod only to remove residents from their cells for showers and yard and take them back afterwards, rather than having to go through the pod once to secure sign-ups, then again for removal, and again for transport, and finally to rehouse residents back into their cells. If the procedure were simplified in his way, the staff can simply skip the cell of any resident who does not want to go to the yard or shower, and save time.

For meals, residents should *always* receive their allotted three meals a day. With its intimate connection to mental and physical health and the possibility of reducing health risks, anger, aggression, violence, and other issues, food should be something residents can depend on. This is challenging for staff who have only a short time to serve hot food hot, drop off the meal trays with residents, allow them time to eat, pick up the trays, and transport them back to the kitchen for cleaning ahead of the next meal service. Efficiency is key, but not at the expense of providing nourishment to residents. Staff commonly complain that they do not have time to awaken sleeping residents for meals, nor do many of them believe this is part of their job. They note that if they pass by a cell with a food tray but the resident is sleeping, they have to go to the next cell in order to have enough time to deliver all the rest of the meals during that service. Staff also note that they do not have time during meal service to circle back to all the resident cells where a resident was sleeping and they cannot provide a tray to a resident for his cellie for fear the resident will eat his and his cellie's food. These reasons are all understandable, but residents oversleep for all kinds of reasons, including prison-prescribed medication, anxiety, stress, and depression, as well as insomnia or other sleeping difficulties in prison and the RHU.

One option for RHUs would be for the kitchen to provide a number of cold bagged meals with each hot tray delivery to RHU units. Staff could keep these between meal services to give to residents who were sleeping during hot meal delivery. Another option would be for prisons to source and contract for meal replacement bars that fit most or all dietary needs. Of course, bagged meals and bars cannot be held indefinitely, and because staff have a host of other duties, they cannot be expected to keep checking on residents who missed meals to see if they are awake. And prison kitchens are already working very hard to produce hot meals, so also preparing cold bagged meals might be challenging. However, the meal replacement bars are an easy option, and they can be distributed by the kitchen or kept on the RHU unit for distribution as needed for missed meals. Yes, there are logistics here that each individual prison and RHU must work out, but feeding and caring for humans is worth the time, effort, and revision to current protocols.

Surviving Solitary

Surviving solitary confinement, or RHUs, currently involves a deep and fervent look into one's soul and an intentional separation from the parts of oneself and one's surroundings that do not belong in this intolerant, inexcusable, and inhumane space. It involves tenacious resilience via various coping mechanisms, coping that at times may be yet another form of masked malignancy as residents hide from themselves and others both literally and figuratively to survive. For both residents and staff, Erving Goffman's "backstage behavior" as a technique for the presentation of self is not possible within RHUs. Backstage is a place where "the performer can relax; he can drop his front, forgo speaking in his lines, and step out of character."[42] Backstage in the RHU is dangerous at best, and at worst it is potentially deadly. In fact, within the RHU there is no backstage.

Both residents and staff within RHUs manage, mitigate, and cope with harm in similar ways. The harm each perceives falls into similar categories and includes potential physical and emotional risk that stems from individual mistreatment, loss of relationships with family and loved ones, and institutional or systemic challenges from unknown or misunderstood policies, practices, rules, and directives. Although the DOC and individual prisons generally purport trying to prevent any harm to residents and staff, they do not always succeed. There are so many ways to harm someone, and some may cause harm to one individual but not to another. Circumstances and contexts dictate perceived and actual harm, and these vary considerably from person to person and even from moment to moment. The masked malignancy of harm includes the hidden and the disguised harms that occur continually, sporadically, and at times, without initial detection. These harms inflict untold damage on both staff and residents—so untold that even the staff and residents often do not know about this harm or are unwilling or unable to admit it, even to themselves.

Yet, despite the rampant harm, there is also hope within RHUs—hope that emerges from facing intense situations and persons and believing in one's own ability to survive and maybe one day to thrive. For some residents and staff, coping mechanisms include trying to stay out of trouble within the RHU, "keeping their head down," and "playing by the rules." For other residents and staff, mitigating harm includes a heavy dose of vigilance and depending on no one but themselves. Resident Lemmer says that he copes by trying "to limit his interaction with the mental health inmates because it really puts a strain on you." Some residents and staff rely on religion and family to get them through. Resident Kennedy says, "I pray, dear God, please give me the strength to deal with this. . . . [My support system is] my religion. My mom. My dad. My whole family. My attorney." Other residents look to physical activity, routine, and books for help coping. For staff, the story is markedly similar. They mostly rely on themselves at work and lean heavily (or not at all) on family and friends to distract or pull their minds from the depths of the hole created by the hole they work in. Some staff go for long drives, take hiking or hunting trips into nature, or sleep and watch TV. Other staff rely on alcohol or other substances for coping.

Neither group accesses or receives the mental and physical health supports they need to learn to cope and deal with the horrors of the RHU. Neither group understands the rules or policies or procedures that govern their every move during every day and night in the RHU. Both groups express dissonance with RHU rules, relating feelings of confusion and ambiguity. Neither group commonly envisions or dares to holistically hope for a world outside the RHU (with the exception of the occasional staff member who discusses retirement). And neither group (although residents seemingly more than staff) offers many real or concrete suggestions on how to improve RHU living or working. While staff get leave the RHU after every shift and residents do not, each carries the RHU with them in perpetuity. Both residents and staff carry the heavy burden of an RHU existence within them and project this onto everyone they know. Both groups struggle, and both find answers that never seem to illuminate.

Charles Dickens once wrote:

> And though he live to be in the same cell ten weary years, he has no means of knowing, down to the very last hour, in what part of the building it is situated; what kind of men there are about him; whether in the long winter night there are living people near, or he is in some lonely corner of the great jail, with walls and passages, and iron doors between him and the nearest sharer in its solitary horrors.[43]

While modern RHUs are not always solitary in the way Dickens evokes, they are indeed lonely for both residents and staff. The events and chaos of the RHU are hard to share with others and even harder to forget. While staff rarely describe the RHU in ways that get at the gut-wrenching images resident narratives conjure, they too, experience great pain and anguish far below the surface of their daily working lives. They feel it in the way they interact with residents. They feel in the way their relationships with their families change after working in the RHU. They feel it in the changes to their own personality and perceptions, often becoming less agreeable and less conscientious.[44] They feel it in the moments, even if fleeting, that they question the purpose their work serves.

Residents are easier to read when it comes to their feelings regarding the RHU. Their words cut deep and expose cavernous wounds and festering sores. "I took down the pictures of my family, because I don't want them to be in this dangerous environment," says resident Epham. "I feel like a piece of dirt here," says resident Gibbs, "a piece of dirt laying on the floor that needs to be picked up."

With their words, perhaps residents paint the RHU picture for the rest of us. They and we are all living in a world where humans are experiencing great suffering inside confined spaces, without help, and without optimism. Both RHU residents and staff feel alone, at risk, and discarded. But if it offers any hope at all, *they still feel*. They are, in fact, surviving. But so much more is needed and so very much more is possible.

Behind the Walls

About This Book

BEHIND EVERY STORY there is a backstory, the part of the story readers sometimes wonder about but only occasionally discover. The backstory contains a mixture of information that helps explain how the story came to be, who the teller is, and how and why the story is told as it is. For me, the backstory for this book is a complex gumbo of several distinct contextual narratives that often compete while occurring simultaneously.

First and foremost, it is a story of and for the people—in this case, the residents living and staff working in RHUs in US prisons. In telling the story in this book, I rely on narratives from residents and staff and hew my analysis of these narratives as tightly to their original and intended meaning as possible. It is true that I am not a mind reader, so I did not always know or comprehend everything that was going on in the thoughts the folks we talked to. However, I truly wanted the people to speak for themselves—and for me to just be the curator and presenter of their lived RHU perspectives and experiences. To accomplish this, I worked diligently to present a preserved narrative from each individual verbatim, or as close to it as our notes allowed.

Second, as the writer and teller, I am indelibly shaped by my own lived experiences, perspectives, understandings, and positionality. As a cisgender, white, middle-aged woman, who lives in an upper-middle-class suburban neighborhood, is a single mom of three boys, grew up in rural upstate New York, has lived in three different states, and is a PhD'd professor at a research-intensive university, these parts of me bleed into my work. I cannot shed them or ignore them. I try, though, to use profound empathy, reflection, and listening when I conduct research with people. I am not perfect when trying to tell someone else's story and make sense of it—I do so from my own positionality. As researchers, we all do this, but we do not all recognize it or discuss it. In this backstory, I will try to illuminate as much of this as I can.

Third, it is not just my individual identities that impact the lens through which I interpret and analyze ethnographic observations and interviews. My professional identity influences these interpretations as well. I am a researcher with a degree in sociology, but my appointment is within a criminology, law, and society department. This positions me as part of the academy. In this role, I must uphold certain standards of academic and research ethics and excellence. This is a tough but privileged position for many reasons, but for me, perhaps most importantly, it includes the struggle within my own discipline and networks to publish and receive recognition for my work. This is already hard for most academic researchers, but as a qualitative researcher, my work is regularly considered "soft science," "not rigorous," or as an anonymous journal reviewer once stated, "not empirical." This means that not only do I work in a business that is filled with rejection (of papers, grants—well, most everything), but I also use a method that at times takes much longer, makes these rejections far more common, and renders my research far less valued (at least by some). The struggles I present here are incomparable to the struggles of RHU residents and staff, and I do not mean in any way to equate the two. I simply offer these three contextual explanations to provide the backstory for the story, *Surviving Solitary*.

I present this background as a way to unpack the backstory for readers and to provide guidance and instruction about doing research in carceral settings. There is an obvious tension here, though, so I will just lay it out. The center of the RHU story is the residents and staff, but as the person bringing their narratives outside the prison walls, I enter the story whether I want to or not—and I enter it with the baggage of my positionality. In the sections that follow, I will pull the tension-filled thread of researching and writing about the experience of RHU residents and staff through for readers in the hope of providing a context for how and why I and the rest of the research team collected, analyzed, and wrote as we did.

In this part of this book, I get to tell you the story of methods. In the great anthropological traditions of ethnography and qualitative work, it is about being able to *see the story* in data, after wrestling with who to collect data from, how, and in what ways. Then, it is about seeing patterns throughout individual narratives without changing them or altering them to meet the researchers' own expectations, biases, or assumptions—as much as possible. It is about piecing together a relatively fractured story from individual people in a way that fairly and accurately represents the people we spoke with and spaces we observed but also includes the overall patterns discovered from looking at the data holistically.

Before I begin, though, I would like to ask readers to bear with me as this part of this book may seem a little long-winded. I want to ensure that I leave for you every morsel of information that I possess to make your qualitative study of prison or jail or probation or parole or wherever it is that you do fieldwork on fruitful and that you find your passion in this work. I will try to present the methods in a chronological order of sorts so that if you are just beginning to think about a project, you will start with this chapter to begin that work. Then, I will walk you through nearly every decision that the research team and I made (and decisions we did not make or should have made) in constructing the study that constitutes the stories in this book. Through learning about my journey and the journey of our research team, I hope you will be inspired to embark on one of your own and find the confidence to do work, which never really feels like work to me, that comes from the heart.

Researcher Background and Project Conception

I knew I was interested in prisons from a really young age. We lived in the country, and I remember my mother driving us into town to go grocery shopping. On our trip each time, we passed a building that did not look like all the other buildings in this small town. There were bars on the windows, and the building was large and brown and ominous. Just looking at it was scary. All the buildings around it had flowers in front and big trees. The library down the street had big white marble steps that you could walk up to get in, but not this building. This building looked like a place that no one wanted to go into, and I imagined if I were inside, I would want nothing more than to get out.

On each trip to town, I asked my mother questions about the people in that building. While I cannot remember her exact answers, she thoughtfully tried to appease her tiny daughter's curiosity, noting that it was a jail, the people in there had done bad things, and they were being punished.

What could they have done? My five- or six-year-old brain spun. When I do bad things, I get sent to my room. I am sure that my mother tired of my questions and that she tried many tactics to get me to stop asking her about the jail (as I now knew it was called), but even in my elementary school years, I was persistent. These were days before internet, so googling it to find out more information was not an option. As our town trips continued, I began asking her to stop at the jail so I could visit with the people in there because I believed they must be lonely living in such a desolate place. She flatly denied all my requests for jail visitation.

In my earliest memories of thinking about carceral spaces, my thoughts centered, as they do now, on how scary it must be (*risk*), how alone they must feel (*relationships*), how different their lives must be (*rules*), how they must long to leave (*reentry*), and how they must want things to change (*reform*). These thoughts have haunted me most of my life. They are the foundation of my studies, my research, my sleepless nights, my advocacy and service, and my career.

I know now that there is very real social distance between me and people living and working inside America's jails and prisons. While I have been studying this world for many years, and my knowledge and understanding grows over time, incarceration has not impacted my life the way it has for staff and residents. I will, though, spend a lifetime trying to understand how it impacts others. This distal difference means that already the language I use is different, who I think is inside and how they got there is often challenged, and many of the situations that brought them there are regularly new to me. It also means that in talking with staff and residents, I am asking people to unpack a trauma in front of me (and, importantly, *for* me) to advance my career. It means that I will get better (I hope) at retelling their narratives over time, but I will never be able to do it from a place of real intimacy with the experience. This is my positionality and I own it. Coming from humble beginnings, a fire ignited inside me to delve into a world I knew nothing about, to try to understand it, and hopefully to inspire others to do the same. When your work is the heart of your life, your life is never work, and your heart is immensely full.

Methodological Concerns for Doing Research with Residents and Staff in Prisons

Although the work starts with people's lived experiences and then formulates in researchers' minds, the first tangible step of any qualitative research project after thinking through the topic and potential questions involves securing access. For some who are studying public spaces, this task is far easier. However, for those needing permission to enter locked, secure, and generally prohibited spaces like prisons, this crucial undertaking means the difference between the bringing to life and the rapid death of a study idea.

For me, this was an easier than expected. In 2013, the research center I co-direct hired a postdoctoral fellow, Dr. Brandy Blasko, to work on various research projects. Although at the time of her hire I did not know or understand the extent of her connection to a state DOC, I certainly benefited from these connections in the coming years. She had worked over a decade before and during her doctoral program as a member of one prison's psychological staff and had used this state's system and data to write her dissertation.

Through her connections, we began a project, The Prison Project, that used mixed methods to examine staff and resident perceptions of issues related to culture and procedural justice (i.e., trust, relationships, confidence, punishment, and fairness). Before that project began, we worked with the DOC to contact and discuss our project with union representatives from five unions to collect data with staff in a way that minimally interferes with their work and does not violate their union agreements. With all the unions' permission, we engaged in the work over the next three-plus years. When that project ended, I had lunch with our DOC contact, who is also the head of its research department. My goal was to thank him for allowing us to do this interesting work in the hopes that we might find a way to continue our collaborative partnership. Then he popped the question. No, he did not ask me to marry him! He asked me what project I wanted to do next.

Throughout The Prison Project, I remained in steady communication with him both when issues came up and when we celebrated successes. We developed a rapport and the beginnings of a friendship that led to the moment when the DOC asked me what I wanted to do and how we might partner in ways that would be mutually beneficial. Nervous, but feeling moderately confident, I pitched my RHU project ideas to him (these emerged from data collected during The Prison Project), and he listened intently. At the end of my ramblings, he smiled, put his elbows on the table, leaned in toward me, and said, "Sure, I think we can make that work." Within just a few short minutes we opened a door to my dream project. For the first time in over thirty years, a research team was going to do qualitative, including ethnographic, work inside RHUs and it was *our* team. We spent the rest of our lunchtime discussing what the DOC would like to get out of this study—what they wanted to learn and how the work might contribute to reform and changes for both those living and working in RHUs.

And it did not end there. The following week I emailed and then called a sergeant I met during The Prison Project and engaged him in the study design process. My point here is that research is and always should be a collaborative process. Although the collaborations described thus far do not indicate a fully participatory action-research project, they do engage practitioners in a participatory way. Research to advance knowledge is of course important, but if you do that *and* assist your research site or sites with learning about their own inner workings in a way that improves systems, processes, and practices, that is a monumental and rewarding feat—one definitely worth pursuing.

Next, we worked with our DOC research partners to decide what prisons to include in the study. In a system the size of the one we work with, conducting rigorous qualitative data collection in *all* prisons and in *every* RHU is resource prohibitive. Although we gained access, in theory, to all the DOC prisons during The Prison Project, we had to choose a subsample from the universe of prisons to do the study. For The Prison Project, we let the DOC secretary of corrections know that we wanted a mixture of six prisons (roughly 25 percent of the prisons in the state) that would provide a maximum variation sample[1] of male and female institutions,[2] institutions at every security level (maximum, medium, and minimum), and institutions with what the secretary perceived had positive and negative cultures. He took a few other things into consideration in choosing our sample, including other research that was occurring at each of institutions and institutions that were currently undergoing audits, court cases, and other challenges. We asked him not to tell us which of the chosen prisons had what he considered positive or negative cultures though, because we wanted to talk with residents and staff without that knowledge and let the people tell us.

Similarly, for the two RHU studies—the Together Alone and the Changing the (w)Hole Mind studies—we worked with the DOC to choose institutions that met our strata but did not overly burden anyone, given the day-to-day challenges that the system, various institutions, and individuals face. For the Together Alone project, we sampled both male (3) and female institutions (1), with a variety of regular and specialty RHUs (e.g., units designed for specific groups of individuals such as those with severe mental health diagnoses), with forty or more daily RHU residents, and with varying security levels (1 maximum and 3 medium). From the first RHU study, Together Alone, we learned that RHUs in female and male prisons are dramatically different in numerous ways. So, for the second RHU study, the Changing the (w)Hole Mind study, we refocused our strata slightly to include only male institutions. For both studies, the DOC again added it its own strata to meet its needs, including not choosing institutions where numerous other research projects were occurring and where recent court or audit events would interfere with data collection and overly burden prison staff. Our strata also included prisons that had RHUs and specialized units for individuals with severe mental health diagnoses as Shannon Magnuson's dissertation looks specifically at those units.

Allowing this type of collaboration between the research team and the DOC yields tremendous benefit to the study, the institutional staff, and the project overall. Of course, the DOC could keep our team away from prisons where they do not want nosy researchers sniffing around—for example, where residents are hugely frustrated and would likely not paint the DOC in a positive light in our interviews. However, in any DOC, all institutions carry the potential to be "that prison," the one under a microscope or the one where things are not going well. Additionally, with a good, collaborative research process in place, the DOC does not view researchers as the enemy; rather, they see us as part of a team of folks working *with* them to improve conditions for the individuals living and working there.

To assist with access at the institutional level, we asked for and received a letter from the state's secretary of corrections that provided an overview of our study and his permission for us to collect data within RHUs. We sent this letter along with our fieldwork scheduling request to our administrative liaison at each of our four institutions. The letter did not imply or mean that staff or residents *had* to talk to us once we were there; it simply gave us permission to access the site with the additional permission of each institution and try to collect data.

Working with People Living and Working in RHUs
Researchers working with carceral staff and residents generally face a bit of an uphill battle to gain approval from Institutional Review Boards

(IRBs)—bodies that oversee and govern all research with people to ensure that researchers adhere to ethical standards that protect the people who are the subjects of research. It is an important part of the research process and one I greatly value. "Prisoners" (as most IRBs call them) are considered a protected class, in part due their perceived vulnerability, the possibility of coercion (because of the extreme power differentials between individuals who are incarcerated and those who are not, such as staff and researchers), and the limited confidential settings for data collection available in prisons. I originally treated the IRB process as a step I had to complete because I did not originally consider this work as "trauma telling." However, now having done this work, I recognize I am asking people to talk about their trauma while they are actively experiencing it. For this reason, the IRB is crucial to helping make sure I am caring for the people I talk with and protecting their emotional labor.

University and DOC IRBs vary greatly, but that is a conversation for another day. For our project, we focused making sure our study design worked within the university's IRB rules but in a way that aligned with our project goals and the practices and procedures that each institution allows.

For the RHU studies, I wanted to do ethnographic data collection (including observations and interviews) with both staff and residents. I also wanted to recruit residents by going cell to cell and pitching our study, because I did not want staff choosing particular residents for us to interview—that might unduly influence who we talked to and our consent process. Then, I wanted staff to immediately transport residents who agreed to participate to a place where we could have a confidential, conversational interview.

When I called my favorite sergeant to discuss my plans for the ethnographic observations, he laughed and said slyly, "Professor, you cannot do that." In this pivotal conversation, I learned a great deal about RHU staffing levels and the structure of day-to-day RHU management. Spending time in the unit to conduct observations of residents would meet a host of insurmountable challenges. Through our conversation, I learned that no one "hangs out" on the pods (groupings of resident cells on the unit). If I dared to ask this of units, the staff would likely consider this a "rookie move" and if it happened—which was seriously unlikely—it would be hugely disruptive to staff and residents.

Although I was disappointed, I also knew that learning the inside story from the people experiencing these units depended on a good relationship with institutional staff. For example, from the first RHU study, we learned that the overnight shift (10 p.m. to 6 a.m.) was not great for data collection. The staff during that shift is a skeleton crew of two or three COs. And most of the COs working the day shifts had once worked the overnight shift. Therefore, interviewing staff on non-overnight shifts would be enough to capture data regarding the overnight shift without having to do it firsthand. Additionally, after 4 p.m. each day, when the maintenance shift (the custodial staff who work 8 a.m. to 4 p.m. to help with extra duties including resident movement) goes home, no resident movement is possible due to limited staffing. So, all data collection with residents needed to occur between roughly 8 a.m. and 4 p.m. but not during institutional count or mealtimes. Interviews with residents would not take place inside the RHU pods and we could not observe residents. We could observe and interview staff anytime as long as we did it in the course of their work or in a private location with permission from their supervisor and their own consent, because an interview would mean stepping away from their post for an hour or so.

After working through these details with an insider (my favorite sergeant), I submitted our study for university IRB approval. For the RHU studies, the human-subjects process involved a lot of back-and-forth between the DOC and the IRB. I was the go-between for these negotiations. The IRB wanted assurances that our team would interview residents and staff in confidential locales. This is challenging in a small RHU that is specifically designed to deny privacy. The approved plan included our team going cell to cell to recruit residents, and the staff moving residents who agreed to participate from their cells and placing them in a confidential location for interviewing. The staff were to move residents to secure locations on the unit, including the psychiatric cage, the strip-search cage, and any other available room where residents could be secured and the audio would not be overheard by staff or other residents. Staff required that they be able to view all interviews, though, from cameras or windows, but did not require being able to hear them. To increase data confidentiality, our team would not write down any resident or staff names. (Because this was not a longitudinal project where we would need to re-interview folks, having their real names was not of any importance to us). We would recruit staff on the unit during their working shift and ask them for consent before each interview. We would gain consent from each resident once we got them to a secure location, just prior to interviewing them. We were set—or so I thought.

During our first RHU visit, we had been on the unit for only about fifteen minutes when I was explaining to the lieutenant what our process would look like. He flatly and sternly denied my request and informed me that repeatedly going cell to cell throughout the day to recruit residents was not possible. This would require staff to be with us continually, and they simply did not have the time for that. So, we discussed other possibilities. At first, the lieutenant wanted to just pull residents one by one for interviews at his and his staff's choosing. I am sure I mumbled something like, "Ah . . . no, that will not work." That was the fear I had initially. I did not want staff choosing who we would interview. I also did not want residents to feel pressured to do an interview, nor did I want them to associate the research team with the carceral staff. Rapport and trust depended on this. Additionally, both were pivotal to us upholding our agreement with the IRB. Participating in an interview had to be a resident's choice.

So, we found a new solution. The team would enter each of the four pods first thing on the morning of the first day. We would go cell to cell recruiting residents for a later interview. The team would keep a running list of residents who agreed to participate, and we would use that list to work with staff throughout the day to pull various residents for interviews (as the staff's other unit duties allowed). To protect confidentiality of the residents, my team would have to keep vigilant watch over the list and destroy it immediately after completing fieldwork. The team had a quick meeting to discuss the new protocol, and I made sure to explain that we would destroy the lists of names as soon as our fieldwork at each prison was complete. This became more complicated because when we returned to the motel each evening, we did not feel comfortable throwing away or even ripping up and throwing away paper with resident names on it in a small, rural prison town where everyone seems to know each other. We agreed we would bring the lists back to the university and shred them—which we do. Our new recruitment approach was approved by the IRB.

One final comment about IRBs pertains to obtaining consent from residents: There is considerable debate among researchers about whether residents are ever really fully able to give consent. This stems from their incapacitated and largely powerless status. Our team generally takes the view that residents are powerless in many regards, but they remain autonomous human beings in many ways, able to make choices when choices are presented to them. We train our team on how to ask staff and residents for consent, and we use only verbal consent processes (rather than written-and-signed forms) so that the consent process is a conversation where the researcher explains and the resident asks questions for clarity and understanding. We also do not want a written record via a signed consent of who participated. Residents are informed how we collect and store their data; they know we do not use their real names or any identifiers that would make them identifiable to readers later; and they know we take this seriously. For example, if a resident uses a specific catch phrase (or a phrase we think is unique to just them), we change that in our data when we write the notes. Despite our interviewing hundreds of residents in several prisons, it is possible that only resident Tyrell Hinks, for example, says, "My mama would not believe the crazy-pants screwbellies in this place." If we left that phrase, in vivo, in our data, anyone who ever met and talked to Hinks would be able to identify him. He deserves confidentiality, and we believe strongly in giving it to him.

We also train our team how to ask residents with a known or unknown mental health diagnosis for consent. We look for signs during the consent process that the resident may be hallucinating, hearing voices, or just generally out of it or confused. Here again, we have a few options if we sense mental health may compromise the clarity and understanding of the consent process. First, we can stop the interview momentarily, excuse ourselves, and go find a psychological staff member to ask if they believe the person is mentally capable of giving consent. If so, we return to the interview. If not, we end the interview by thanking the resident and then we destroy any collected data (not use it). Second, we can use the same processes above where we assess the resident for mental capacity and clarity, but without the assistance of the psychological staff, instead relying on our own judgment. We try not to enlist custodial staff for mental health evaluations because they are not clinically trained and may have ulterior motives for allowing or stopping an interview. These are challenging choices, but we do our best to make every resident feel heard and important while also holding up our ethical agreements for consent and destroying data if we have any questions about a resident's consent at any point during the interview. For example, some residents may provide what appears a clear and lucid consent at the start of an interview, but during the course of the interview become less lucid or clear. Our goal is never data at any cost; it is data when it makes sense and does not harm anyone, either the researcher or the subject.

Preparing and Training the Research Team

Before conducting any fieldwork or data collection within RHUs, I co-designed a training program with a doctoral student, Shannon Magnuson, and we trained our team. The team for this project included two faculty from the GMU Sociology Department, Dr. Earl Smith and Dr. Angela Hattery (Women and Gender Studies Center),[3] me, Shannon Magnuson, and a host of graduate and undergraduate students for one or both years. These folks included graduate students Taylor Hartwell, Sydney Ingel, Lindsay Smith, Heather Toronjo, Cait Kanewske, Esther Matthews, Lina Marmolejo, Kristen Huete, and Cassie Wright and undergraduate students Casey Tabas, Liz Rosen, Kaley Regner, Karlie Berry, Liana Shivers, Sewit Beraki, Sabrine Baiou, Beau Coleman, Taylor Whittington, Cady Balde, Heather Pickett, Bryce Kushmerick-McCune, Dakota Daughtry, and Elizabeth Schray. For any given prison trip, we took a team of roughly nine to twelve folks, and the remaining team members stayed behind reading, coding, analyzing, and preparing for our return with more data. The team consisted of individuals who identify as white, Black, and mixed race; at least three identify as LGBTQ+; and at least one identifies as Latinx. The team ranged in age from the low 20s to over 60 years, and they had varying experiences, backgrounds, and training.

Our training program included a thorough overview of the project, study design, and goals, followed by more specific information, including professionalism, what to wear for prison fieldwork, what to expect in RHUs, and other travel logistics. Although some but not most of our staff had qualitative-data-collection experience, we also engaged in a qualitative methods workshop that included practice taking fieldnotes and learning to interview. We specifically tailored this training to custodial fieldwork settings. The training included specific instruction in how to recruit residents at their cell door (e.g., where to stand), where to position yourself in a room (between a resident and the door), and how to look for exits so if anything should happen, the researchers know the quickest way to safety. We also engaged in a longer conversation about mental health for researchers doing this type of work.

We openly and candidly discussed the toll this emotional labor sometimes takes on researchers (although this is likely different from the toll prison takes on residents and staff). It is not a world most researchers are ever really ready to enter, and it can have numerous and sometimes long-lasting effects. The two stories I tell from personal experience include the first time I saw a grown man with leg irons, belly chains, and handcuffs (with hands behind his back) walking steps ahead of several custodial staff, with one of them holding a leash that was tethered to the man's belly chains in the back. I was immediately overcome with a profound sense of sorrow and shame. It was hard to watch, and I remember holding back tears as he walked by and thinking to myself that I had to get used to seeing this but I hoped I would *never* get used to seeing this. The second story is about the unanticipated effects I felt after interviewing women RHU residents. While I had interviewed literally hundreds of residents, it was not until I interviewed women that I fully engaged with the fact that my prior interviews had all been men. The women tore at my heartstrings as a woman and as a parent in ways I was not prepared for. The trauma they discussed and the fear and intense guilt they exuded overwhelmed me. All the way home from that fieldwork trip, I cried alone in my car, sometimes uncontrollably, and had to pull the car over to calm myself down. For several weeks after the trip, I found it difficult to motivate myself—which is not a problem I typically experience. I was lethargic, sad, and moody. I kept hearing the women's voices and the words from some of the interviews echoing in my head. The stories of their pain, of their children, of their longing for a different life cut me deeply. Still, several years later, even writing this, I have difficulty managing the emotional toll this took on me.

I wanted our team to be prepared for the unexpected, to be ready to talk to each other and to me to process what they experienced and to not be ashamed of feeling any kind of way. We also provided information about the university's mental health and psychological services that are available free of charge to all students, and we encouraged team members to use those services if and when they were needed. For these reasons, we also built in debriefings with the whole team after each fieldwork day where we could discuss sensitive topics (or any topics) to process them together. We sometimes debriefed again fully after we returned to the university and we did frequent check-ins with the team throughout the project. We also housed undergraduate research assistants in shared motel rooms away from graduate students and faculty so they would have some private alone time with just members of their group to talk through things as needed. While in the prison, one of the more senior members of the team (usually myself, Shannon, or Angie) play a sort of facilitator role, coordinating interviews and observations and checking in on the team to make sure everyone was doing all right.

Our training was not perfect however, and in retrospect there are few things we neglected and will change for subsequent trainings and projects. These include our lack of in-depth attention to specifically talking about how the emotional labor of fieldwork in RHUs would be experienced differently across team members. We talked about taking care of their mental health, but we did not name this additional layer of what it would mean for those in our group who identify as Black or Muslim, or who have incarcerated family members, or are parents. We did not train on how the intersectionality of our research staff could and *would* make it extremely hard to do data collection.

We did train our team about what to do in uncomfortable or overwhelming situations while in the RHU. Our practice is that if an interview takes an emotional toll on a researcher and they feel like they can finish it after a break, they will find me, Shannon, or Angie and ask for a pause to collect themselves. Once we are in the RHU, we cannot leave because we are locked into the unit, and leaving or going anywhere else requires a staff escort. This is not possible during fieldwork because the staff are fully engaged in their day-to-day duties. Also, the RHU is nearly entirely devoid of privacy. Our instructions to our team are to go into the staff bathroom (the only place they can be alone), lock the door, and stay in there as long as they need to regroup. In serious situations, one of the team members may come with them, but we try to avoid this if possible, so that the rest of the team may continue collecting data. When the team member is ready to return to the interview, they do so. If they determine they cannot return, one of the other available team members completes the interview.

There are also other types of challenging situations that require training and open dialogue. For example, at times during interviews residents and staff act in ways that are uncomfortable for researchers or say and do things to shock us. Sometimes it is relatively mundane and a researcher may overlook it and move on—for example, the multiple times residents asked me to marry them or told me we would make beautiful children together. Sometimes, it is more serious, such as when staff make sexually, racially, ethnically, or otherwise inappropriate comments to researchers or to each other in a researcher's presence or when a resident masturbates or touches themselves during an interview or during the recruitment process.

With insensitive comments, we instruct our research team to stay calm, not to engage, not to try to educate or chastise the other person, but instead to focus on making mental notes of what is said for later recording. It is not our job (during fieldwork) to judge the residents or staff or bring our values to them. We are guests in their world, there to collect stories and information and learn. This is challenging for many researchers, especially in light of the current Black Lives Matter and #MeToo movements. We recognize that and talk it through when necessary. However, as researchers, inserting ourselves into the scene and changing the dynamics is not our goal, but with a large research team, it absolutely does happen. We do hope that any inappropriate language or behaviors presented in our analysis, reports, and other writings helps inform DOCs about resident and staff views and contributes to training and policy changes to address any shortcomings.

In the case of inappropriate touching or masturbation, our team members know that they have two main choices, but they are not to ignore the act and keep interviewing the resident. First, they may acknowledge the act and ask the resident to stop doing it during the interview or recruitment process, letting them know we will not continue until their hands are on a table or in plain sight. This requires direct confrontation and action, and some researchers have understandable difficulty with this. Second, they may simply stop the interview by saying, "Thank you for talking to me" and leave the room. Again, they do not chastise, belittle, or scold the resident. Instead, they must set clear boundaries for each interview and adhere to and uphold those boundaries as they go. Our next iteration of training will also include discussions about what witnessing acts like these may mean for researchers who have previously experienced sexual assault or other traumas and what that might bring up for them.

Team Science: All for One
One unique facet of our research team is that we take a team-science approach to every part of our projects. A team-science approach is one that is interdependent and collaborative, where team members work together toward common goals. In our team, I define the overarching project goals. I wanted to do research in RHUs. Year one's study questions, foci, and direction were based on my preferences, and Year Two's were a collaborative effort between Shannon and me. However, while the entire team works toward overall project goals, they also work toward their

own goals. While some team members collect and analyze data for the overarching project and then subsequently work on papers, presentations, and reports from this work, many team members develop their own research questions—ones that may be answered within RHUs using the approved methods for the broader project. In a parallel, simultaneous project, Shannon asked several crucial research questions for her dissertation work in specific RHUs designed for residents with severe mental health diagnoses. The team asked these questions for Shannon, and she "owns" that part of the data. Likewise, the undergraduate researchers in teams of two asked their own research questions regarding, for example, staff and resident perceptions of empathy, identity, and coping. This data is later used for their projects and papers, but if at some point they do not wish to continue analysis, their data becomes part of the broader project data available for analysis by all members of the team. During fieldwork, all members of the team collect data for the whole team; this means everyone asks everyone else's questions. This way, each team member accesses a variety of residents and staff (a larger total number of interviewees and observations) and makes the best use of diverse researchers with varying interviewing styles to collect data. The project data is then shared among the team members, with each member using the parts of the data they collected within the broader context of the whole project for analysis.

This approach is not for everyone. There are many lone wolf researchers out there who would shun this approach and prefer the ease and independence of solo work. I get it. But while the projects tend to take longer, some of the data collection is better than others, and the analysis and production of publications takes a lot longer, the benefits of a team far outweigh the drawbacks. I always tell the team that "many brains make the project better." We share ideas, we wrestle with difficult questions, and we explore questions we did not even know we were interested in by engaging with the work, the people, the scene, the data, and each other. It is definitely a labor of love, but the yield far surpasses original project goals every single time.

We also take less from the prisons, staff, and residents by combining our projects and fieldwork to minimize our intrusions into their lives and work. As a qualitative researcher, I have always struggled with the idea that I take so much via resource extraction. I learn so much from the people we talk with, but rarely am I able to give back in what I consider meaningful ways. For example, in our prison settings, we cannot compensate residents or staff in any way—no gift cards, no cash on their commissary accounts, no cool swag from our research center like pens or water bottles, and not even any home-baked goods. Working as a team, we embrace gratitude, and we remind ourselves and each other often that we are lucky to have this insider's view and it is our job, our duty, to make the most of each experience and "give back" by telling the narratives and opening this closed world to others in the hopes they will hear the narratives and work toward change and improvement. Of course, I also give back in other ways by volunteering for a local nonprofit that helps individuals released from prisons and jails with reentry, and I frequently donate time and money to causes that align with my values, but for the specific people we engaged with for this study, the telling of the narratives and the hope for eventual change is all I am able to really give back. I just hope it is enough.

Research Procedures

In designing the RHU studies, I thought carefully and intensely about sampling. To some qualitative researchers, this statement may sound antithetical to all that we know and understand about fieldwork, and I do not disagree. In a traditional sense, qualitative work involves deep immersion into the lived experiences of others. During the Park and Burgess Chicago School days of early sociology, ethnography meant being open to and explorative with the world. As such, strict methodological guidelines and constructs were ill-advised. The old-school qualitative studies were about discovery, so having pre-established sampling guidelines might limit (in countless ways) the events, people, places, and interactions good fieldworkers engage and learn from. However, fast forward some eighty-plus years, and I find myself firmly grounded in some gripping positivistic traditions (even against my better judgment at times) within the field of criminology.

In much of criminology, quantitative methods reign, and sound and rigorous attention to methodological details matters greatly. This entails producing studies that meet reviewers' bars for positivistic and largely quantitative standards such as reliability, generalizability, and validity (not qualitative method constructs) and often quantifying qualitative data in various ways. While the sociologist in me longs for the Chicago School roots and framework I learned in graduate school—how I would love to just go out and see what I find—the intense structure of science and academia, particularly in criminology, has a firm hold on my ability to remain employed, get promoted, and, frankly, survive my career path. This tension regarding method is in large part due to the positionality struggles mentioned earlier in the chapter. Over my years as a scholar, I adapted and found a way to make it work. For me, this is largely through sampling.

Sampling. The RHU studies began on the heels of their precursor, The Prison Project, so we already had a firm understanding of prison life and institutional norms, structures, rules, and practices. We also knew that while some prior work uses interviews and observations in prison settings, very little examines RHU living and working, save the occasional survey or secondary data analysis of administrative data. We had a chance here to enter this world and discover the hidden narratives of those within it. We wanted to do it as thoroughly, thoughtfully, and as representatively as possible. To do this, we designed a sampling strategy that we believed would yield a rich and informative data set that would not privilege one or just a few voices and would not ignore key components of day-to-day institutional life that many researchers either do not understand or simply do not take the time to include in their studies. This includes attention to the finer details of RHU living and working, including conducting fieldwork in various pods, units, on various shifts and days, and using inclusive recruitment strategies to garner consensual participation.

Our first step involved choosing the prisons for data collection. As described above, we worked with our DOC partner to ensure maximum variation sampling, find RHUs with at least forty individuals (average daily), in a mix of security levels, with the specialized units Shannon was studying for her dissertation, and where our research would minimally interfere with the work of other researchers currently engaged within our state of study. We chose four prisons for each RHU study.

Second, considering our available resources and timeline, we conducted the first year of study spending just two days at each RHU, but we expanded to four days per RHU in the second study to accommodate Shannon's dissertation fieldwork and to yield additional RHU data. We knew we wanted multiple days because a Monday in any prison may look dramatically different from a Tuesday. One day may include taking residents for showers or yard while another may include razor distribution for in-cell shaving. We learned after year one that two days was just not enough; we needed a bit more variation. Perhaps our most important considerations for sampling include the factors we call interorganizational and individual level. These involve structural and institutionally specific factors such as buildings, units, and shifts and personal factors such as age, race, tenure, position or role, and experience or history. To ensure a rich, diverse, and representative sample, we gathered administrative data from the DOC so that we had some idea of the universe of both residents and staff within RHUs to eventually compare our sample to. We also spent considerable time mapping out our sampling strategy for both staff and residents to ensure we traveled to prisons when specific events we wanted to see occurred (such as the performance review committee) and to make sure we would have access to the full range of staff who work in RHUs (which varies by shift, unit, prison).

For staff, we wanted to engage as many (ideally all) within the RHU as possible, knowing that some staff would refuse an interview. We decided that to wholly understand the RHU, we needed to gather data from custodial (lieutenants, sergeants, and COs) and noncustodial (psychological and program) staff, and we were open to interviewing or observing anyone else who came onto the RHU during our visit including deputies, clergy, and the warden. During the course of each staff interview, we recorded information about the staff's demographics, including their age, race, job tenure, education, experience, training, position or role, race, and their interpretation or perception of each question topic we posed. To observe staff and to create rapport, we accompanied them anywhere within the RHU where they would allow us and throughout their duties. We observed them delivering meals, moving residents to yard and shower, during resident interactions and altercations, and in both the staff and lieutenant's office and the bubble (control room).

For resident interviews, we spent the first several hours of the first day of fieldwork at each prison going cell to cell to recruit every RHU resident into our study. We also doubled back to residents (when possible) who were not in their cell or were asleep during our first pass. We recruited residents from every RHU in every prison in our study, including specialty RHUs for those with severe mental health diagnoses, those in behavioral or gang-related units, and those in units designed for individuals with substance-use disorders. At the end of each interview, we recorded information about the resident's demographics, including age, race, tenure in this unit, this prison, and in custody overall, race, and their interpretation or perception of each question topic we posed.

We also informed ourselves, prior to data collection, about any intra-organizational factors that might play a role in gathered data. To do this, we read local newspapers about the goings-on within our state's prisons; we kept abreast of recent federal and state rulings that might affect staff and residents during our fieldwork; and we asked a lot of information-gathering questions of our prison liaison about what was happening in and around each prison. I also regularly followed up with my favorite sergeant to ensure we were clued in on what might be troubling or exciting staff or residents so that we could prepare for each fieldwork day with this knowledge in hand. For example, around the time of our fieldwork, a CO died in a prison in the state of study after being struck by a resident, and the DOC had intense and well-publicized challenges with illegal drugs entering institutions. These inevitably affected the data we collected from the staff and residents as either or both were likely were on their minds at the time of interview.

Recruitment and Interviews. Recruiting staff and residents for interviews was a ground-up process that took some finessing. At the start of each fieldwork trip, day one, after entering the gates and clearing security, our team would, if possible, meet with a team of staff from the warden's office and others from around the prison. Usually, our entire team and the large prison staff group would congregate in a conference room. where the supervisors welcomed our team and I said a few words about our study. I had three goals for these meetings: (1) tell staff and supervisors enough about the project so that they would have some understanding of it, but not so much that they would judge it; (2) provide an explanation about the project that showed what was in it for them, what they gain from the study and participating in it; and (3) engender their trust and confidence in our team by extolling our vast experiences in prisons and thanking them profusely for allowing us to do this important work with them. These meetings were usually quite short, but their importance cannot be understated. Starting off on the right foot with prison staff is a tremendous door-opener for the remainder of the fieldwork. To help with their assessment of us, we regularly and purposefully used language from the system as code-switching (using the jargon of the scene even when it is not your personal language). This included calling units by the colloquial names staff and residents used and using words like *kicks* to describe when a resident is released from the RHU rather than saying "is released." We did this to garner legitimacy for our team and to prevent (or at least lessen) any staff judgment of our study or study team.

Once on the unit, our team engaged a divide-and-conquer strategy that included a lead person (usually me, Shannon, or Angie) talking to the lieutenant or the sergeant (if the lieutenant was not there) about expectations and goals. During these conversations, we enlisted their help to reach our data collection goals. When it seemed like a competition among prisons for the most or the best participation and when they felt they had a stake in the process, data collection generally yielded more. While this was occurring, our team would break into groups of two or four so that COs could escort them into pods for resident recruitment. If a team of four entered a pod, one group would take the upper tier of cells while the other research team took the lower tier, going cell to cell talking with residents about the study and asking if they would like to be interviewed.

To talk to RHU residents in their cells, we had to first get their attention through the small window in the door, sometimes knocking on it, and then talk to through the door. For residents who agreed, we wrote their name on a list and explained that we would be pulling names from this list randomly over today and the next one or more days for an interview (outside their cell and unit) that would take roughly forty-five minutes to an hour. We explained that participation was voluntary and they could change their mind at any time and they did not have to answer any of our questions that made them uncomfortable. Although this was not the full consent process, we wanted to doubly ensure they felt under no pressure to agree to an interview or to do an interview later if they initially agreed to do so. Before moving on to the next cell, we slid a study-information sheet through the gap in the door. This document contained an overview of the study and procedures and my name and university address in case they wanted to contact me later. We also let them know that if they were unable to complete an in-person interview with us (e.g., if they were unavailable when it was their interview time or if we ran out of time during this visit to interview everyone who had volunteered), we would happily provide them a copy of the interview questions and they could fill it out, if they want, and send it to us. We would de-identify that data and add it to our data for analysis. If they chose this option later on, we also included a full informed-consent document in our packet so that they understood both the risks and benefits of participating in this project.

Interviews with staff occurred throughout each shift. Although some were a full sit-down interaction where the researcher and staff member went to a private, confidential location to talk, other times staff agreed to interview over the course of all or part of a shift as they completed their work. This might mean that a researcher could hang out with the same staff member for several hours, observing them doing their work while sprinkling in interview questions as time allowed, or it might mean spending some time with a particular staff member, ending that time before completing a full interview because their shift ended or they needed to do other things, and then returning on a subsequent fieldwork day to finish the interview while again observing them work. Our team remained extremely flexible in order to garner staff trust and build rapport, but also to minimally interrupt staff work. We always recognize that our access is a privilege and one we do not take for granted.

Data Capture. Because the prisons in our study did not allow audio or video recording equipment, each researcher received a folder at the start of each fieldwork trip. The folder contains several copies of the IRB informed-consent document (we do these verbally, but have paper copies on hand for anyone who wants a copy for their records), several copies of the study recruitment-information sheet (as extras), a copy of the full interview focal areas, a set of blank guided notetaking pages that truncate each focal area to just a few words and leave ample space for the researcher to take notes (these are optional, but some researchers prefer using this method), a notebook, and several pens. Our team is trained to take minimal notes during interviews so as to maintain eye contact with interviewees and provide minimal distraction. However, the researchers did take shorthand jottings during interviews to refresh their memories later on and occasionally wrote down verbatim quotes from staff and residents to ensure they would get the language exactly right during later transcription. This is a standard and accepted practice in qualitative fieldwork.[4]

Following all IRB protocols, our team stores all de-identified data on password-protected computers in password-protected files. We keep all project-related folders in an electronic project file with subfolders for data (staff and resident) (i.e., interviews, letters, observations), team training materials, analysis documents, and scholarly literature, as well as a separate folder for each paper we write (again with more subfolders specific to each paper). We also maintain two Excel spreadsheets that provide a thumbnail overview of data collection. I have been using documents like these on projects since graduate school. For one thing, it helps keep track of important information such as fieldwork hours and total interviews. But perhaps more importantly, it reminds me that I am productive (something academe tends to beat out of researchers).

Our first Excel spreadsheet is called "People, Places, and Events." In this spreadsheet, we detail in numerous columns all the interview facts (minus names). Columns include interviewee's position, role, training/education (for staff), age, institution, race, RHU, day we interviewed/observed them, and other information that we may need to easily retrieve for papers, reports, or presentations. The content of these Excel sheets varies considerably by project but generally serves as a quick snapshot of the project's methods and sample. The second spreadsheet we create contains similar information but focuses on the number of interviews and observations and the total fieldwork hours. We call this one "Hours and Activities." Within our files, all interview and observational notes are titled similarly with the institutional pseudonym, number or letter, the interviewee number, and the researcher's initials. Although when we write papers and reports, we give each research subject a pseudonym, when we record data for analysis we just give everyone a number and every institution a number or a letter. This ensures that no one who might steal our data might think that someone named Sam Jones is actually named that. Sam Jones's data may be in an interview file just called Staff 435.

The research team is managed by a project manager. In this case, it was Shannon Magnuson followed by Taylor Hartwell. That person keeps track of our IRB deadlines for continuing review, keeps the files organized, harangues researchers who are late turning in their typed fieldnotes, and generally keeps everything organized. They also maintain folders in our project file for any news articles, DOC documents, reports, or other information we find or obtain as the project progresses that may matter to our team as we analyze data and write up findings.

The team constructs all typed fieldnotes and interview notes from handwritten jottings in two ways. First, if time allows between interviews while inside the RHU, they tuck themselves into a somewhat private location (such as a visiting room) and fully hand-write on notebook paper as much of the interview as they can remember. Writing down the interview while it is still fresh in their mind and before they do another interview keeps the data robust and rich. Second, after our debriefing and dinner, the team heads back to the motel for a night of frantic note-typing. This is difficult since we usually do ten- to fourteen-hour days and we are mentally and physical exhausted each night. But the work must go on. We do cut the team some slack here though, and ask that they at least handwrite fuller notes for any they did not have time to do while in the RHU. Then, the team delivers fully typed observational and interview notes to the shared computer files within forty-eight hours after we return from our prison trip. As with any good ethnography, we ask that the interviewer capture (even for residents whom we are not officially observing) verbal statements and nonverbal behaviors in their notes.

When coding begins largely depends on each project, but generally we try to code after the first or second prison trip and not save it all for after the final trip of each project. We use Glaser's Constant Comparative Method[5] to continually improve our fieldwork as we learn from coded data by refining questions and pursuing answers to questions unanswered or discovered in prior fieldwork. To code, we use a qualitative software program called Atlas.ti. This program provides a way of coding and organizing data, but it by no means does the work for us. All the brainpower that goes into qualitative coding and analysis comes from our team, not the software. All fieldwork files are linked to Atlas as project files, and then we are ready to begin coding.

Data Coding. Our team generally codes in several stages or phases, which begin with creating a starter code list of the key interview focal areas or questions we asked. So, in our RHU projects, starter code lists included codes for punishment, mental health, physical health, rules, relationships, reform, and so on. For now it seems orderly, but it gets more complex as we go and becomes a bit unruly at times, with the final code list containing hundreds, if not thousands, of codes. There are many ways to code data, but our team takes the long route because my qualitative training ingrained the vast benefits of this approach in me many years ago. We begin with a process that qualitative researchers call line-by-line or primary coding.[6] This inductive process includes coders reading every *line* (not sentence) of text and coding it with as many codes as needed. Coding is really categorizing, labeling, or grouping data together in ways that simplify by labeling what was said or observed. We code for demographics, substance, and context/interpretation. So, for example, in this excerpt from a fieldnote, demographic codes will include this CO's race, age, role/title/position, the RHU, the prison, and job tenure; substantive codes might include resident entitlement, property, meals, clothing, mail, and intake process; and contextual/interpretive codes might include sarcasm, disagreement/questioning of, and rule following.

> ***Sample Interview Excerpt from a CO***: "The inmates come down here are entitled to things [said slightly sarcastically]. That includes their property, but only a specific amount, meals, a jumper exchange—which is where they get an orange jumper to identify them as a RHU inmate instead of their browns, and their legal mail."

As coding continues, the process becomes more evaluative or interpretive. This occurs as patterns start to emerge in the data between and among various interviews and when coders further classify the data to organize, synthesize, or even place codes within thematic or hierarchical structures. This is sometimes referred to as thematic, secondary, or axial coding.[7] For example, something that looked mundane the first time you read it may begin to take on new meaning as you realize forty people said something similar and all with sarcasm or distaste. So, you have to go back. But this is not analysis yet, just coding, so we do not do too much interpretation during this process, just the interpretation necessary to label and categorize data.

In the full project coding phase, when the team is coding, we also conduct checks for intercoder reliability (ICR) among coders. We do this when two or more coders are coding the same data set and need to ensure that each coder is coding similarly to the other so that the data is coded the same way throughout. To do this, the coders meet and discuss how they will code the data (typically, we do it by hard returns in the notes—where the typist hits the return/enter key). That piece of data is called a chunk. The coders use their starter code list to code one randomly selected data file using just the starter codes. They do this together, discussing their decision-making along the way. Then, they take a second randomly selected data file and independently complete the same process so that they can compare one coder document to the other. If they reach 90 percent consensus on the coding (via chunks), they move on. If they do not, they keep doing this until they reach 90 percent coding consensus. As they add codes, they use the Comment feature of Atlas.ti to create a code dictionary, and they write memos or emails to each other describing what added codes are and mean. Periodically, throughout the coding they do more ICR checks, using the process described above. Each time they reach 90 percent coding consensus, they continue; when they do not, they discuss every code with non-agreement, make joint decisions about how to proceed, and keep trying until they reach 90 percent. This process is an absolute must for multiple coders coding the same data set.

However, there are two times when research teams can avoid this process. First, the coders could decide to divide the code list, with each coder only coding for certain things rather than dividing up the files and each coding for everything. When they divide the code list, there is automatically 100 percent ICR (of sorts) because each coder is consistent in their coding throughout the coding process. They still, however, discuss any coding challenges they face and their codes overall to affirm they are interpreting the data in similar and understandable ways. Second, and as is the case for this book, I was the only coder (similar to the first example), so I was 100 percent reliable in my coding. I hand-coded every document in the entire data set of interviews and observations for both years of the RHU studies, all policy documents, all handbook and training materials, and all letters from residents. I kept notes on all my coding decisions and frequently referred to them or updated them as needed to keep coding consistent throughout the process.

At times, academic life gets the better of us and we cannot do the full coding. We may be on a deadline to submit a paper or a chapter, or we may be headed to a conference to present on our work. Other times, we have a report to the DOC due and fieldwork just concluded, so we need to speed things up a bit without sacrificing the quality of our coding. In these cases, we may simply apply the same rigor to coding but without the full line-by-line approach. Instead, we read and code only the data for the specific research question or questions we want to answer at this point. Our team does this sometimes, but we always then return to the full data set and start anew with a full coding endeavor.

For this book, I took a bit of an old-school approach to coding to ensure I really understood the data and could write a book-length manuscript that stayed aligned with the resident and staff narratives. While the research team split into three smaller groups of two to fully code (line by line) the men's prison data from year one (coding group 1), the women's data from year one (coding group 2), and the data from year two (all men's, coding group 3), and I read each project file including their codes, I also wanted to code the data for myself. To do this, I channeled my qualitative-methods training (thank you Drs. David Snow and Calvin Morrill) and started by reading every fieldnote, interview note, and letter in our data set.

Next, I coded on big themes for the book chapters—risk, rules, relationships, reentry, and reform—by using Microsoft Word to read every piece of data and cut and paste the parts of each note that explained or discussed each key theme into a new document (I also attached all demographic and institutional information to each data chunk). Then, I hand-coded each new document, using various colored markers and highlighters and an elaborate series of sticky notes. To me, this felt real. I was fully immersed in the data and the coding process through the tangibility of hand-coding it. I read and reread the words on the page and labeled, categorized, and in fact, coded them many times until I could not find anything else to code.

Data Analysis. When coding feels complete—and it is never really complete; it just comes to an understandable stopping place for the time being—analysis begins. The process for both me and our team is similar (though mine was by hand and theirs is generally within Atlas.ti). Qualitative analysis includes the next logical step after coding: interpretation. We use a semi-grounded-theory approach that in part squares with Glaser and Strauss's (1967), Strauss and Corbin's (1978), and Charmaz's (2014) conceptualization of grounded theory as a research tool and analysis framework that allows meaning to emerge from the collected data. Relying on a symbolic interactionist approach, grounded theory, for us, provides, as Charmaz suggests, an "interpretive portrayal of the studied world, not an exact picture of it."[8] It is a way for researchers to construct reality, while relying on their collected data to do so as the people and places in their study see it, experience it, and understand it.

Analysis, then, includes the scholar moving back and forth between the data and existing scholarship and theory to try to explain what is happening, why, and how. I tell our team continually that qualitative data answers two main questions: (1) Under what conditions does something occur? (2) What are the mechanisms by which that something occurs? So, if I have numerous codes that explain perceptions and views from both staff and residents on a particular RHU policy, I begin to interrogate or query the data to ask those two questions. My thinking might go something like this:

Codes suggest this finding: Staff and residents do not understand X policy.

My data queries begin something like this:

- What do they understand about it?

- What do they not understand about it?
- What does the policy actually say?
- Where did they learn about this policy in the first place? Where did they get information? Did they read about it? Read the actual policy? Where? How? Can they read? Did they hear about it from someone else? Who? And how did that person learn about the policy? Etc.

And my data queries continue something like this:

- What do staff and residents do when they use or cite this policy?
- How do they behave regarding this policy or when this policy is involved/invoked?
- Does the policy interpretation vary depending on demographics (age, race, role, etc.)?
- Does policy interpretation vary depending on shift, unit, prison?
- Does policy interpretation ever change? How? In what ways? By whom?
- And so on.

This is the type of process I used when analyzing the data for this book. As I went back through the data multiple times to recheck and clarify my coding, I also added notes-to-self that resembled analytic memos (a common tool among qualitative researchers for working out the details of their interpretive thinking as they go). Something rather magical happens during this phase—or at least it always does for me. As the stories start to hang together and I am able to make contextual and interpretive sense out the data, the story (from the perceptions of the studied people) literally jumps off the page. After that, it becomes a matter of double-checking myself to make sure I have not taken any misguided interpretive leaps or misunderstood anything. Again, for qualitative researchers, this process may include more analytic memoing and even some negative case analysis (searching the data for bits that do not fit with the story you are telling and trying to explain). I used this analytic, interpretive analysis process for the narratives in this book.

Writing

The writing process for books and journal articles is slightly different, but it follows some general conventions. Unlike our quantitative counterparts in academe, qualitative researchers (particularly those who work within an inductive or grounded-theory framework) write in a bit of a mixed-up order. To write a qualitative paper, the researcher must start with the findings. Then, they build the rest of the paper around those findings to create a holistic argument. This occurs because the findings of a qualitative paper drive everything else. The data speaks for itself (with a little interpretive help from the researcher) and tells a story. When incorporating or presenting quotes or fieldnote excerpts, the researcher reads all the data within a particular code and chooses what is commonly called a "representative" quote or excerpt. It signifies or is illustrative of the whole data within that quote and is not vastly different—not an outlier. Then, the researcher describes how they gathered, coded, and analyzed the data used in the story (the methods), tells the readers what others have already found regarding this topic or finding and how it is currently explained (literature review), sets up the argument within a general or specific context (introduction), and discusses what it might mean, to whom, and why and how it matters (discussion).

For this book, I engaged a similar writing process, starting with the findings within each substantive chapter (risk, rules, relationships, reentry, and reform) and then building the rest of the book around those findings. All quotes and fieldnote excerpts are representative of the whole data set, except in cases where I noted something was indeed an outlier (e.g., only one person said something or a quote was vastly different from others). This chapter about the book is foreshadowed in the introduction, but I wrote the full rendering (as you are reading it here) last.

When writing papers or books using qualitative data, especially verbal interview or focus group data, researchers present a three-part model that includes the quote set-up (to set the scene for what is being said and by whom), the quote (verbatim if possible, or paraphrased when necessary), and the quote interpretation (the researcher's interpretation of the quote in the context of the argument and the complete data set). The data in this book mostly conform to this structure.

The final section of any paper or book generally includes a discussion and conclusion where the researcher tries to make sense of what they found within the broader empirical, theoretical, or everyday living world. Chapter 7, "Reversal and Revision," attempts this for readers and offers policy recommendations as an accompaniment.

Additional Project Concerns

In addition to the above methodological concerns, readers may be interested in a few other notes regarding generalizability, validity, reliability, working with people, giving back, following up (member checking), and sustaining researcher-practitioner partnerships. I present these, in turn, below.

Despite the positivistic approach to sampling to appease my criminological colleagues in the academy and to produce sound science that highlights the lived experiences of the RHU staff and residents, I do hold tight to some major differences between qualitative and quantitative work that bear some discussion here. Quantitative data is judged, if you will, based on a series of methodological standards such as generalizability, validity (both internal and external), and reliability. Generalizability is the degree to which the data or study may represent or be "generalizable" to the broader population. Validity is the degree to which a construct is measuring what it is supposed to be measuring and is not unduly influenced by something internal or external to the study. Reliability is the degree to which another researcher who does the same work might come to the same conclusions. All these methodological goals are far easier in quantitative studies (particularly ones with large sample sizes), where sampling allows for representative groups, and statistical adjustments may accommodate or adjust for any differences between groups. However, in qualitative work, generalizability, validity, and reliability are not, I repeat, *not*, the goal. Those standards are not an appropriate way to judge qualitative work for many reasons, most of which stem from the fact that they were the target in the first place.

In qualitative research, the goal is *trustworthiness*—or the degree to which the data is believable, authentic, and realistic. Ethnographers Yvonna S. Lincoln and Egon G. Guba[9] discuss how qualitative work, particularly ethnography, seeks four things:

1. *Credibility* as a substitute for quantitative methods' desire for internal validity. In qualitative studies, this is achieved through time in the field, observational methods, and triangulation (using multiple data sources to collect and verify information).

2. *Transferability* as the goal instead of external validity. This is achieved through rich, thick description in interview and observational notes capturing as much as possible about both verbal utterings and perceptions and nonverbal actions and behaviors.

3. *Dependability* as a substitute for reliability. Qualitative researchers achieve this by accounting for instability and change and using overlapping methods and replication within their fieldwork.

4. *Confirmability* as the replacement goal instead of objectivity. This is possible for qualitative researchers via auditing processes that carefully examine captured data and fill in missing information when and where needed with additional data.

In the data collection, coding, and analysis for this book we embodied every possible angle to achieve trustworthiness including ample time in the field—or what my graduate school mentor, Dr. Calvin Morrill,[10] calls the "sweat quotient, " rich and purposive sampling to obtain narrative and observational data with a representative sample of staff and residents at multiple prisons, and via thick, rich description, member checks, and triangulation with various other sources such as policies, handbooks, signs, memos, and pamphlets on prison walls and bulletin boards, and the RHU training program called RHU School. We also interrogated, queried, analyzed, and audited our data in as many diverse ways as possible.

Working with staff and residents in prisons involves a collaboration in the form of a partnership. It is not just about asking questions and receiving answers. It is not just about observing scenes and events and taking notes. Instead, it is a mutually beneficial alliance or relationship where the researcher asks permission to enter another world and the people in that world (it is hoped) grant that permission free of coercion or pressure. In numerous textbooks and scholarly writings about qualitative methods, one recurring theme notes that this type of research should dismantle researcher assumptions through a process that illuminates the values, cultures, and norms at work in the subject's world, the place of study. However, researchers may achieve this only by taking inventory of their own positionality and social distance from what and who they are studying.

In prison research there are plenty of assumptions researchers and others make regarding what life is like inside for residents and staff. In my work, this book included, I try to push aside my own assumptions (as much as possible) during fieldwork and remain fully open to the experiences, feelings, behaviors, and perceptions of the folks who are kind enough to engage in research with me. This is a tall order in many regards because setting aside all preconceived notions is impossible. However, when researchers partner, truly partner, with the people, places, and events they study move closer toward (but never really achieve) objectivity. This partnership is a driving force of the research process; it enables researchers such as me to learn about another world and from the very people who know that world best: those encompassed by it. If, and it is a big if, the partnership is truly relational, both the studied and the studier may potentially reap benefits. Without that communal experience, though, the people being interviewed and observed may feel objectified, used, or even left out of a process they so intimately are a part of. And the researcher may feel omnipotent, powerful, or perhaps shameful about all the taking and not realize they also have the power to give.

Second, because I feel this guilt often, and my research team often feels the same, we work to creatively find ways to reward and honor the generous folks who let us into their world and their lives. One way researchers do this is through compensating or incentivizing research participation. In our prisons, as previously noted, this is disallowed. Of course we are gracious and thankful during fieldwork visits, but this somehow never feels like enough. My amazing graduate student, Shannon Magnuson, had the wonderful idea of writing personalized thank-you notes to each institution to formally acknowledge their role in the research partnership and to express sincere gratitude for the many gifts they bestowed upon us, including time, energy, and information. Within the RHU studies, she designed an individualized letter to each institution after our fieldwork. The letters are thoughtful and positive, naming particular individuals (whom we may or may not have specifically interviewed, so as not to violate their confidentiality), to thank them for their help and their acceptance of our presence in their RHU and to recognize what they did to help the research team during the research process. We sent these to the warden of each prison so the staff's highest-level supervisor sees them. We also sent them to the RHU lieutenants so they could share our praise and appreciation with staff. Additionally, we forwarded a copy to the DOC central office and the secretary of corrections at the state level. We do not want micro-level and physically and emotionally taxing RHU work with us to go unnoticed. To date, we have received many emails and correspondence about how much our letters meant to them, how seen and heard they felt. It may not seem like much, and perhaps it is not, given all we received from the partnership, but it is a small token of our immense gratitude. Additionally, as most researchers would attest, my team and I work extra hard to tell staff and resident stories in the most real, raw, and honest way possible. We do not take our relationship for granted; we are grateful and we try in every way we can think of to honor the heroes of our work: the staff and residents of every prison we enter and those outside of prison who love them and support them, as well as those who read this work and begin thinking of ways to reform a system in need of tremendous kindness and attention.

Third, whenever necessary and possible, we follow up with residents and staff for member checks. Due to the design of our study, a full rendering of member checking (in its truest form) is not possible. As previously noted, we do not keep information containing the real names of any staff or residents in our data set. However, during subsequent trips to the same or different prisons, we often talk through findings with staff and residents to get feedback and perceptions. We then adjust our interpretations accordingly. We also elicit feedback from the DOC central office staff by sharing our thoughts, reports, presentations, and papers. We maintain our academic freedom—a decision we jointly made with the DOC's full support—but we provide them anything we write or present as not only a courtesy (so that they know what information we are disseminating about their system, prisons, units, staff, and residents), but also as part of our sustained and respectful partnership. When we develop new study ideas, we approach them (generally first), and when they have ideas for research they would like completed, they pitch their ideas to us. To date, the DOC we work with has not funded any of our research (we are self-funded with university funds and grants), but the DOC provides a perfect canvas where we may collaboratively paint a picture of living and working inside *with* staff and residents. Again, in our mutually beneficial relationship, we get access, partnerships, and a place to learn, grow, and perhaps affect change. The DOC gets thoughtful, considerate, and rigorous researchers conducting research about topics they are interested in studying but do not have the time or resources to undertake. And when the research is done by "outsiders," it carries a bit of perspective not available if DOC staff were to try to research themselves.

Concluding Thoughts: Living and Telling Stories

The work of retelling and making sense of individuals' lived experiences and their perceptions of those experiences is wonderful, and challenging, and exuberating, and frustrating. It is indeed work, but not the kind of work that the people who qualitative researchers often study are doing simply to live. I am immensely aware of and passionately reflective about my own positionality in this endeavor, and I work to wrestle with both the luck and luxury that comes with academic research. I am a white, middle-aged, middle-class woman with a PhD (something only roughly 2 percent of the US population possesses). I live in a comfortable, moderately diverse, fairly upper-class neighborhood in suburban Virginia. I am a single mom. I struggle to pay our bills sometimes, but my children never go hungry and they want for very little (save some fancy new technological equipment that I hesitate to buy both for its cost and ramifications on their lives). I do have a diversity of experiences, having lived in many places including growing up rural upstate New York around tractors, hay bales, stockcar races, mud bogs, beer bellies, big belt buckles, and countless days making mud pies by the creek with skinned knees and a cane pole over my shoulder. I also attended both a community college and a state college in my home state before packing up my hatchback with $1,000 and moving to New Orleans to experience city life in the South—a world of cultures and experiences away from my pastoral childhood. In my first year in New Orleans, broke and alone, I slept on a mattress on the floor without other furniture, often without electricity, stalked by palmetto bugs (really large cockroach relatives) and I was the only white woman living in my neighborhood just one block away from the famous St. Thomas housing projects. I worked as a restaurant server for fifteen years throughout high school, college, and beyond in greasy truck stops and in destination restaurants in touristy locales such as the French Quarter. I also worked in San Francisco's Mission District as a vocational instructor, teaching and training folks experiencing some of life's hardest realities, including substance use, homelessness, and probation and parole. Then, due to my family situation, my privilege, and a move to California, my socioeconomic situation improved. In graduate school, I lived just a mile from a gorgeous Southern California beach and spent my time reading, doing yoga, conducting ethnographic fieldwork with parole officers, and playing by the pool with my children.

I take these experiences with me during fieldwork, and in some ways they define me, my perspective, and how I understand the world. I also, though, try to see the world through the eyes of the wonderful people I interview and observe, and I teach our team to do the same. We are who we are; we bring our past into our research, but we try to approach each fieldwork experience with as open a mind as possible. It is true that I have never experienced prison as a staff member nor as a resident. But, as any good qualitative researcher knows (or learns), people's narratives are powerful tools for unlocking perspective. You do not always have to live something to begin to understand it, but you do have to really listen and observe without judgment. Of course, it is not the same, but it can be illuminating and heart-wrenching nonetheless.

The narratives in this book represent the lives of staff working and residents living in RHU units in seven adult prisons in one US state. They are not meant to be generalizable to the totality of the RHU population of staff and residents in the United States, but they are meant to open a door to inquiry and understanding for readers. I made a conscious and reflective choice in presenting the narratives to omit myself and my team from the stories as often as possible in the main chapters of this book. These are *not* our stories. I put myself in this chapter to pull back the curtain for readers regarding how and why the work was done and what challenges and limitations we faced because these inform the work whether we want them to or not. The narratives in this book represent real lives, real perceptions, real trauma, and real experiences. Whether things happened exactly as folks remembered is not the point. Memories have a way of taking on new shape over time and in the telling and retelling of accounts. However, the stories that we heard, wrote down, and I presented are the perceptions the people who engaged in our study with us. It is what they remember, and it is their truth.

I also made a reflective decision to focus on the overall human experience here and not focus on race and ethnicity or gender as a primary target of my analysis or inquiry. This is not to say that race, ethnicity, and gender do not matter in these settings or do not matter to me. Both are absolutely not true. In fact, a large part of the reason I first engaged several colleagues to join our team was their vast expertise and experience researching and writing about race, ethnicity, and gender. Although these areas of research are imperative to understanding carceral life, I have not explicitly focused on them for this book. As part of our team-science approach, the specific data on race, ethnicity, and inequality more generally was not my story to tell. I have included race, ethnicity, and gender in the narratives in this book when they help explain or are a large part of the conversations we had with staff and residents. However, my colleagues and dear friends Drs.

Angela Hattery and Earl Smith are now writing a book using the race, ethnicity, and inequality data from the larger data set collected for both RHU studies. I leave those important topics and analyses to them. They are experts in these areas, and these critical topics deserve a full rendering and a place of their own.

I also made a determined decision to vehemently protect the identities of the residents and staff who participated in this study. This changes the story just a bit but does not weaken or contort the overall message. Each time I used an interview quote or a fieldnote excerpt, I carefully acknowledged who said it and who was involved. However, each time I gave the speaker a new name. In a state like ours where residents move around from prison to prison frequently, and staff, although less frequently, do the same, I was intensely concerned that a reader with inside knowledge of this state, the prisons we visited, and the people within them would be able to easily identify individuals based on stories they told or the way they told them. This writing decision means that readers do not get to know the staff and residents in the book as intimately as perhaps they would in other retellings. Readers do not get a chance to see how, for example, resident Anders views both rules and relationships because his name never appears twice even though he may have spoken about several topics that are presented in various chapters. However, it gives the staff and residents an extra layer of protection and confidentiality. For all that they gave and are giving, I, too, must do my part to give, and this is one small way I can do that.

The entirety of this book is a story about the harm that the carceral system and the people living and working within it do to themselves and others in a structure that not only manifests these harms but at times encourages them. However, it is also a story of resilience and the powerful and often unnoticed ways humans survive and at times thrive in unrelentingly challenging situations. It is not ground-breaking in that, through television, film, news, and the popular press, many people may feel they already know the prison world and the treachery within. However, this book yields value. There are real people living and working in a situation that is in many ways unnecessary. If the book does nothing else, I hope it illuminates the dark inner corners of the RHU in a way that suggests more questions than it answers. I hope it is at times unsettling in ways that prompt desire for and actions toward change.

In his autobiography, *The Long Walk to Freedom*, Nelson Mandela recalls: "I found solitary confinement the most forbidding aspect of prison life. There is no end and no beginning; there is only one's mind, which can begin to play tricks. Was that a dream or did it really happen? One begins to question everything." To this, we say, please yes, *question everything* and let those questions help you find the pathway toward and the heart to change.

NOTES

Chapter 1: Living and Working in the RHU
1. Kiebala and Rodriguez, 2018.
2. Calavita and Jenness, 2015.
3. The quotes are by resident, staff, staff, resident, resident.
4. Wacquant, 2002.
5. Haney, 2003, Guenther, 2013; Rhodes, 2004; Herbert, 2019; Grassian, 2006; Gendreau and Bonta, 1984.
6. Reiter, 2016; Richards, 2015; Kupers, 2017; Jackson, 2019; Shalev, 2013; Reiter and Koenig, 2015; Eastaugh, 2017.
7. Casella, Ridgeway, and Shourd, 2016; Polizzi, 2017; Pendergrass and Hoke, 2018.

Chapter 2: Risk
1. Tuan, 1979.
2. Renn, 1998.
3. Grassian, 2006; Haney, 2003; Haney and Lynch, 1997; Reiter et al., 2020; Suedfeld et al., 1982; Liebling, 1999.
4. Haney, 2003; Brodsky and Scogin, 1988.
5. Haney, 2019, 292.
6. Poole and Regoli, 1981.
7. Greene, 2013.

8. US Department of Labor, OSHA, n.d., https://www.osha.gov/SLTC/workplaceviolence/.
9. Lanctôt and Guay, 2014.
10. Boudoukha et al., 2013; James and Todak, 2018.
11. Maier and Ricciardelli, 2019.
12. Bottoms, 1999; Crewe 2011.
13. Garbarino, Kostelny, and Dubrow, 1991, 377.

Chapter 3: Relationships

1. Lincoln, 2000.
2. Beach et al., 1993; Gurung, Sarason, and Sarason, 1997.
3. Steptoe and Fancourt, D., 2020.
4. Klinger, 1977.
5. This varies from system to system. Seventy-two hours is an example of the rule in one system.
6. In Hochschild's (1983) conceptualization, emotional labor is the relational aspect of jobs (typically in service or client-based industries), where individuals face deeply personal, and at times draining, expectations to be nice, comforting, or soothing to their customers or clients above and beyond the task-based aspects of their jobs.
7. Hochschild, 1983, 7.
8. Christian, 2005; Tewksbury and DeMichele, 2005.
9. Tracy and Scott, 2006, 30.

Chapter 4: Rules

1. Rudes, Magnuson, Ingel, and Hartwell, 2021.
2. A senior management staff member notes that hard cells are cells with cameras and are reserved for residents who were destructive to their prior cells and are sometimes used to prevent self-harm. There is no specific hard-cell policy, but the staff members generally use the guidance found in the cell assignment policy and their own discretion after that.
3. If a resident who identifies as transgender completes the central office paperwork, they receive an "accommodation." This means that even in the RHU, a staff member who matches that resident's gender identity must do that resident's strip searches. So, for trans-residents with accommodations, women staff are requested to come to the RHU and do strips. This is the only policy that specifically supports women in the RHU.

Chapter 5: Reentry
1. Ingel, Smith, Magnuson, and Rudes, 2021.
2. Bishara, 2019; Baird, 1991.
3. Overmier and Seligman, 1967.
4. Martinko and Gardner, 1982.

Chapter 6: Reform
1. Because this book considers only residents and staff within the RHU and not specialty-unit residents and staff like those in the DTU, we note only how RHU residents and staff feel about D-codes and the DTU but do not offer specifics from inside the DTU. For more on that topic, see Magnuson's dissertation work (in progress) at George Mason University.
2. Rubin and Reiter, 2018.

Chapter 7: Reversal and Revision
1. King, Mauer, and Huling, 2003.
2. Many correctional staff openly and readily relate their work in prisons to "parenting" and "babysitting." Thus, the family analogy, even if it involves mixing children, youth, and teens with adults seems particularly fitting in this context.
3. Frost and Monteiro, C. E.,2016.
4. Spock and Parker, 1946/1976; Sears and Sears, 2001.
5. Haney, 2003.
6. Flannery, 2017; Hervas, Ruiz-Carrasco, Mondejar, and Bravo, 2017, 395–404; Bolton, Dimant, and Schmidt, 2020.
7. Meyer, Brooks, and Goes, 1990.
8. Obama, 2016.
9. Dart, 2019.
10. Kiebala, 2019.
11. TCR Staff, 2021.
12. Raemisch, 2014.
13. Cipriano, 2021.
14. Quandt, 2020.
15. Kim, 2020.
16. Kelly, 2016.
17. Corley, 2018.
18. Solitary Confinement Study and Reform Act of 2019, H.R. 4488, 8.
19. DiMaggio and Powell, 1983.
20. Liebling, 1999.

21. Glisson, 2007, 737.
22. Bouffard, 2019.
23. Andvig, Koffeld-Hamidane, Ausland, and Karlsson, 2020.
24. Corley, 2018.
25. Bouffard, 2019, n.p.
26. Reiter, Sexton, and Sumner, 2018.
27. Smoyer and Kjaer, 2015.
28. Herbert et al., 2012.
29. Huertas and Herrara, 2020.
30. Gesch et al., 2002.
31. Gesch et al., 2002.
32. Cohn, 2018.
33. Darmon et al., 2005.
34. Rudes, Taxman, Portillo, Murphy, Rhodes, Stitzer, et al., 2012.
35. Gendreau et al., 2014, 1043.
36. Cullen, Jonson, and Eck, 2012.
37. Heaphy and Dutton, 2008, 157, 140.
38. Koper, 1995.
39. Meis and Kashima, 2017.
40. Think about signs like proper lifting procedures to avoid back injuries placed near heavy materials at a job site or signs that encourage handwashing to prevent disease placed above a bathroom sink.
41. Austin et al., 1993; Bickman, 1972; Craig and Leland, 1983; Crump et al., 1977; Geller et al., 1973; 1977; Kurtz and Walker, 2005.
42. Goffman, 1956.
43. Dickens, 1874, ch. 7, 117.
44. Einat and Suliman, 2021.

Behind the Walls: About This Book

1. Coyne, 1997; Palinkas et al., 2015.
2. Institutions in the state of study assign individuals to prisons based on a variety of factors including their sex assignment at birth. Residents may later apply for, and some receive, an accommodation for prison assignment based on gender identity.
3. Dr. Hattery and Dr. Smith are now at the University of Delaware.
4. Emerson, Fretz, and Shaw, 2011.
5. Glaser, 1965.

6. See Charmaz, 2014; and Tracy, 2019 for more information on qualitative coding/analysis.

7. Again, see Tracy, 2019.

8. Glaser and Strauss, 1967; Strauss and Corbin, 1978, Charmaz, 2014, 10.

9. Lincoln and Guba, 1985.

10. Dr. Morrill was my mentor at the University of California, Irvine, but is now at the University of California, Berkeley.

REFERENCES

Andvig, E., Koffeld-Hamidane, S., Ausland, L. H., and Karlsson, B. (2020). "Inmates' Perceptions and Experiences of How They Were Prepared for Release from a Norwegian Open Prison." *Nordic Journal of Criminology*, 1–18.

Austin, J., Hatfield, D. B., Grindle, A. C., and Bailey, J. S. (1993). "Increasing Recycling in Office Environments: The Effects of Specific, Informative Cues." *Journal of Applied Behavior Analysis*, 26(2), 247–53.

Baird, C. (1991). "Building More Prisons Will Not Solve Prison Overcrowding." In *America's Prisons: Opposing Viewpoints*, edited by Stacey L. Tipp, 118–24. Farmington Hills, MI: Greenhaven Press. https://www.ojp.gov/ncjrs/virtual-library/abstracts/building-more-prisons-will-not-solve-prison-overcrowding-americas.

Beach, S. R., Martin, J. K., Blum, T. C., and Roman, P. M. (1993). "Effects of Marital and Coworker Relationships on Negative Affect: Testing the Central Role of Marriage." *American Journal of Family Therapy*, 21(4), 313–23.

Bickman, L. (1972). "Environmental Attitudes and Actions." *Journal of Social Psychology*, 87(2), 323–24.

Bishara, H. (2019, September 27). "'If They Build It, They Will Fill It': Prison Abolitionists Protest outside the Ford Foundation." *Hyperallergic*. https://hyperallergic.com/519794/if-they-build-it-they-will-fill-it-prison-abolitionists-protest-outside-the-ford-foundation/.

Bolton, G., Dimant, E., and Schmidt, U. (2020). *When a Nudge Backfires: Combining (Im)Plausible Deniability with Social and Economic Incentives to*

Promote Behavioral Change. CESifo Working Paper Series 8070. Munich: CESifo. https://www.cesifo.org/en/publikationen/2020/working-paper/when-nudge-backfires-combining-implausible-deniability-social-and.

Bottoms, A. E. (1999). "Interpersonal Violence and Social Order in Prisons." *Crime and Justice*, 26, 205–81.

Boudoukha, A. H., Altintas, E., Rusinek, S., Fantini-Hauwel, C., and Hautekeete, M. (2013). "Inmates-to-Staff Assaults, PTSD and Burnout: Profiles of Risk and Vulnerability." *Journal of Interpersonal Violence*, 28(11), 2332–50.

Bouffard, K. (2019, October 11). "States Put Norway-Style Prison Reform to Work in U.S." *Detroit News*.

Brodsky, S. L., and Scogin, F. R. (1988). "Inmates in Protective Custody: First Data on Emotional Effects." *Forensic Reports*, 1(4), 267–80.

Calavita, K., and Jenness, V. (2015). *Appealing to Justice: Prisoners Grievances, Rights, and Carceral Logic*. Berkeley: University of California Press.

Casella, J., Ridgeway, J. and Shourd, S., eds. (2016). *Hell Is a Very Small Place: Voices from Solitary Confinement*. New York: New Press.

Cavan, R. S. (1983). "The Chicago School of Sociology, 1918–1933." *Urban Life*, 11(4), 407–20.

Charmaz, Kathy. (2014). *Constructing Grounded Theory: A Practical Guide through Qualitative Analysis*. Los Angeles, CA: Sage.

Christian, J. (2005). "Riding the Bus: Barriers to Prison Visitation and Family Management Strategies." *Journal of Contemporary Criminal Justice*, 21(1), 31–48.

Cipriano, A. (2021, April 12). "Colorado Bill Proposes Curbs on Use of Solitary in Jails." *The Crime Report*. https://thecrimereport.org/2021/04/12/colorado-bill-proposes-curbs-on-use-of-solitary-in-jails/.

Cohn, M. (2018, December 5). "To Lower Prison Health Care Costs, Maryland Is Trying Something New: Serving Healthier Food." *Washington Post*.

Corley, C. (2018, July 31). "North Dakota Prison Officials Think Outside the Box to Revamp Solitary Confinement." *NPR News*. National Public Radio. https://www.nepm.org/post/north-dakota-prison-officials-think-outside-box-revamp-solitary-confinement#stream/0.

Coyne, I. (1997). "Sampling in Qualitative Research. Purposeful and Theoretical Sampling; Merging or Clear Boundaries?" *Journal of Advanced Nursing*, 26(3), 623–30.

Craig, H. B., and Leland, L. S., Jr. (1983). "Improving Cafeteria Patrons' Waste Disposal." *Journal of Organizational Behavior Management*, 5(2), 79–88.

Crewe, B. (2011). "Depth, Weight, Tightness: Revisiting the Pains of Imprisonment." *Punishment and Society*, 13(5), 509–29.

Crump, S. L., Nunes, D. L., and Crossman, E. K. (1977). "The Effects of Litter on Littering Behavior in a Forest Environment." *Environment and Behavior*, 9(1), 137–46.

Cullen, F. T., Jonson, C. L., and Eck, J. E. (2012). "The Accountable Prison." *Journal of Contemporary Criminal Justice*, 28(1), 77–95.

Darmon, N., Darmon, M., Maillot, M., and Drewnowski, A. (2005). "A Nutrient Density Standard for Vegetables and Fruits: Nutrients per Calorie and Nutrients per Unit Cost." *Journal of the American Dietetic Association*, 105(12), 1881–87.

Dart, T. (2019, April 4). "My Jail Stopped Using Solitary Confinement. Here's Why." *Washington Post*.

Dickens, Charles. (1874). *American Notes*. London: Chapman and Hall. http://xtf.lib.virginia.edu/xtf/view?docId=legacy/uvaBook/tei/DicAmer.xml.

DiMaggio, P. J., and Powell, W. W. (1983). "The Iron Cage Revisited: Institutional Isomorphism and Collective Rationality in Organizational Fields." *American Sociological Review*, 48(2), 147–60.

Eastaugh, C. (2017). *Unconstitutional Solitude: Solitary Confinement and the US Constitution's Evolving Standards of Decency*. Cham, Switz.: Springer/Palgrave Macmillan.

Einat, T., and Suliman, N. (2021). "Prison Changed Me—and I Just Work There: Personality Changes among Prison Officers." *Prison Journal*, 101(2), 166–86.

Emerson, R. M., Fretz, R. I., and Shaw, L. L. (2011). *Writing Ethnographic Fieldnotes*. Chicago: University of Chicago Press.

Flannery, M. (2017). "Self-Determination Theory: Intrinsic Motivation and Behavioral Change." *Oncology Nursing Forum*, 44(2), 155–57.

Frost, N. A., and Monteiro, C. E. (2016). *Restrictive Housing in the U.S.: Issues, Challenges, and Future Directions*. Washington, DC: National Institute of Justice. NCJ 250316.

Garbarino, J., Kostelny, K., and Dubrow, N. (1991). "What Children Can Tell Us about Living in Danger." *American Psychologist*, 46(4), 376–83.

Geller, E. S., Farris, J. C., and Post, D. S. (1973). "Prompting a Consumer Behavior for Pollution Control." *Journal of Applied Behavior Analysis*, 6(3), 367–76.

Geller, E. S., Mann, M., and Brasted, W. (1977). "Trash Can Design: A Determinant of Litter-Related Behaviour." Paper presented at American Psychological Association, San Francisco.

Gendreau, P., and Bonta, J. (1984). "Solitary Confinement Is Not Cruel and Unusual Punishment: People Sometimes Are." *Canadian Journal of Criminology*, 26, 467–78.

Gendreau, P., Listwan, S. J., Kuhns, J. B., and Exum, M. L. (2014). "Making Prisoners Accountable: Are Contingency Management Programs the Answer?" *Criminal Justice and Behavior*, 41(9), 1079–102.

Gesch, C. B., Hammond, S. M., Hampson, S. E., Eves, A., and Crowder, M. J. (2002). "Influence of Supplementary Vitamins, Minerals and Essential Fatty Acids on the Antisocial Behaviour of Young Adult Prisoners: Randomised, Placebo-Controlled Trial." *British Journal of Psychiatry*, 181(1), 22–28.

Glaser, B. (1965). "The Constant Comparative Method of Qualitative Analysis." *Social Problems*, 12(4), 436–45.

Glaser, B. G., and Strauss, A. L. (1967). *The Discovery of Grounded Theory: Strategies for Qualitative Research*. Chicago: Aldine.

Glisson, C. (2007). "Assessing and Changing Organizational Culture and Climate for Effective Services." *Research on Social Work Practice*, 17(6), 736–47.

Goffman, E. (1956). *The Presentation of Self in Everyday Life*. New York: Doubleday.

Grassian, S. (2006). "Psychiatric Effects of Solitary Confinement." *Washington University Journal of Law and Policy*, 22, 325.

Guenther, L. (2013). *Solitary Confinement: Social Death and Its Afterlives*. Minneapolis: University of Minnesota Press.

Gurung, R., Sarason, B., and Sarason, I. (1997). "Close Personal Relationships and Health Outcomes: A Key to the Role of Social Support." In *Handbook of Personal Relationships: Theory, Research and Interventions*, edited by S. Duck et al., 2nd ed., 547–73. New York: Wiley.

Haney, C. (2003). "Mental Health Issues in Long-Term Solitary and 'Supermax' Confinement." *Crime & Delinquency*, 49(1), 124–56.

Haney, C. (2019). "Solitary Confinement, Loneliness, and Psychological Harm." *Solitary Confinement: Effects, Practices and Pathways towards Reform*, edited by J. Lobel and P. Scharff Smith, 129–52. New York: Oxford University Press.

Haney, C., and Lynch, M. (1997). "Regulating Prisons of the Future: A Psychological Analysis of Supermax and Solitary Confinement." *New York University Review of Law & Social Change*, 23, 477.

Heaphy, E. D., and Dutton, J. E. (2008). "Positive Social Interactions and the Human Body at Work: Linking Organizations and Physiology." *Academy of Management Review*, 33(1), 137–62.

Herbert, S. (2019). *Too Easy to Keep: Life-Sentenced Prisoners and the Future of Mass Incarceration*. Oakland: University of California Press.

Herbert, K., Plugge, E., Foster, C., and Doll, H. (2012). "Prevalence of Risk

Factors for Noncommunicable Diseases in Prison Populations Worldwide: A Systematic Review." *Lancet*, 379(9830), 1975–82.

Hervas, R., Ruiz-Carrasco, D., Mondejar, T., and Bravo, J. (2017). "Gamification Mechanics for Behavioral Change: A Systematic Review and Proposed Taxonomy." In *Pervasive Health '17: Proceedings of the 11th EAI International Conference on Pervasive Computing Technologies for Healthcare*, 395–404. New York: Association for Computing Machinery. https://doi.org/10.1145/3154862.3154939.

Hochschild, A. R. (1983). *The Managed Heart*. Berkeley: University of California Press.

Huertas, T., and Herrara, J. (2020, March 6). "Local School District Partners with Farmers to Bring Fresh Vegetables and Fruit to Campuses." KSAT.com.

Ingel, S., Smith, L., Magnuson, S., and Rudes, D. (2021). "Strain and Gain: From Deprivation to Innovation within Restricted Housing Units." *Deviant Behavior*, 1–19. https://doi.org/10.1080/01639625.2021.1913453.

Jackson, M. (2019). *Prisoners of Isolation*. Toronto: University of Toronto Press.

James, L., and Todak, N. (2018). "Prison Employment and Post-Traumatic Stress Disorder: Risk and Protective Factors." *American Journal of Industrial Medicine*, 61(9), 725–32.

Kelly, J. (2016, September 28). "California Restricts Use of Solitary Confinement Practices at Juvenile Facilities." *The Imprint*.

Kiebala, V. (2019, December 17). "Sheriff Tom Dart Says Cook County Jail Is the First to End Solitary Confinement. Here's What It Looks Like from the Inside." *Chicago Reporter*.

Kiebala, V., and Rodriguez, S. (2018). "FAQ." Solitary Watch. https://solitarywatch.org/wp-content/uploads/2019/05/Solitary-Confinement-FAQ-2018-final.pdf.

Kim, C. (2020, July 11). "Solitary Confinement Isn't Effective. That's Why New Jersey Passed a Law to Restrict It." *Vox*.

King, R. S., Mauer, M., and Huling, T. (2003). *Big Prisons, Small Towns: Prison Economics in Rural America*. Washington, DC: Sentencing Project.

Klinger, E. (1977). *Meaning and Void: Inner Experience and the Incentives in People's Lives*. Minneapolis: University of Minnesota Press.

Koper, C. (1995). "Just Enough Police Presence: Reducing Crime and Disorderly Behavior by Optimizing Patrol Time in Crime Hot Spots." *Justice Quarterly*, 12(4), 649–72.

Kupers, T. A. (2017). *Solitary: The Inside Story of Supermax Isolation and How We Can Abolish It*. Berkeley: University of California Press.

Kurz, T., Donaghue, N., and Walker, I. (2005). "Utilizing a Social-Ecological Framework to Promote Water and Energy Conservation: A Field Experiment 1." *Journal of Applied Social Psychology*, 35(6), 1281–1300.

Lanctôt, N., and Guay, S. (2014). "The Aftermath of Workplace Violence among Healthcare Workers: A Systematic Literature Review of the Consequences." *Aggression and Violent Behavior*, 19(5), 492–501.

Liebling, A. (1999). "Prison Suicide and Prisoner Coping." *Crime and Justice*, 26, 283–359.

Lincoln, K. D. (2000). "Social Support, Negative Social Interactions, and Psychological Well-Being." *Social Service Review*, 74(2), 231–52.

Lincoln, Y. S., and Guba, E. G. (1985). "Establishing Trustworthiness." In *Naturalistic Inquiry*, 289–331. Beverly Hills, CA: Sage.

Magnuson, S. (in progress). "Solitary Diversion: Reforming Restricted Housing Units for Severely Mentally Ill Inmates." PhD diss., Criminology, Law and Society diss., George Mason University.

Martinko, M. J., and Gardner, W. L. (1982). "Learned Helplessness: An Alternative Explanation for Performance Deficits." *Academy of Management Review*, 7(2), 195–204.

Maier, K. H., and Ricciardelli, R. (2019). "The Prisoner's Dilemma: How Male Prisoners Experience and Respond to Penal Threat while Incarcerated." *Punishment & Society*, 21(2), 231–50.

Meis, J., and Kashima, Y. (2017). "Signage as a Tool for Behavioral Change: Direct and Indirect Routes to Understanding the Meaning of a Sign." *PloS One*, 12(8), e0182975.

Meyer, A. D., Brooks, G. R., and Goes, J. B. (1990). "Environmental Jolts And Industry Revolutions: Organizational Responses to Discontinuous Change." *Strategic Management Journal*, 11(special issue), 93–110.

Morrill, C. (1995). *The Executive Way: Conflict Management in Corporations*. Chicago: University of Chicago Press.

Obama, B., (2016, January 26). "Unnecessary Solitary Confinement Is an 'Affront to Our Common Humanity.'" *Washington Post*.

Overmier, J. B., and Seligman, M. E. P. (1967). "Effects of Inescapable Shock upon Subsequent Escape and Avoidance Learning." *Journal of Comparative and Physiological Psychology*, 63, 28–33.

Palinkas, L., Horwitz, S., Green, C., Wisdom, J., Duan, N., and Hoagwood, K. (2015). "Purposeful Sampling for Qualitative Data Collection and Analysis in Mixed Method Implementation Research." *Administration and Policy in Mental Health*, 42(5), 533–44.

Pendergrass, T. and Hoke, M., eds. (2018). *Six by Ten: Stories from Solitary*. Chicago: Haymarket Books.

Polizzi, D. (2017). *Solitary Confinement: Lived Experiences and Ethical Implications*. Bristol, UK: Policy Press.

Poole, E. D., and Regoli, R. M. (1981). "Alienation in Prison: An Examination of the Work Relations of Prison Guards." *Criminology*, 19(2), 251–70.

Quandt, K.R.. (2020, October 23). "Inside One Lawyer's Quest to End Solitary Confinement." *Rolling Stone*.

Raemisch, R. (2014, February 20). "My Night in Solitary." *New York Times*.

Reiter, K. (2016). *23/7: Pelican Bay Prison and the Rise of Long-Term Solitary Confinement*. New Haven, CT: Yale University Press.

Reiter, K., and Koenig, A., eds. (2015). *Extreme Punishment: Comparative Studies in Detention, Incarceration and Solitary Confinement*. New York: Palgrave MacMillan.

Reiter, K., Sexton, L., and Sumner, J. (2018). "Theoretical and Empirical Limits of Scandinavian Exceptionalism: Isolation and Normalization in Danish Prisons." *Punishment & Society*, 290(1): 92–112.

Reiter, K., Ventura, J., Lovell, D., Augustine, D., Barragan, M., Blair, T., et al. (2020). "Psychological Distress in Solitary Confinement: Symptoms, Severity, and Prevalence in the United States, 2017–2018." *American Journal of Public Health*, 110(S1), S56–S62.

Renn, O. (1998). "The Role of Risk Perception for Risk Management." *Reliability Engineering & System Safety*, 59(1), 49–62.

Rhodes, L. A. (2004). *Total Confinement: Madness and Reason in the Maximum Security Prison*. California Series in Public Anthropology, vol. 7. Berkeley: University of California Press.

Richards, S. C. (2015). *The Marion Experiment: Long-Term Solitary Confinement and the Supermax Movement*. Carbondale: Southern Illinois University Press.

Rubin, A. T., and Reiter, K. (2018). "Continuity in the Face of Penal Innovation: Revisiting the History of American Solitary Confinement." *Law & Social Inquiry*, 43(4), 1604–32.

Rudes, D. S., Magnuson, S., Ingel, S. N., and Hartwell, T. N. (2021). "Rights-in-Between: Resident Perceptions of and Accessibility to Rights within Restricted Housing Units." *Law & Society Review*, 55(2), 291–319.

Rudes, D. S., Taxman, F. S., Portillo, S., Murphy, A., Rhodes, A., Stitzer, M., et al. (2012). "Adding Positive Reinforcement in Justice Settings: Acceptability and Feasibility." *Journal of Substance Abuse Treatment*, 42(3), 260–70.

Sears, W., and Sears, M. (2001). *The Attachment Parenting Book: A Commonsense Guide to Understanding and Nurturing Your Baby*. Boston: Little, Brown/Spark.

Shalev, S. (2013). *Supermax: Controlling Risk through Solitary Confinement*. New York: Routledge.

Smoyer, A. B., and Kjaer Minke, L. (2015). *Food Systems in Correctional Settings: A Literature Review and Case Study*. World Health Organization Regional Office for Europe. https://www.euro.who.int/__data/assets/pdf_file/0006/292965/Food-systems-correctional-settings-literature-review-case-study.pdf.

Spock, B., and S. J. Parker. (1946; 1976). *Dr. Spock's Baby and Child Care*. New York: Simon & Schuster.

Steptoe, A., and Fancourt, D. (2020). "An Outcome-wide Analysis of Bidirectional Association between Changes in Meaningfulness of Life and Health, Emotional, Behavioural, and Social Factors." *Scientific Reports*, 10(1), 1–12.

Suedfeld, P., Ramirez, C., Deaton, J., and Baker-Brown, G. (1982). "Reactions and Attributes of Prisoners in Solitary Confinement." *Criminal Justice and Behavior*, 9(3), 303–40.

TCR Staff. (2021, April 1). "New York Adopts 'Nelson Mandela' Rules Curbing Use of Solitary." *Crime Report*. https://thecrimereport.org/2021/04/01/new-york-adopts-nelson-mandela-rules-limiting-use-of-solitary/.

Tewksbury, R. and DeMichele, M. (2005). "Going to Prison: A Prison Visitation Program." *Prison Journal*, 85(3), 292–310.

Tracy, S. J. (2019). *Qualitative Research Methods: Collecting Evidence, Crafting Analysis, Communicating Impact*. Hoboken, NJ: John Wiley & Sons.

Tracy, S. J., and Scott, C. (2006). "Sexuality, Masculinity, and Taint Management among Firefighters and Correctional Officers: Getting Down and Dirty with 'America's Heroes' and the 'Scum of Law Enforcement.'" *Management Communication Quarterly*, 20(1), 6–38.

Tuan, Y.-F. (1979). "Fear of Disease." In *The Landscapes of Fear*, 87–104. New York: Pantheon Books.

Wacquant, L. (2002). "The Curious Eclipse of Prison Ethnography in the Age of Mass Incarceration." *Ethnography*, 3(4), 371–97.

Websites

Prison Policy Initiative [nonprofit, nonpartisan group that produces research about criminal justice reform]. https://www.prisonpolicy.org/.

Solitary Watch [nonprofit national watchdog group that investigates, documents, and disseminates information on the use of solitary confinement in US prisons and jails] www.SolitaryWatch.com.

US Department of Labor, Occupational Safety and Health Administration (OSHA). (n.d.) Workplace Violence. https://www.osha.gov/SLTC/workplaceviolence/https://www.osha.gov/SLTC/workplaceviolence/.

Vera Institute of Justice [nonprofit group that works with government and civic leaders to improve justice systems in over forty states]. https://www.vera.org.

Court Cases

Delaney v. Detella, 256 F.3d 679 (7th Cir. 2001).
Gillis v. Litscher, 468 F.3d 488, 493–94 (7th Cir. 2006).
O'Brien v. Moriarty, 489 F.2d 941, 944 (1 Cir. 1974).
P. D. v. Middlesex County, Superior Court of New Jersey, Docket No. MID-L-3811–14.
Peoples v. Fischer, 898 F. Supp. 2d 618 (S.D.N.Y. 2012).
Quintanilla v. Bryson, et al., No. 17-14141 (11th Cir. 2018).
Rhodes v. Chapman, 452 U.S. 337 (1981).
Sheley v. Dugger, 833 F.2d 1420, 1428–29 (11th Cir. 1987).
Weems v. United States, 217 U.S. 349 (1910).
Wilson v. Seiter, 501 U.S. 294 (1991).

Laws

Prison Rape Elimination Act (PREA) of 2003
Solitary Confinement Study and Reform Act of 2019, H.R. 4488
US Constitution, Eighth Amendment, § 1983
US Constitution, Fourteenth Amendment

FURTHER READING

Surviving Solitary is just one book in a library of important and relevant readings about living and working in restricted housing units. The list below will get you started on learning more.

Ahalt, C., Haney, C., Rios, S., Fox, M. P., Farabee, D., and Williams, B. (2017). "Reducing the Use and Impact of Solitary Confinement in Corrections." *International Journal of Prisoner Health*, 13(1), 41–48.

Aranda-Hughes, V., Turanovic, J. J., Mears, D. P., and Pesta, G. B. (2021). "Women in Solitary Confinement: Relationships, Pseudofamilies, and the Limits of Control." *Feminist Criminology*, 16(1), 47–72.

Arrigo, B. A., and Bullock, J. L. (2008). "The Psychological Effects of Solitary Confinement on Prisoners in Supermax Units: Reviewing What We Know and Recommending What Should Change." *International Journal of Offender Therapy and Comparative Criminology*, 52(6), 622–40.

Association of State Correctional Administrators and The Liman Center for Public Interest Law. (2018). *Working to Limit Restrictive Housing: Efforts in Four Jurisdictions to Make Changes*. https://law.yale.edu/sites/default/files/documents/pdf/Liman/asca_liman_2018_workingtolimit.pdf

Beck, A. J. (2015). *Use of Restrictive Housing in U.S. Prisons and Jail, 2011–12*. Washington, DC: Bureau of Justice Statistics.

Butler, H. D., and Steiner, B. (2017). "Examining the Use of Disciplinary Segregation within and across Prisons." *Justice Quarterly*, 34, 248–71.

Clark, V. A., and Duwe, G. (2019). "From Solitary to the Streets: The Effect of Restrictive Housing on Recidivism." *Corrections*, 4(4), 302–18.

Cloud, D. H., Drucker, E., Browne, A., and Parsons, J. (2015). "Public Health and Solitary Confinement in the United States." *American Journal of Public Health*, 105(1), 18–26.

Cloyes, K. G., Lovell, D., Allen, D. G., and Rhodes, L. A. (2006). "Assessment of Psychosocial Impairment in a Supermaximum Security Unit Sample." *Criminal Justice and Behavior*, 33(6), 760–81.

Cochran J. C., Toman, E. L., Mears, D. P., and Bales, W. D. (2018). "Solitary Confinement as Punishment: Examining In-Prison Sanctioning Disparities." *Justice Quarterly*, 35, 381–411.

Digard, L., Sullivan, S., and Vanko, E. (2018). *Rethinking Restrictive Housing: Lessons from Five U.S. Jail and Prison Systems*. Vera Institute of Justice. https://www.vera.org/rethinking restrictive-housing.

Fathi, D. C. (2015). "United States: Turning the Corner on Solitary Confinement." *Canadian Journal of Human Rights*, 4, 167–77.

Fenster, A. (2020, October 13). "New Data: Solitary Confinement Increases Risk of Premature Death after Release." *Briefings* (blog), Prison Policy Initiative. https://www.prisonpolicy.org/blog/2020/10/13/solitary_mortality_risk/.

Galford, G. (2021). "Prison as Home: Characteristics of Control within General Prison and Solitary Confinement Environments." *Journal of Interior Design*, 46(2), 35–53.

Garcia, M., ed. (2016). *Restrictive Housing in the U.S.: Issues, Challenges, and Future Directions*. Washington, DC: US Department of Justice, Office of Justice Programs, National Institute of Justice.

Haney, C. (2018). "Restricting the Use of Solitary Confinement." *Annual Review of Criminology*, 1, 285–310.

Hagan, B. O., Wang, E. A., Aminawung, J. A., Albizu-Garcia, C. E., Zaller, N., Nyamu, S., . . . and Fox, A. D. (2018). "History of Solitary Confinement Is Associated with Post-Traumatic Stress Disorder Symptoms among Individuals Recently Released from Prison." *Journal of Urban Health*, 95(2), 141–48.

Kaba, F., Lewis, A., Glowa-Kollisch, S., Hadler, J., Lee, D., Alper, H., et al. (2014). "Solitary Confinement and Risk of Self-Harm among Jail Inmates." *American Journal of Public Health*, 104(3), 442–47. https://doi.org/10.2105/AJPH.2013.301742.

Kupers, T. A. (2008). "What to Do with the Survivors? Coping with the Long-Term Effects of Isolated Confinement." *Criminal Justice and Behavior*, 35(8), 1005–16.

Labrecque, R. M., and Mears, D. P. (2019). "Prison System versus Critics' Views on the Use of Restrictive Housing: Objective Risk Classification or Ascriptive Assignment?" *Prison Journal*, 99, 194–218.

Labrecque, R. M., and Smith, P. (2019)." Assessing the Impact of Time Spent in Restrictive Housing Confinement on Subsequent Measures of Institutional Adjustment among Men in Prison." *Criminal Justice & Behavior*, 46, 1445–55.

Mears, D. P., Hughes, V., Pesta, G. B., Bales, W. D., Brown, J. B., Cochran, J. C., and Wooldredge, J. (2019). "The New Solitary Confinement? A Conceptual Framework for Guiding and Assessing Research and Policy on 'Restrictive Housing.'" *Criminal Justice and Behavior*, 46, 1427–44.

Mears, D. P., Pesta, G. B., Aranda-Hughes, V., Brown, J. M., Siennick, S. E., Cochran, J. C., and Bales, W. D. (2020). *The Impacts of Restrictive Housing on Inmate Behavior, Mental Health, and Recidivism, and Prison Systems and Personnel*. Research report submitted by Florida State University to the National Institute of Justice. https://www.ojp.gov/pdffiles1/nij/grants/256000.pdf.

Mears, D.P, and Reisig, M.D. (2006). "The Theory and Practice of Supermax Prisons." *Punishment & Society*, 8, 33–57.

Metcalf, H., Morgan, J., Oliker-Friedland, S., Resnik, J., Spiegel, J., Tae, H., Work, A., and Holbrook, B. (2013, January). "Administrative Segregation, Degrees of Isolation, and Incarceration: A National Overview of State and Federal Correctional Policies." *SSRN Electronic Journal*. https://www.researchgate.net/publication/272243318_Administrative_Segregation_Degrees_of_Isolation_and_Incarceration_A_National_Overview_of_State_and_Federal_Correctional_Policies.

Metzner, J. L., and Fellner, J. (2013). "Solitary Confinement and Mental Illness in US Prisons: A Challenge for Medical Ethics." In *Health and Human Rights in a Changing World*, edited by M. Grodin, D. Tarantola, G. Annas, and S. Gruskin, 316–323. New York: Routledge.

Meyers, T. J., Infante, A., and Wright, K. A. (2018). "Addressing Serious Violent Misconduct in Prison: Examining an Alternative Form of Restrictive Housing." *International Journal of Offender Therapy and Comparative Criminology*, 62, 4585–608.

Morgan, R. D., Gendreau, P., Smith, P., Gray, A. L., Labrecque, R. M., MacLean, N., . . . and Mills, J. F. (2016). "Quantitative Syntheses of the Effects of Administrative Segregation on Inmates' Well-Being." *Psychology, Public Policy, and Law*, 22, 439–61.

Morris, R. G. (2016). "Exploring the Effect of Exposure to Short-Term Solitary Confinement among Violent Prison Inmates." *Journal of Quantitative Criminology*, 32, 1–22.

O'Keefe, M. L., Klebe, K. J., Metzner, J., Dvoskin, J., Fellner, J., and Stucker, A. (2013). "A Longitudinal Study of Administrative Segregation." *Journal of the American Academy of Psychiatry and Law*, 41, 49–60.

Rocheleau, A. M. (2015). "Ways of Coping and Involvement in Prison Violence." *International Journal of Offender Therapy and Comparative Criminology*, 59(4), 359–83.

Sakoda, R. T., and Simes, J. T. (2021). "Solitary Confinement and the US Prison Boom." *Criminal Justice Policy Review*, 32(1), 66–102.

Salerno, L. M., and Zgoba, K. M. (2020). "Disciplinary Segregation and Its Effects on In-Prison Outcomes." *Prison Journal*, 100(1), 74–97.

Shames, A., Wilcox, J., and Subramanian, R. (2015). *Solitary Confinement: Common Misconceptions and Emerging Safe Alternatives*. Vera Institute of Justice. https://www.vera.org/publications/solitary-confinement-common-misconceptions-and-emerging-safe-alternatives.

Smith, P. S. (2006). "The Effects of Solitary Confinement on Prison Inmates: A Brief History and Review of the Literature." *Crime and Justice: A Review of Research*, 34, 441–528.

Strauss, A., and Corbin, J. M. (1997). *Grounded Theory in Practice*. Thousand Oaks, CA: Sage.

Strong, J. D., Reiter, K., Gonzalez, G., Tublitz, R., Augustine, D., Barragan, M., et al. R. (2020). "The Body in Isolation: The Physical Health Impacts of Incarceration in Solitary Confinement." *PloS One*, 15(10), e0238510.

Suedfeld, P., Ramirez, C., Deaton, J., and Baker-Brown, G. (1982). "Reactions and Attributes of Prisoners in Solitary Confinement." *Criminal Justice and Behavior*, 9(3), 303–40.

Sundt, J. (2016). "The Effect of Administrative Segregation on Prison Order and organizational Culture." *Restrictive Housing in the US: Issues, Challenges, and Future Directions*, 297–330.

Wacquant, L. (2002). "The Curious Eclipse of Prison Ethnography in the Age of Mass Incarceration." *Ethnography*, 3(4), 371–97.

Way, B. B., Sawyer, D. A., Barboza, S., and Nash, R. (2007). "Inmate Suicide and Time Spent in Special Disciplinary Housing in New York State Prison." *Psychiatric Services*, 58(4), 558–60. https://doi.org/10.1176/ps.2007.58.4.558.

Wildeman, C., and Andersen, L. H. (2020). "Long-Term Consequences of Being Placed in Disciplinary Segregation." *Criminology*, 58(3), 423–53.

Woo, Y., Drapela, L., Campagna, M., Stohr, M. K., Hamilton, Z. K., Mei, X., and Tollefsbol, E. T. (2020). "Disciplinary Segregation's Effects on Inmate Behavior: Institutional and Community Outcomes." *Criminal Justice Policy Review*, 31(7), 1036–58.

Wynn, J. R., and Szatrowski, A. (2003). "Hidden Prisons: Twenty-Three-Hour Lockdown Units in New York State Correctional Facilities." *Pace Law Review*, 24(2), 497–526.

INDEX

AC-status (administrative custody) residents: cell assignments, 92; defined, 2, 77, 144; personal property allowed for, 11, 143; visitations and phone calls, 12, 44, 62, 63
administrative segregation (AdSeg), 1. *See also* RHU (restricted housing unit)
Ahalt, Cyrus, 167
alcoholism, 32, 73, 127–28
Amend: Changing Correctional Culture, 166–67
Anvig, Ellen, 166
Atlas.ti, 208, 209, 211

Baiou, Sabrine, 196
Balde, Cady, 196
Beraki, Sewit, 196
Berry, Karlie, 196
bid posts, 3, 95, 147
BIU (Behavioral Intervention Unit), 163
Blackmun, Harry, 82
Blasko, Brandy, 189

books, access to, 12, 98, 121, 139–40
"the bubble" (control room), 13, 75, 96, 97, 103
burning (denied opportunities, rights, privileges), 50, 56, 86, 88–89, 90, 91, 97–99, 104

California, carceral reform, 162, 168
cameras, 10–11, 23, 224n2 (chap. 4)
case law, 81–83
Castro, Jennifer, 7
cell assignments, 35, 45–46, 91–92, 104–5, 107–8, 124–25
Certified Peer Specialists (CPS workers), 54–55
chains and handcuffs, 12, 22–23, 43, 87, 161, 175
Changing the (w)Hole Mind study, 190–91
Charmaz, Kathy, 211
chemical munitions (OC), 24, 25, 34, 57–58, 68, 99, 101–3, 133, 138
civil rights, 81–82
clothing, 88, 135, 138

CM (Contingency Management) programs, 170–71, 172
code-switching, 204
coding procedure, 208–11
Coleman, Beau, 196
Colorado, carceral reform, 162
consent process, for interviews, 192, 193, 194–95, 205
Constant Comparative Method, 208
constitutional rights, 81–82
contraband, 2, 30, 46, 105–6, 169
control room ("the bubble"), 13, 75, 96, 97, 103
Cook County (Chicago), carceral reform, 161
coping strategies, 74, 75, 120–21, 182–83
Corbin, J. M., 211
count time, 11, 84
CPS workers (Certified Peer Specialists), 54–55. See also peer assistant; peer advocate
criminology research methods, 201–2
cruel and unusual punishment, 81–82
Cullen, Francis, 172
cultural reform, 133, 145–46, 165–67
Cuomo, Andrew M., 162

Dart, Tom, 161
data analysis procedure, 211–12
data capturing procedure, 206–8
data coding procedure, 208–11
Daughtry, Dakota, 196
DC-status (disciplinary custody) residents: cell assignments, 92; defined, 2–3, 77, 144; personal property allowed for, 11; visitations and phone calls, 12, 44, 62, 63
death row, 7, 18
dehumanization, 24, 57–59, 68, 133, 148–49

Delaney v. DeTella (2000–1), 83
Denmark, prison model, 167
Dickens, Charles, 183
diet. *See* food
dignity and humanity, 24, 55, 57–59, 68, 133, 148–49, 163
divorce, 32, 72, 73
double shifts, 74
drug addiction, 26, 118, 127–28
drug searches, 23
DTU (Diversionary Treatment Unit), 131, 225n1 (chap. 6)
due process, 81
Dutton, J. E., 174

Eck, John E., 172
education: resident access to, 2, 120, 121, 174; staff background, 3–4, 153
Eighth Amendment, 81–83
email. *See* mail/email
emotional labor, 59–60, 73, 224n6
empathy, 61, 67, 74
England, carceral reform, 169

family: parenting analogy, 121–22, 155–56, 158–59, 225n2 (chap. 7); of residents, 62–64, 117–18, 174; of staff, 32–33, 71–75, 119
fear. *See* risks
female staff, 60–61, 92, 96–97, 224n3 (chap. 4)
fishing, 12–13, 50, 51
food: choices, 30–31, 78; hunger strikes, 24; reform, 136–38, 168–70; serving procedure, 11–12, 89, 98, 100, 179–81; withheld, 21, 58, 88, 89, 98
Fourteenth Amendment, 81, 83

gangs, 45, 50, 51, 52, 53, 162
Gardner, W. L., 127

gender. *See* sexuality and gender
Gendreau, Paul, 170–71
general population: handbook, 83–84, 86, 89, 90, 91, 92, 97, 109; movement in, 86–87; programs, opportunities, and privileges in, 120, 121, 139, 143; reentry in, 113–14, 115–17
Gillis v. Litscher (2006), 82
Glaser, B. G., 208, 211
Glisson, Charles, 165
Goffman, Erving, 182
gossip, 55–56, 62
grounded theory, 211
Guba, Egon G., 214
Gumm v. Jacobs (2015), 83

haircuts, 90–91
handbooks, 83–84, 85–86, 88, 89, 90, 91, 92, 97, 99–100, 105, 109, 178
handcuffs and chains, 12, 22–23, 43, 87, 161, 175. *See also* leash and tether
hard cells, 91, 224n2 (chap. 4)
Hartwell, Taylor, 196, 207
Hattery, Angela, 196, 197, 198, 205, 220
health. *See* medical care; mental health; physical health
Heaphy, E. D., 174
helplessness, learned, 127
help-seeking behavior, 149–51
Hochschild, A. R., 59, 224n6
housing assignments, 35, 45–46, 91–92, 104–5, 107–8, 124–25
Huete, Kristen, 196
humanity and dignity, 24, 55, 57–59, 68, 133, 148–49, 163
hunger strikes, 24
hygiene, 135–36. *See also* showers

ICR (intercoder reliability), 209–10
incentives, 34, 140, 170–73
Ingel, Sydney, 120, 196

interview procedure, 14–15, 192–95, 204–6
IPC (interpersonal communication) skills, 39
IRB (Institutional Review Board), 21, 191–92, 193, 194, 206

Johnson, Robert, 7
Jonson, Cheryl Lero, 172

Kanewske, Cait, 196
Klinger, Eric, 43
Koper curve, 176
Kushmerick-McCune, Bryce, 196

landscape of fear, 17–18. *See also* risks
learned helplessness, 127
leash and tether, 12, 32, 63, 87, 197
LGBTQ+, 22, 196, 224
Liebling, Alison, 164–65
lieutenant's office, 13–14
Lincoln, Yvonna S., 214
Loneliness, 19, 76, 174, 183

mace, 24, 25, 34, 57–58, 68, 99, 101–3, 133, 138. *See also* OC; pepper spray
Magnuson, Shannon, 191, 196, 197, 198, 199, 200, 202, 205, 207, 216
mail/email: policies sent to staff via, 109; resident access to, 44, 64, 138–39, 174
Mandela, Nelson, 221
Marmolejo, Lina, 196
Marshall, Thurgood, 82
Martinko, M. J., 127
Maryland, carceral reform, 169
masculinity, 75, 177
masked malignancy, 8–9, 18, 54, 58, 74, 152, 181–2
Matthews, Esther, 196
meals. *See* food

Mears, Daniel, 7
medical care: prescription delivery procedure, 12, 137; reform, 175; resident access to, 23, 24, 25, 26–27, 58, 61, 68, 98, 116, 134–35; staff access to, 36, 75
mental health: and AC status, 77; and cell assignments, 45, 131, 147; and consent process for interviews, 195; and criticism, 148; and ongoing traumatic stress, 40–41; policies on, 35–36; psychological assessment of staff, 95–96, 138; of researchers, 196–98; of residents, 21–22, 24, 26–27, 54, 60–61, 115, 119–20, 132–35; of staff, 31–32, 36, 75–76, 177; studies on negative effects of RHUs on, 18–19, 35; training for staff on, 38, 39, 176–77. *See also* suicide
military, 146–47, 154
Morrill, Calvin, 210, 215, 227n10
movement procedures, 12, 22–23, 43, 86–87

Nelson Mandela Rules, 160–61, 162
New Jersey, carceral reform, 162
New Mexico, carceral reform, 162
New Start program, 168–69
New York, carceral reform, 162
NIC (National Institute of Corrections), 5
North Dakota, carceral reform, 163, 167
Norway, prison model, 166–67

Obama, Barack, 161
O'Brien v. Moriarty (1974), 82
OC (chemical munitions), 24, 25, 34, 57–58, 68, 99, 101–3, 133, 138. *See also* mace; pepper spray

ongoing traumatic stress, 40–41
Oregon, carceral reform, 167
OSHA (Occupational Safety and Health Administration), 40
overcrowding, 1, 44
Overmier, J. B., 127

parenting analogy, 121–22, 155–56, 158–59, 225n2 (chap. 7)
PC status (protective custody). *See* AC-status (administrative custody) residents
P.D. v. Middlesex County (2015), 83
peer assistant, 5
peer advocate, 68
Peoples v. Fischer (2015), 83
pepper spray, 24, 25, 34, 57–58, 68, 99, 101–3, 133, 138. *See also* mace; OC
performance review committee (PRC), 3
Petersilia, Joan, 112
phone calls, 12, 44, 62, 63, 138, 139, 140
physical health: of residents, 21–26, 53, 56, 57–58, 65–66, 101–3; of staff, 28–31, 53, 103; studies on negative effects of RHUs on, 19
Pickett, Heather, 196
policies. *See* rules, procedures, and policies
PREA (Prison Rape Elimination Act), 37–38, 97, 105, 106
The Prison Project, 189, 190, 202
privacy, 48, 49, 61–62
privileges, 56, 63, 87, 114–15, 124, 126, 140, 142–43, 146, 148, 153, 155, 167, 170–71
procedures. *See* rules, procedures, and policies
property: allowed for residents, 11, 105; confiscation, 38, 105, 106; and contraband, 2, 30, 46, 105–6, 169;

sharing among residents, 12–13, 50, 51
protective custody (PC status). *See* AC-status (administrative custody) residents
psychological staff: medicine delivery, 12; mistreatment of female, 92; numbers, 5; and rehabilitation *vs.* punishment, 144; resident access to, 61, 116, 134–35; resident criticism of, 59; RHU spaces for, 14; and suicide policies, 107–9; volunteers, 175
PTSD, 32, 40
punishment: burning, 50, 56, 86, 88–89, 90, 91, 97–99, 104; cruel and unusual, 81–82; as RHU goal, 123–25, 129, 141–45. *See also* rules, procedures, and policies

qualitative *vs.* quantitative research methods, 6–7, 201–2, 212–13, 214–15
Quintanilla v. Bryson (2018), 82

race, and cell assignments, 45, 92
radios, 11, 106
Raemisch, Rich, 162
reading materials, access to, 12, 98, 121, 139–40
recidivism, 166, 169, 172
reentry, 112–29; defined, 15, 112; intracarceral, 113–14, 115–17; lack of thinking about, 126–28; paradox of, 121–23; post-carceral, 114–15, 117–19; preparation and self-improvement for, 118, 119–21, 146–47; staff views on, 123–26; studies on, 112–13
reform, 130–51; book access, 139–40; communication opportunities, 138–39; cultural, 133, 145–46, 165–67; food, 136–38, 168–70; hygiene, 135–36; incentives, 34, 140, 170–73; lack of thinking about, 148–50; limiting time served and resident numbers, 160–63; lowering perceptions of risk, overview, 164–65; policy revisions, 34, 68, 102, 107–9, 138, 178–81; punishment perspective of, 141–43; reentry preparation, 146–47; as risk for staff, 34, 37–38; second-order *vs.* first-order change, 159–60; social interactions, 173–75; of staff, 132–35, 145–46, 175–77
Regner, Kaley, 196
rehabilitation, absence of, 77, 118, 128–29, 141, 173
Reiter, Keramet, 141, 167
relationships, 42–79; resident-CPS worker, 54–55; resident-family/friends, 62–64, 117–18, 174; resident-resident, cellies, 43, 44–48; resident-resident, non-cellies, 43, 48–54; staff-DOC and management, 34–35, 36, 67–69; staff-family/friends, 32, 71–75; staff-resident, 43–44, 55–62, 65–67, 70, 147; staff-staff, 44, 70–71; studies on, 42–43
research methods: acknowledging competing contextual narratives, 185–86, 217–19; data analysis procedure, 211–12; data capturing procedure, 206–8; data coding procedure, 208–11; identity protection, 193, 194, 195, 207, 220; interview procedure, 14–15, 192–95, 204–6; IRB approval, 191–92, 193, 194; mutually beneficial partnerships, 215–17; obtaining access

research methods (*continued*)
to prisons, 5–6, 188–91; project conception, 187–88; qualitative *vs.* quantitative research methods, 6–7, 201–2, 212–13, 214–15; research team preparation and training, 196–99; sampling procedure, 202–4; team-science approach, 199–201; writing process, 212–13

residents: circumstances for entering RHU, 2–3, 153; living conditions, overview, 10–13; staff-to-resident ratio, 4–5. *See also* AC-status (administrative custody) residents; DC-status (disciplinary custody) residents; reentry; reform; relationships; risks

resilience, 9, 52, 128, 152, 181, 220

Rhodes v. Chapman (1981), 82

RHU (restricted housing unit): as convenient, 155–58; defined, 1; living conditions, overview, 10–13; malignancy and resilience in, 8–9; as repeated history, 158–59; scholarship on, 5–7; working conditions, overview, 113–14. *See also* reentry; reform; residents; risks; rules, procedures, and policies; staff

RHU School, 5, 38–39, 84–85, 95, 97, 98, 100, 101, 103–4, 106

risks, 17–41; to family life, of staff, 32–33, 119; lowering perceptions of, overview, 164–65 (*see also* reform); from managerial decisions and policies, 34–40; mental health, of residents, 21–22, 24, 26–27, 54, 60–61, 115, 119–20, 132–35; mental health, of staff, 31–32, 36, 75–76, 177; as ongoing, 40–41;

physical health, of residents, 21–26, 53, 56, 57–58, 65–66, 101–3; physical health, of staff, 28–31, 53, 103; studies on, 17–19

Rosen, Liz, 196

Rubin, Ashley, 6–7, 141

rules, procedures, and policies, 80–111; bending and breaking, by staff, 60, 86, 93, 106–7; for book borrowing, 12, 98; case law on, 81–83; for cell assignments, 35, 45–46, 91–92, 104–5, 107–8, 124–25; as confusing and inconsistent, 23, 24–25, 57–58, 87, 89–97, 102, 104, 106–7, 109–10, 177–78; for count time, 11; for haircuts, 90–91; handbooks on, 83–84, 85–86, 88, 89, 90, 91, 92, 97, 99–100, 105, 109, 178; institutional changes to, process, 107–9 (*see also* reform); for meal delivery, 11–12, 89, 98, 100; for movement of residents, 12, 22–23, 43, 86–87; for property, 11, 105–7; as risk and hindrance for staff, 34–38, 67–69, 94, 100–101, 103, 104–6; as safety and control measures, 94, 97–100, 101–2, 106; for shower time, 12, 43, 50, 87–88, 97–98, 99; for suicide, 24, 35–36, 57–58, 68, 101, 102, 107–9; training staff on, 5, 38–40, 43, 84–85, 95, 97, 98, 100, 101, 103–4, 106, 176–77, 178–79; for visitations and phone calls, 12, 44, 62, 63, 66; for yard time, 12, 43, 50, 57, 88, 97–98

safety. *See* risks; violence
sanitation, 135–36. *See also* showers
Scalia, Antonin, 81–82
Schray, Elizabeth, 196
Scott, Clifton, 75

SEAP (State Employee Assistance Program), 36, 75
Sears, William, 159
self-harm, 36, 132, 133. *See also* suicide
self-improvement, 120–21, 139–40
Seligman, M. E. P., 127
Sexton, Lori, 167
sexual abuse, 21, 37, 57. *See also* PREA (Prison Rape Elimination Act)
sexuality and gender: and AC status, 2, 77; and cell assignments, 45, 226n2; female staff, 60–61, 92, 96–97, 224n3 (chap. 4); masculinity, 75, 177
sexual relationships, 60–61
shackles and handcuffs, 12, 22–23, 43, 87, 161, 175
Sheley v. Dugger (1987), 82
Shivers, Liana, 196
showers: after being pepper sprayed, 25, 58, 102; assault in, 57; location, 10; procedure for, 12, 43, 50, 87–88, 97–98, 99; reform, 135; sharing property in, 51
SHU (security housing unit), 1. *See also* RHU (restricted housing unit)
sleep deprivation, 24–25
Smith, Earl, 196, 220
Smith, Lindsay, 196
SMR (Standard Minimum Rule) for the Treatment of Prisoners (1955/1957/2015), 160–61, 162
SMU (Special Management Unit), 161
Snow, David, 210
solitary confinement, as term, 1
Solitary Confinement Study and Reform Act (2019), 163
Spock, Benjamin, 158–59
staff: backgrounds, 3–4, 153–54; criticism of management and policies, 34–39, 67–69, 94, 100–101, 103, 104–6, 145–46; female, 60–61, 92, 96–97, 224n3 (chap. 4); as incarcerated, 78–79; personality changes, 33–34, 72, 73; reentry, views on, 123–26; reform, ideas for, 141–47; reform of personnel and culture of, 132–35, 145–46, 165–67, 175–76; staff-to-resident ratio, 4–5; training, 5, 38–40, 43, 84–85, 95, 97, 98, 100, 101, 103–4, 106, 176–77, 178–79; working conditions, overview, 113–14. *See also* psychological staff; relationships; risks; rules, procedures, and policies
Standard Minimum Rule (SMR) for the Treatment of Prisoners (1955/1957/2015), 160–61, 162
State Employee Assistance Program (SEAP), 36, 75
Stevens, John Paul, 82
Stitzer, Maxine, 170
Strauss, A. L., 211
strip searches, 14, 23, 43, 87, 96, 97, 224n3 (chap. 4)
suicide: cases and rates of, 27, 32, 36, 54, 105, 133, 141; policies on, 24, 35–36, 57–58, 68, 101, 102, 107–9; prevention efforts, 1, 10, 11, 35, 44, 107; thoughts of, 21, 22, 26
suicide watch, 10, 11, 35, 44, 107
Sumner, Jennifer, 167

Tabas, Casey, 196
tablets, 11, 83, 106, 120, 138–39, 142, 174
Taxman, Faye, 170
team-science research, 199–201
television, 11, 21, 51, 106, 107, 131, 142
time-out, 121–22, 155
Together Alone study, 190–91

Toronjo, Heather, 196
Tracy, Sarah, 75
training, staff, 5, 38–40, 43, 84–85, 95, 97, 98, 100, 101, 103–4, 106, 176–77, 178–79
traumatic stress: ongoing, 40–41; PTSD, 32, 40
Travis, Jeremy, 112
trust: of residents toward CPS workers, 54–55; of residents toward residents, 47, 52–53; of residents toward staff, 22–25, 55–58, 60, 61–62; of staff toward residents, 66
trustworthiness, in qualitative research, 214–15
Tuan, Y. F., 17–18
TV, 11, 21, 51, 106, 107, 131, 142

understaffing, 61, 103, 145
use-of-force policy, 101–2

victims' rights, 143
violence: resident-to-resident, 53, 65–66; resident-to-staff, 28–30, 53, 103; sexual, 21, 37, 57; staff-to-resident, 22–23, 25, 56, 57–58, 101–3; workplace, defined, 40
visitations, 12, 44, 62, 63–64, 66, 140
volunteer staff, 175

Wacquant, Loïc, 6
weapons, 11, 29, 53
Weems v. United States (1910), 81
White, Byron, 82
Whittington, Taylor, 196
WHO (World Health Organization), 168
wickets, 18, 31–33, 77, 84, 107, 109, 120, 156, 199
Williams, Brie, 166
Wilson v. Seiter (1991), 81–82
women as RHU staff, 60–61, 92, 96–97, 224n3 (chap. 4)
Wright, Cassie, 196

yard: assault in, 53; procedure for, 12, 43, 50, 57, 88, 97–98; sharing property in, 51